FACULTY REQUEST

Learning Resources Center
Collin County Community College District
Spring Creek Campus
Plano, Texas 75074

OTH
PRO

OTHER PEOPLE'S PROPERTY

A SHADOW HISTORY
OF HIP-HOP
IN WHITE AMERICA

JASON TANZ

BLOOMSBURY

Published by Bloomsbury USA, New York
Distributed to the trade by Holtzbrinck Publishers

All papers used by Bloomsbury USA are natural, recyclable products made from wood grown in well-managed forests. The manufacturing processes conform to the environmental regulations of the country of origin.

Library of Congress Cataloging-in-Publication Data

Tanz, Jason.
    Other people's property : a shadow history of hip-hop in white America / Jason Tanz.
        p. cm.
    Includes bibliographical references and indexes.
    ISBN 1-59691-273-1 (alk. paper)
    1. Whites—United States—Attitudes.   2. Youth—United States—Attitudes.   3. Hip-hop.   4. Rap (Music)   5. Youth—United States—Social life and customs.   6. United States—Race relations.   7. Tanz, Jason—Travel—United States.   8. United States—Description and travel.   9. United States—Social life and customs—1971–   I. Title.

    E184. A1.T36 2007
    305.235089'00973—dc22

                                                                    2006021165

First U.S. Edition 2007

1 3 5 7 9 10 8 6 4 2

Typeset by Westchester Book Group
Printed in the United States of America by Quebecor World Fairfield

CONTENTS

For Denise
and
for Mom, Dad, and Laura

"Who's down with O.P.P.?"
—Naughty By Nature, "O.P.P."

PREFACE

Hip hop could care less what White people have to say.
　　　　　　—**Todd Boyd**, *The New H.N.I.C.: The Death of*
　　　　　　　　　Civil Rights and the Reign of Hip-Hop

Let's start with a deceptively simple question: What is hip-hop?

If you're a casual listener, or someone with a passive interest in popular culture, you probably think of hip-hop as a form of music, also known as rap, consisting of beats and rhymes. If you are well-versed in hip-hop's history, you may use the doctrinal definition of hip-hop as a collection of four elements: MCing (or rapping), DJing, graffiti, and breaking (the form of street dance also known as b-boying, rocking, or breakdancing). If you are less rigid, hip-hop may refer to a broad swath of cultural expression, a collection of slang, fashion, music, marketing, art, and ethos. And if you are deeply invested in hip-hop, you may not even think of it as a noun but rather as an adjective that describes a mind-state, a confidence, a swagger, a commitment. It shows itself in the way you wear your clothes, and in the way that you walk, and in the attitude with which you slur your words. It is more than a music. More than a culture. It is a mode of being.

But however you think of hip-hop, you probably think of it as black. Ever since hip-hop first came barreling out of the Bronx a quarter century ago, it has been seen as a unique vehicle to express the hopes, dreams, fears, and trials—the "reality," to offer an oft-used buzzword—of African American life. Hip-hop's favored mode has been gritty social realism, a sometimes nihilistic, sometimes joyous, sometimes angry depiction of the inner city. The white rock journalist Dave Marsh has said that when he first heard hip-hop music, his immediate thought was "Finally, something white people can't steal." *Spin* magazine agreed: "Hip-hop will not be consumed," read a 1988 article in its pages. "This is a music that television, my parents, and any institution with a stake in protecting the old discourse simply cannot fuck with."

Well, perhaps not. *Spin* was using "fuck with" as a synonym for "interact with," and over the past couple of decades, just about every element of mainstream American culture has, in one way or another, fucked with hip-hop. Network television shows are spiced with hip-hop humor, presidential candidates drop knowing references to the Atlanta hip-hop duo OutKast, and the gangsta rapper Snoop Dogg appears next to Lee Iacocca in advertisements for Chrysler automobiles. Just like previous paradigm shifters—from jazz to rock to punk—hip-hop culture, which once felt alien and potentially revolutionary, has been fully integrated into American life.

It is, in a sense, an old story. The artistic expression of black struggle has always captivated white listeners, ever since groups of slaves converted their plantation woes into musical lamentations. The urge of sheltered suburban kids to turn to abrasive, foreign music—from rock to punk to techno—as an outlet for their own frustrations and fantasies is almost as old as the suburbs themselves. And every generation has discovered new technology by which to infuriate and befuddle its parents, a goal that rap music has proved singularly successful at achieving. But despite the many parallels, hip-hop is a unique phenomenon. Unlike rock, which did not gain a foothold in popular culture until Elvis Presley gave a white face to its potentially threatening rhythms, rap's performers and narratives have remained defiantly black for more than two decades. Even more important, hip-hop is seen, even by its detractors, as something beyond mere entertainment. More than any other musical form before it, hip-hop promises to provide insight into the lives and thoughts of an entire community of black Americans.

If our culture is an expression of our deepest fears, anxieties, and fantasies, then what does it mean that hip-hop has become our national soundtrack? In 1970, Tom Wolfe coined the expression "radical chic" to describe a cadre of moneyed white elites whose members entertained themselves by throwing dinner parties for the Black Panthers. Today, that prospect seems neither radical nor particularly chic. To an unprecedented degree, our popular culture consists of white people entertaining themselves with, and identifying with, expressions of black people's struggles and triumphs. Racial dissonance has become an immutable fact of our everyday life. The rappers Method Man and Redman shill for Right Guard deodorant; soccer moms shout, "You go, girl!" at one another; white kids wear FUBU, a black-owned label whose name stands for "For us, by us." *Other People's Property* examines how we got here, and what it means. It is a book about hip-hop's mainstream white audience, the assumptions and subtexts and emotions that bubble just under the surface of our fandom.

In many ways, it is surprising that hip-hop has survived and thrived for so long. It is no secret that Americans are a wildly anxious people when it comes to race. In our post-PC, post–welfare reform age, the issue is deemed too sensitive or intractable to merit much discussion. In the 1950s, 1960s, and 1970s, civil rights activists sought political responses to the forces that segregated the country. Today we remain separated, but apart from an occasional affirmative action dustup or limp presidential commission, Capitol

Hill and City Hall don't have much to say about the matter. In universities and office buildings, race is discussed only in the blandest terms; anything with the potential to cause offense can result in expulsion or lawsuits.

But the national conversation about race has not ended; instead, it has been coded into beats and rhymes. Many of the most important race-related discussions of the last two decades have concerned hip-hop music directly: anti-Semitic statements attributed to a member of the rap group Public Enemy in 1989; the 1992 controversy over "Cop Killer," a song by Ice-T's heavy-metal band; the criticism by presidential candidate Bill Clinton of Sister Souljah in 1992; the flap in 2001 over the rap CD made by Cornel West. The ongoing crack epidemic, the 1992 L.A. riots, inner-city gang warfare—even the semantics of the word "nigger"—have all been passionately analyzed and discussed through rap music. Small wonder that Public Enemy's Chuck D memorably referred to rap as "black America's CNN," an alternative news source for those shut out of mainstream discourse. Hip-hop, and white America's reactions to it, also shows us how the old racial verities of the 1960s and '70s have transformed, and provides a fruitful avenue through which to examine a complicated and confusing new world.

Hip-hop has also precipitated a radical shift in the racial self-image of the United States, providing a link between picket-fenced suburbia and the drive-by ghettos of the Bronx and Compton. At its best, the desire of white teenagers to identify themselves with the African American struggle represents an urge to connect and to overcome the artificial separations of our past. At its worst, it is a fantasy that equates garden-variety suburban alienation with the struggle of ghetto life, and that defines the black experience by the cartoonish swagger of paid entertainers. This book is about how hip-hop is consumed once it moves outside the inner cities that birthed it, away from the black community that has provided the bulk of its inspiration and artists, and into the furthest reaches of suburbia. It is an outsider's history, a look at how and why white people, and white culture at large, have consumed, interacted with, and used the narratives of young African American men.

I love hip-hop, the noun, but I am not hip-hop, the adjective. If I were hip-hop, I would not much care whether people misunderstood this book, or took things the wrong way, or were offended. But the fact is that I am not hip-hop, and I do care, and so I feel compelled to offer the following clarifications and disclaimers.

Because this is a book about how hip-hop has been consumed, it necessarily reflects some of the oversimplifications and misunderstandings of that consumption. For instance, the notion that hip-hop is fundamentally black can obscure the contributions of members of all ethnicities—black, white, Asian, and Latino—who have played major roles throughout hip-hop's history. (By the time breakdancing grew into a national dance craze in 1984, for instance, many of its practitioners were Latino, not black.) Similarly, the characterization of "suburban" or "mainstream" or "middle-class" America as white is another imprecise shorthand. Of course, black, Asian, and Latino Americans make up a vibrant and growing segment of that population. Furthermore, blanket terms such as "white" and "black" overlook the many different ethnicities and identities that can operate within those categories. For instance, I treat Jews—such as the Beastie Boys, Rick Rubin, MC Serch, and myself—as white, despite the fact that there are surely relevant dynamics that are unique to the Jewish experience, and the involvement and interest of Jews in black music has its own rich and complicated history. But my aim is to discuss how hip-hop and race have been understood by the country at large, and I think the loose terms "black" and "white" accurately represent that understanding.

This is also why I tend to focus on hip-hop as a male phenomenon. To be sure, there have been a number of prominent woman rappers, and I've met many, many devoted female hip-hop fans. But I worried that writing about female fans and artists would raise issues of gender that, while undeniably worthwhile and important, would require another book's worth of research and writing. For the purposes of this book I've limited my scope to men.

Throughout this book I write about the way that white people, including myself, have thought about hip-hop and race. I hope it will be clear that my purpose is to air and critique those views, not necessarily to endorse them. For instance, when I write, in chapter 2, that hip-hop represented to me "a purity of authentic suffering and egoless existence," I am not celebrating that belief, but naming it as a topic of discussion and analysis. This will hopefully be clear in the writing, but the subjects of race and culture are so sensitive that I want to err on the side of overclarification.

And speaking of sensitive topics, a word on the "n-word": you will find it—in its unexpurgated form—in this book. I never use the word myself, but when others do, or when it is used in an artist's song, I do not censor it. That word, offensive and terrible as it can be, is an integral part of hip-hop, and a symbol of its racially fraught overtones. It symbolizes one of the most important and difficult dynamics of hip-hop: it means one thing when black people use it and another when white people do. To abbreviate or otherwise avoid it would be to ignore one of the music's most explosive elements. I sympathize with anyone who is offended by my decision but hope that it does not detract from my book.

Finally, hip-hop fans tend to distinguish between rap and hip-hop music: "hip-hop" refers to all the music that bears an organic tie to the culture and community from which it sprang, whereas "rap" refers to the music's more commercial manifestations. I don't make that distinction in this book, but use the two terms basically interchangeably.

CHAPTER ONE
White Like Me: An Introduction

German klezmer may be evolving into the ground for a sort of proxy dialogue, a process through which Germans address not Jews, who largely avoid the concerts, but other Germans about their common past and their relationship to a Yiddish world that was destroyed. How far that dialogue progresses will probably depend on the willingness of the musicians and audiences to probe beyond the surface of the music, rather than merely contenting themselves with the feel-good "Jewish" flavor that the genre can provide . . . "The assumption that you can overcome history by using culture or music is just wrong," [the German clarinettist Christian Dawid] said.

—**Jeremy Eichler, "Klezmer's Final Frontier"**
New York Times, **August 29, 2004**

I have been called "nigga" at least once a week for the past fifteen years of my life. Black people have threatened me with murder and rape, and invited me to family barbecues. They've brought me along to witness church ceremonies, marriage proposals, weddings, births, and suicides. They have greeted me as a brother and shunned me as an intruder. But none of these interactions took place in the physical world. They all occurred in the fantasy realm of rap music.

Most paeans to hip-hop begin with an epiphany, the moment the author first hears rap's booming beats, chaotic samples, and street poetry, and falls instantly in love. When I first heard rap music—blasting from the tinny speakers of a boom box that a scrawny black kid had smuggled on to my school bus—I was terrified. I don't recall the song or the year, but I can remember the deep-throated machismo and apocalyptic drums that muscled their way down my hot-pink ear canal. Had I grown up in the swaggering alleys of New York or the blasé cloverleafs of Los Angeles, perhaps I would have been better prepared for rap's naked aggression and in-your-face racial provocation. Instead, I was raised in the piney suburbs of Tacoma, Washington, where rough-hewn musical depictions of ghetto struggles seemed as hypothetical and threatening as an extraterrestrial invasion.

From such inauspicious beginnings was a lifelong obsession born. I have now listened to rap music for half of my life; have purchased hundreds of tapes, CDs, and MP3s; have spent countless hours decoding lyrics, waiting in line for underwhelming concerts, and—yes—recording my own rap songs. Hip-hop has been an undeniable force in my life, influencing my personal relationships, my politics, my worldview, and my self-image. Picturing my life without rap music is like imagining who I'd be if my parents had never met. And, to paraphrase Eminem's "The Real Slim Shady," there are millions of people just like me. In October 2003, rap and rhythm-and-blues artists held every spot on *Billboard*'s Top 10 singles chart. Later that year, seven of the ten Grammy nominations for song and album of the year went to hip-hop or hip-hop-inflected R&B acts. In 2005, the two top entrants on *Billboard*'s year-end Top 200 artists list were both rappers. An oft-repeated mantra is no less true for its ubiquity: rap is my generation's rock and roll. We introduce our children to A Tribe Called Quest's *The Low End Theory* or Nas's *Illmatic* with the same reverence and wistfulness with which baby boomers view *Blonde on Blonde*.

The story of how suburbanites like me fell in love with hip-hop

2

culture has all the makings of a blockbuster Hollywood romance in which two crazy kids from different sides of the tracks face down parental disapproval and fall desperately in love. Rap music was born in the cauldron of the South Bronx in the 1970s, a time when urban policies with such Orwellian names as "benign neglect" and "urban renewal" had turned the neighborhood into a haven for roving street gangs. I, on the other hand, grew up playing kickball in the street, setting up a lemonade stand with my next-door neighbor, and riding my bicycle to the candy store across town for Pop Rocks and jawbreakers. But despite our differences, today hip-hop and I have grown inseparable, together forever. Love conquers all.

It's a great story, one I've told myself many times. But of course movie romances are not realistic, and the relationship between hip-hop and white America is not that seamless or uncomplicated. Instead, like all relationships, it is fraught with historical resonances and moments of mistrust and unease. As Tricia Rose, a professor of American Studies at the University of California at Santa Cruz, writes, "Young white listeners' genuine pleasure and commitment to black music are necessarily affected by dominant racial discourses regarding African Americans, the politics of racial segregation, and cultural differences in the United States." In other words, we don't consume hip-hop in a vacuum. When we listen to black music, we are doing more than just listening to music. We are participating in a moment that is informed by centuries of racial history. Nor are we passive consumers; as with jazz, or rock, or soul, our listening becomes a part of the hip-hop phenomenon, changing its context and meaning. Call it the hip-hop Heisenberg uncertainty principle: every time we observe hip-hop, we change that which we are observing.

That's why the loose amalgamation of listeners, artists, and producers known as the "hip-hop community" has zealously guarded hip-hop's borders throughout its history, trying to preserve the music and culture's power as a unique vehicle of black expression. That's also why many fans are so quick to cluck their tongues at the current state of hip-hop—a commercialized, homogenized pop-music form—and declare it dead. And as the white audience for rap has grown over the decades, so has the anxiety in some circles over its corrupting influence. Today, some embittered hip-hop fans want to wrest the means of production from white-run corporations. "[H]istory repeats itself," concludes an essay by Minister Paul Scott that appeared in the *Final Call*, the official newspaper of the Nation of Islam. "The slaves fight one another while the slave master laughs all the way to the bank." In 2003, the *Source*, a magazine that has long been the bible of hip-hop journalism, declared war on Eminem. The publication had championed the rapper before, but now it argued that his success represented the front line in a battle between rap purists and interloping white co-opters. "We've got to remember where we came from," David Mays, the *Source*'s cofounder, summed up the argument. "We've got to remember the history and the struggle and the culture." (The fact that Mays himself is a white Harvard graduate is emblematic of the kinds of racial complications that are common in the world of hip-hop.)

It is easy to see why the specter of white folks dabbling in hip-hop culture might raise some hackles: we tend to colonize whatever we touch. In 1923 the cultural critic Gilbert Seldes declared that jazz would never grow into a true art form until white musicians took it away from black artists. Twelve years later, America had crowned Benny Goodman the King of Swing. As Nelson George writes in his *Death of Rhythm and Blues*, white jazz stations refused to hire black on-air personalities, although they occasionally enlisted a few African Americans to help the white DJs craft more authentic patter. And then there is rock and roll, the epitome of cultural theft. Fifty years after Elvis brought his hip-swiveling to the American public, the music that Chuck Berry and Little Richard created is primarily the domain of white performers and audiences. Small wonder, then, that the prospect of white-bread rap fans is almost as offensive to many culture cops as cork-faced minstrelsy was to an earlier generation. Once you go white, you never go back.

And it is not only the hip-hop community that has qualms: plenty of white critics seem to think there's something, well, improper about the enthusiasm of suburban white hip-hop fans. The video for the surf-punk band the Offspring's 1998 song "Pretty Fly (For a White Guy)" shows a blond twerp in baggy clothes; the song's lyrics describe the wannabe as clueless and mired in denial. Television viewers laugh at Ali G, a buffoonish character created by the white British comedian Sacha Baron Cohen, for clinging to his hip-hop-inspired wardrobe and incomprehensible speech patterns as a way to mask his staggering cluelessness.

Still, not everyone thinks that white hip-hop fans should be discouraged. "White folks tend to worry about this in a way that seems curious," says Bill Adler, the white man who served as the original director of publicity for Def Jam, the groundbreaking rap label, from 1984 to 1990. He has worked with the Beastie Boys, LL Cool J, Public Enemy, and Run-DMC, among others, and produced and wrote a five-part documentary series on hip-hop history for VH1. "This whole idea that 'I'm white, so I guess I can't like something that's black' seems slightly retarded to me," he says. He sees hip-hop as a way to break down such false distinctions. "I believe that the average white kid is going to be cooler about these questions of race. In effect, he is going to be less racist than his parents because of hip-hop."

It may seem odd that, decades after Chuck Berry, Miles Davis, and Motown, the prospect of popular black music could still fill white Americans with such fear and promise. But there has never been a music quite like hip-hop. Despite its mainstream popularity, and despite its vast white fan base, hip-hop's underlying theme has never shifted: the celebration and documentation of the lives of black Americans. How can a generation of kids raised on explicit musical tales of black people's triumphs and misfortunes *not* feel differently about race than their parents do?

To judge by surveys, hip-hop's rise has coincided with an unprecedented improvement in American race relations. A poll taken by the *New York Times* in 2000 found that 57 percent of all Americans described race relations as "generally good," up 16 points from 1990; 63 percent of whites said they favored interracial marriage, up from 44 percent nine years earlier; 93 percent of whites said they would vote for a qualified black presidential candidate; and 85 percent of whites said they did not care whether their neighbors were white or black. (It is impossible to know how much of this attitudinal shift can be credited to hip-hop, and how much is the function of a healthy economy, low crime rates, the country's changing demographics, and other factors.) But despite our seemingly universal desire to live in an integrated world, in fact we still do not. The *New York Times* poll found that 85 percent of white respondents—the same percentage who said they did not care what color their neighbors were—lived in areas with few or no black neighbors. According to the U.S. Census, the American population is 13 percent black and 67 percent white. But a study by Harvard's Civil Rights Project found that the average white public school student attends schools that are 78 percent white and only 9 percent black; the average black student attends schools that are 30 percent white and 53 percent black. Between 1991 and 2003, the percentage of black public school students attending majority nonwhite schools rose from 66 percent to 73 percent. The Lewis Mumford Center at SUNY–Albany has reported that the average white American lives in a neighborhood in which 80 percent of residents are white and only 7 percent are black, while the average black person lives in a neighborhood that is 33 percent white and 51 percent black.

I want to use hip-hop as a lens to explore this distance between what our ideals tell us we are and what our lives show us that we are. "Yeah, hip-hop has brought people closer together, but so has McDonald's," a hip-hop journalist, Gabriel Alvarez, says. "It's easy for everybody to say, 'Hey, this is great music. Let's enjoy it together.' I don't think hip-hop has made people sit down and have discussions." The history of hip-hop's spread through the suburbs is the story of what happens when one of our most deeply held fables—America as color-blind melting pot where we can all just get along—is contradicted by unrelenting reality.

Why do so many white kids love hip-hop so much? Does our appreciation foment understanding and communication, or reinforce stereotypes and substitute a cheap commercial transaction for significant cultural exchange? How has our consumption of rap influenced the music itself, and the communities from which it springs? These are all just polite ways of asking the Big Question, what we *really* are talking about when we talk about hip-hop: Can we live together? Or are the combined forces of history and our own weaknesses just too strong? Hip-hop's trajectory through white America is really the continuing story of the complicated legacy of race in our country, of the forces that pull us together even as they pull us apart.

To write this book, I traveled across the country to talk to a wide array of hip-hop-loving white kids, trying to nail down where their fandom comes from and what it means. But here's a tougher question to answer: Why has hip-hop been so attractive to *me*? Every journey starts at home, as they say. And before I headed out on the road, it seemed only fair to turn my microscope on myself, to try to examine my own life for its racial subtext, to try to understand my own obsession with hip-hop and black culture.

I can't rule out simple genetics. As much as I love hip-hop, my grandfather loved jazz even more. I never met my mother's father—he died when I was young—but from what I can piece together, he was not a very good guy. He was an alcoholic and abusive and a deadbeat and probably brilliant, in the way that guys whose minds are too cranked to hold down a job are often said to be brilliant. In 1956, he left my grandmother with three young children and no source of income (not that he had ever provided much of one anyway). It's tempting to say that my grandfather didn't love anything outside himself, but that's not entirely true: he loved jazz. I don't know whether he smoked reefer or played the bongos or wrote poetry like the era's Beats, but I do know that he followed Duke Ellington the way future generations of hackey-sackers would trail the Grateful Dead. According to my grandmother's (perhaps embellished) recollections, the admiration was mutual. Three weeks before graduating from the University of Chicago, the story goes, my grandfather dropped out of college to tour with Ellington as a paid hanger-on. In later years, Ellington and his musicians would stop in at my grandparents' whenever they passed through Indianapolis. Billy Strayhorn once helped bathe my uncle Michael when he was a baby.

I don't know if my grandfather was drawn to blackness for the same reasons as the narrator of Jack Kerouac's *The Subterraneans*, who put his ear up to his black girlfriend's belly and "listened to the rumbling underground." But that's a pretty fair description of the function that my grandfather played in my life, his legend providing a dull, growling counterpart to the bland safety of my childhood. My mother, seeking escape from the tumult that defined her youth, raised my sister and me with a deep aversion to conflict and a theory of interpersonal relationships that mirrored my surgeon-father's Hippocratic Oath: first, do no harm. Despite spending the summer of 1968 in Berkeley, my parents made it through that decade with minimal drug experimentation, zero race rioting, and (as far as I know) a complete absence of free love. They suffered through a stint in Los Angeles in the mid-1970s until my father finished his medical residency in 1980. We fled to Tacoma, where my parents found a home at the end of a cul-de-sac and converted the downstairs bar into a shelving unit for our board games. On the rare occasions when my sister and I fought, my mother wouldn't yell at us; she'd get teary-eyed, which was infinitely worse. To me—a walking-on-eggshells, consensus-seeking, eager-to-please kid—my scotch-swigging, Negro-loving, self-immolating grandfather became a mythic figure.

My parents' lifestyle was echoed in their musical taste. I was not raised on the complex cacophony of bebop or the angry provocation of the Rolling Stones' "Street Fighting Man" or Jefferson Airplane's countercultural experimentation or Jimi Hendrix's whammy-barring or James Brown's sweaty exhortations of racial pride, but on the acoustic strummings and canned righteousness of easy-listening folkies like Judy Collins and Joan Baez, soft-voiced chanteuses who to my mind seemed to believe that the world could be cured and racial divisions healed if we all behaved just a little more . . . gently.

It was a theory that I did not have much occasion to test. For the most part our exposure to African Americans was limited to our locked-door drives through Hilltop, the crime-riddled district that we had to traverse to get to the waterfront eateries in Tacoma's North End. I went to a technically integrated "magnet" elementary school, but those of us in the accelerated program attended class in our own special building, on the other side of a block-long playground that separated us from our fellow students. The only time we would meet our black schoolmates was during recess, when we would lose athletic contests and fights to them. And so I depended upon my schooling to tell me about the African American experience, which was usually spoken of in the past tense: as a struggle for civil rights that had been successfully and resoundingly won. Black America meant Martin Luther King Jr. and Rosa Parks, members of a noble race seemingly handpicked by God to enlighten white people through their suffering. Meanwhile, racists wore the hoods of the Klan and flew the flags of the Confederacy; they were a group of anachronisms as easily relegated to the past as the pilgrims and colonialists that we learned about in history class.

None of this helped me make much sense of my contemporary inability to commune with black people. The mere sight of a black man was enough to trigger a series of conflicting emotions: fear, admiration, guilt, envy, desire, dread. The old civil rights slogan stated that if you weren't part of the solution you were part of the problem, and I sure as hell didn't feel like part of the solution. What's more, I was convinced that black people could sense my anxiety—that they not only knew me better than I knew them, but knew me better than I knew myself. One day, I suggested to my father that he ask a coworker, a black man about whom he often spoke fondly, over for dinner. My dad, who had never invited any of his other coworkers to our house, responded by introducing me to the concept of tokenism, asking if I wasn't really attracted to the idea of having a black family friend as a way of feeling better about myself. This awakened in me a crippling new level of self-consciousness, the sense that I was inevitably tainted by bad faith.

Usually I funneled these impulses into what I took to be the socially acceptable language of race-conscious liberalism. When I was about twelve, I was with my family in one of the many chain restaurants outside Disneyland, and the sight of a black waiter got me thinking about racial injustice. As he poured our water I turned to my parents and loudly mentioned how terrible I thought it was that then secretary of the interior James Watt had a couple of years earlier referred to the members of his staff as "a black, a woman, two Jews and a cripple" (I had read about the line in a "Bloom County" comic). Instead of clapping me on the back and taking me to an underground meeting of some secret society of the Anaheim African American community, as I'd hoped, the waiter continued to pour our water and walked off as if he hadn't heard a word. And instead of beaming with pride at her son's sensitivity, my mother hissed at me to knock it off and finish my shrimp boat.

That's not to say that I didn't know any black people whatso-ever. In fact, one of my best friends was black, as the saying goes. I'll call him Marcus. At recess Marcus would recite Eddie Murphy standup routines and I would laugh and laugh, even though I didn't understand them. Marcus lived about a half hour away, in a dingy part of town where the houses weren't stained a deep-woodsy brown, like ours, but were slathered in dirty beige paint that peeled off the wood in long, fat strips. I only went to his house once, for a slumber party. The next morning, I got my first peek at a dirty magazine when Marcus's mom left to run errands and we scram-bled upstairs and dug under his bed and passed around the photos he had stashed there, gaping goonily and pointing out every nipple and pubic hair. Marcus and I got along pretty well for a while there, although every time I was with him a mantra looped through my brain: "He'sblackhe'sblackhe'sblackhe'sblackhe'sblackhe'sblack-he'sblackhe'sblackhe'sblackhe'sblackhe'sblackhe'sblackhe'sblack-he'sblackhe'sblack."

Apparently Marcus had a similar mental soundtrack because one day we got in a fight and he passed me a note in which he offhand-edly remarked that I was a Jew, and when I returned it I pointed out that he was black, and then he responded that he would pass my comments along to some of his bigger, stronger black friends from another school, and they wouldn't be too happy about it. And that was the end of our communication.

After Marcus and I fell out, Mr. T became my new favorite

black person. Apart from his skin color, Mr. T bore no resemblance to the then-popular TV star whose nickname he had appropriated. He was a wiry bus driver with a stringy, perennially moist Jheri curl and sleepy eyelids. He also spoke with a pronounced jivey inflection, which my classmates and I all revered. Just the sound of him saying my name felt like he was stamping my passport to some far-off, imaginary land. But that relationship didn't last either, ending when I was in fifth grade, on the Friday before the long Presidents' Day weekend. My teacher had suffered through a grueling afternoon filled with our anticipatory fidgeting, and she nearly fell on Mr. T when she saw him enter our room, grateful for the distraction. Mr. T stood in the doorframe and, with his usual enthusiastic drawl, asked about our weekend plans. I was the first to answer, by jumping out of my chair and announcing, in my best Buckwheat voice, "I be goin' skiin'!"

I sat down triumphantly to the laughter and applause of my fellow students, and Mr. T slid quickly out of the room. It wasn't until my teacher approached my desk and whispered to me that Mr. T's ever-present smile had vanished when he'd heard my comment and that, as one of Tacoma's few Jews, I should be more sensitive to the feelings of other ethnic minorities, that I felt sick to my stomach. Waiting for my school bus to leave that afternoon, I looked out the window and saw Mr. T directing traffic, and I knew that I would never hear him say my name again. I audibly mouthed the words "I'm sorry, I'm sorry, I'm sorry," over and over again. What I meant was: "Please, black man, don't make me feel like a bad guy."

"Too black. Too strong."

I was neither of these things. But the sample of a Malcolm X speech that poured out of my stereo in 1989 seemed to implicate me by association.

"Too black. Too strong."

I had just purchased my first rap CD, Public Enemy's *It Takes a Nation of Millions to Hold Us Back*. I flipped through the liner notes, past photos of Chuck D in a jail cell. He stood on an American flag, surrounded by a five-member black militia, and snarled into the camera. I could not tell if his sneer was a sign of anger or of camaraderie—an appraising look that communicated, "Yeah, you're with us."

I was a sophomore in high school, and most of my friends had been listening to rap for years. By the time I hit junior high—the school was closer to home and whiter than my elementary school experience—hip-hop's influence had spread far enough to invade even my cocooned consciousness. The opening bars of the Beastie Boys' "Fight for Your Right" at a school dance sent the entire crowd into an unironic, fist-pumping panic, but like a good son I disapproved of the band's sexism and overall mookishness. Most of my cohorts had begun experimenting with Run-DMC, De La Soul, and DJ Jazzy Jeff & the Fresh Prince, but for the most part I remained aloof.

But Public Enemy seemed to offer something greater than teenage aggression: absolution. I entertained fantasies of a gaggle of armed black men wearing army fatigues and shimmering 1970s-era Afros, storming our neighborhood with their fists in the air, only to retreat, impressed, when I held up a copy of my new CD. I made cassette copies to play in my car with the windows cracked so that everyone driving by would know how "down" I was. I was thrilled beyond belief when, after purchasing a copy of Public Enemy's *Fear of a Black Planet* at the Tacoma Mall, I was hounded by two hulking white guys who trailed me out of Sam Goody, calling me a "race traitor" who wanted to "shut the white people down." (I was also thrilled when they got bored with me after a few minutes and wandered off.)

I knew that some of my friends were just in this for the beats and attitude, that the words merely served as aggressive placeholders. But to me, the lyrics were the whole point. When rappers boasted of their incomparable God-given "skillz," I dutifully shook my head in wonder and thought, "I could never do that." While I was staying up nights strategizing the best way to win over the good graces of college admissions officers, Ice Cube was reveling in his status as "the nigga you love to hate." Listening to hip-hop provided me with more than a shot of cheap adrenaline. To paraphrase Naughty by Nature's pop-rap hit "O.P.P.," the experience felt like partaking in other people's property, with all the fascination, danger, and guilt that implied. A popular T-shirt boasted, IT'S A BLACK THING, YOU WOULDN'T UNDERSTAND; Dres, of Black Sheep, derided my pigment-mates for fetishizing suntans " 'cause you cannot be it"; and Naughty By Nature's Treach told me in "Everything's Gonna Be Alright" that if I hadn't been to the ghetto I shouldn't ever show up there, because "you wouldn't understand the ghetto." The members of Cypress Hill informed me that I could never understand how they could just kill a man. "That's a lovely sentiment," my friend Kim scoffed upon hearing that lyric at a drunken pregraduation party, and she immediately fell several notches in my esteem. To me, the song represented a challenge—such as getting into college—that I knew I could pass. I could understand! I was smart, and I was sensitive, and I was trying so very very hard.

Then again, maybe not. I started college at Brown University, fell in with a circle of lovely (and mostly white) classmates and neighbors, and immediately began annoying them with hardcore rap acts such as N.W.A. and Da Lench Mob. I papered my walls with posters of Public Enemy and Denzel Washington as Malcolm X. I read *Native Son* and felt overwhelmed by my renewed exposure to the idea that all black people contained a raging, violent beast inside them that white people like me had created. I ran sobbing to a black friend and apologized for everything. I heard that a black student was working to create a Brown chapter of the NAACP, and I gave her a call and asked if I could help.

But I was waiting for an epiphany that never seemed to come. The people who showed up at the NAACP meetings were nice enough, but they looked at me with amusement and never invited me to hang out afterward. During my freshman year, I ran across a black classmate while I was wearing a Malcolm X cap. He looked at me, clearly troubled, and started to ask, "Why do you—" but then stopped. "Forget it," he said, and walked away. His dismissal, combined with the authority of his blackness, devastated me. Some friends and I attended a dance at the Third World Center, but we left in the middle of Dr. Dre and Snoop Doggy Dogg's "Deep Cover" when we realized that the entire room of black people was derisively mimicking our moves. During a campus performance by the Digable Planets, the group's female MC, Ladybug, frowningly changed a lyric stating that she was "93 million miles above these devils" to "93 million miles above you devils." The overwhelmingly white audience made a collective silent pact to pretend that we had not heard her.

And then, one day, it ended. I was attending one of the countless protest rallies that were regularly held on the campus green. The crowd was largely black, and they cheered as a white woman stood up, grabbed the microphone, and denounced racism in all its forms. That looked good to me, so I added my name to the list of speakers. The rally ended immediately before they reached my name, but not before another speaker took the microphone to announce that "We don't want your white guilt." It took me a while to accept that white guilt was pretty much all I had been offering, but when I did grasp it, a couple of weeks later, I gave up. I hung up the Malcolm X hat and stopped attending the NAACP meetings. Like the rest of the white world, I clucked my tongue and shook my head at the photographs of African Americans celebrating the verdict in the O.J. Simpson case. I started to admit that there may be something to this welfare-reform idea. I felt a small twinge of failure, as though I was proving every black person's doubts about me correct, that my commitment was a phase that I would grow out of once I wearied of the challenges, that in the end I was just like almost every white person before and after me, full of talk and good intentions but not prepared to make the necessary sacrifice or effort to really change anything. In the same way that the rapper Marky Mark morphed back into Mark Wahlberg, I became white again.

In 1997 I moved into a rent-stabilized apartment in New York City with my friend Daniel, got my mail forwarded, secured a job, signed up for a subscription to the *New York Times*, picked up a New York driver's license, ordered cable, and started seeing my first therapist. Every Thursday afternoon I left work for a couple of hours and took the subway to East Eightieth Street where my therapist, a white-haired full-throated fiftyish guy, listened solemnly to my standard-issue insecurities and counseled me to "Fake it until you make it." That is: Pretend you are what you want to be until you eventually become it.

From what I could see, it was a fitting message for life in New York during the waning days of the go-go 1990s. Everywhere I looked, geek-hipsters were reinventing themselves as a combination of new-economy money minters and paradigm-toppling bad boys. I ran into a college friend, a former member of the International Socialist Organization, who proudly told me that she was working for a San Francisco startup that published nightclub calendars on the Internet and was seeking a second round of venture-capital funding. While hosting a party, some friends of mine tacked up a sheet of butcher paper and encouraged their guests to scrawl graffiti all over it. The most prominent message, in thick, black ink, read "My IPO gives me a hard-on." My friend Lukas—a semiotics major who seemed particularly well prepared for this moment—moved to town, bought Apple stock, spent his paper profits on three-hundred-dollar Prada shoes, and boasted of his accomplishments in an online column called "MacCommunist." (Sample text: "It's a good thing that MacCommunist is so good at manipulating the capitalist system he professes to despise!")

Hip-hop had provided me with a righteous soundtrack for my earnest undergraduate days; now, rap lent the perfect aural backdrop to this era of filthy lucre and countercultural machismo. Sean "Puff Daddy" Combs rocketed to stardom with "I'll Be Missing You," a lamentation of the murder of his friend The Notorious B.I.G., then recorded songs boasting of his check-writing abilities; hosted Wall Street executives and real estate tycoons at his Hamptons compound; and launched a clothing line that won him the Menswear Designer of the Year award from the Council of Fashion Designers of America. Jay-Z wore a Che Guevara T-shirt for his MTV Unplugged performance, just three months after the *New Yorker* described him as "the greatest of the corporate rappers." The *New York Times* informed me that the business suit had replaced the tracksuit as the hip-hop uniform du jour. It quoted a sales clerk at a clothing store who announced that hip-hop was "becoming more Wall Street." Her coworker agreed: "A lot of rappers now aren't as much street as they used to be."

By day, I was working at a personal-finance magazine, spending much of my time reading the *Wall Street Journal*, and conducting uneasy telephone interviews with stock market analysts. By night, I was rapping. Lukas, Daniel, and I recreated ourselves as a hip-hop trio called Commodore 64 and spent hours every week recording our "geeksta-rap" album. Technology's march had resulted in cheap software that allowed us to piece our songs together on our home computers, self-publish our own CD, and then sell it on Amazon.com. Of course, we didn't have quite the passion of the previous generation of rising young microphone fiends, who hoped that a successful demo might lift them out of poverty. Our songs were, quite simply, jokes—usually about decidedly un-hip-hop topics such as fruit salad and pep assemblies. Daniel, a Ph.D. candidate in mathematics at New York University, adopted the name MC Squared and put together an instrumental track entitled "Proof of the Riemann Mapping Theorem." In contrast to most rappers, who tended to boast of their skills, our songs were filled with *Mad* magazine–style disavowals.

The subtext to all of these songs was "We are very white," so it came as a bit of a shock when we saw one of our tracks, "Straight Outta CompUSA," climb to the top of the mp3.com hip-hop charts, which in this brief and deluded moment of dot-com dominance seemed a more relevant indicator of popular appeal than the *Billboard* Hot 100. "CompUSA" blasted past entries from such legitimate luminaries as Busta Rhymes and Eminem. Our CD, *The K-Minus Initiative*, sold fairly briskly on Amazon.com, and before we knew it we had generated an international fan base. "It's albums like this that make hip-hop worth listening to," gushed one disconcerting customer review. "The best thing to come out of hip-hop since . . . well, ever," asserted another.

To think that just a few years earlier, in college, Lukas, while moderating a panel to discuss hip-hop, was angrily denounced by a black student for daring to profess expertise about a fundamentally African American art form. We had clearly come a long way; now, we cavalierly laughed at the kind of jokes that would have gotten us expelled if we had made them at school. Sarah Silverman, a Jewish comic, quipped that she was dating a half-black man who dumped her for being a loser, immediately castigated herself for being overly negative, paused, and then closed with the shocker: "He's half *white*." Chris Rock delivered a famous routine that delineated the differences between black people and "niggers." One of the founders of *Vice* magazine defended the hipsters swarming into his Brooklyn neighborhood by joking to the *New York Press*, "At least they're not fucking niggers or Puerto Ricans. At least they're white." To my postcollege self, these racist jokes didn't really seem racist; I received them as metaracist, comments on my own caution, discomfort, and hypersensitivity, as a knowing recognition that most of my seemingly earnest efforts had proven hopelessly flawed and self-serving. Now I looked back at my sincere college years with something like shame, and slid effortlessly into the bulletproof stance of knowing irony.

There was Lenny Bruce–ish liberation here, in the belief that even the most explosive social problems could be magically undercut through brash humor. But nothing felt as liberating as a good rap concert. New York afforded me the opportunity to see a different act every night if I so chose, and there were moments—seeing Black Star open for the Beastie Boys at Hammerstein Ballroom, or People Under the Stairs at S.O.B.'s, or the DJs Z-Trip and Q-Bert at the Bowery Ballroom—when a crowd of blacks and whites and Asians and Latinos shared one set of ears and one body, listening raptly to an intricate freestyle or bouncing euphorically every time the DJ dropped a new beat. After a show, I walked to the subway station filled with my share of the concert's collective goodwill, and it seemed that, if hip-hop could bring a sheltered kid from Tacoma to downtown Manhattan and throw him into a community of people of every hue, then its powers must truly be unlimited. For brief stabs in time, I was convinced that hip-hop could still save me.

But those moments felt harder to come by as the 1990s bled into the next millennium. More and more, instead of communing with members of different races and classes, I went to concerts only to find myself surrounded by people who looked exactly like me—scrawny white guys from suburbia. One evening Lukas, Daniel, and I hit Nowbar, a smoky haunt beneath the West Village that hosted a weekly night of rap music. The place was mobbed with brawny black and Latino guys in baseball hats and ski jackets, with whom I immediately set about trying to make conspiratorial eye contact. My efforts fell on stony faces, so instead, Lukas, Daniel, and I formed a tight circle and spent the rest of the night staring at one another and gigglingly reciting our own lyrics. A few weeks later, we learned that the event had been discontinued, presumably because it had been discovered by too many undesirables—that is, people like us.

One morning a short while back I was getting ready for work. With a half decade of financial-journalism experience behind me, I had become an editor. I worked in a flashy building in midtown and spent most of my time poring over writers' copy, making sure that they had properly analyzed their subjects' businesses, that their calculations of annual revenue growth checked out, that they had accurately described a company's new supply-chain-management technology. Heading across the street to a cash machine, I heard a familiar song, one I couldn't quite place, blasting from a delivery truck at the stoplight on the corner. Once I recognized the tune, from a relatively obscure New York–based hip-hop group, I made eye contact with the African American driver, rapping along with the lyrics so that he could witness firsthand my knowledge. He smiled and nodded. It was a brief moment of connection, and, overcome with a sense of brotherhood, I threw my fist up into the air. I wanted this guy to know that I was on his side, that we weren't so different, that even though I was wearing a crisp white button-down shirt and he was wearing a sweat-stained T-shirt, even though

OTHER PEOPLE'S PROPERTY

I was five years younger and probably made twice as much money as he did, even though I spent my day in front of a computer and he spent his hauling cargo around the city, even though most of my friends—still—were white and upper middle class and well educated, even though our lives were unquestionably different in so many ways, we still had a common cause, symbolized by our shared love of hip-hop. But before the driver could see me, the light changed and the truck pulled away. I dropped my fist and headed in to work.

CHAPTER TWO
Touring the 'Hood: Hunting for Reality
in New York City

> In order for ethnology to live, its object must die; by dying, the object
> takes its revenge for being "discovered" and with its death defies the
> science that wants to grasp it.
>
> —**Jean Baudrillard,** *Simulacra and Simulation*

The first thing I hear when I board the tour bus is LL Cool J's 2004
song "Hush." The Queens-based rapper is best known as a lady-
pleasing Lothario, and this track being pumped over the bus's
public-address system shows why. After a silky introduction, in
which a guest singer, 7 Aurelius, implores me to stay quiet and assures me that everything will be all right, LL commences his sweet-
talking. He tells me how good I make him feel, that he wants to
protect me, and that if he had his way he'd whisk me out of the
'hood—a contraction of "neighborhood" that refers to the hard-
scrabble inner city—forever. But my fellow travelers and I have gotten on a bus in midtown Manhattan to do precisely the opposite: we
are headed *into* the 'hood. Not only that, as customers of a private
tour company called Hush Tours, we have paid seventy-five dollars
for the privilege. Every Saturday, Hush offers a Legends of Hip-Hop
Tour that guides its visitors through Harlem and the South Bronx,
pointing out significant landmarks of hip-hop history.

OTHER PEOPLE'S PROPERTY

The words "guided tour" and "South Bronx" may seem like an unlikely combination for anyone who still remembers the neighborhood by the reputation it earned in the 1970s and '80s as the very epitome of urban blight. Back then, the nightly news broadcast images of a postapocalyptic wasteland where fearsome gangs roamed the streets and children played in the ashen hulls of burned-out automobiles. If any visitors came to the South Bronx, it was usually as part of the occasional noblesse-oblige-y presidential motorcade or dumbstruck news team. Not only would tourists not spend seventy-five dollars to visit the Bronx, they'd probably pay twice as much if you could promise them that you'd never make them go there. But rap fans hold different associations with the South Bronx. To them, it is the legendary birthplace of hip-hop, the place where disc jockeys, street dancers, and graffiti artists, despite the dismal surroundings, created what would become the dominant American popular cultural force of the late twentieth century.

This is what led Debra Harris—a Bronx native, hip-hop fan, and legal secretary—to create Hush Tours in June 2002. "So many people were into rap music," she told me in a phone interview in 2005. "I figured this would be a good opportunity for them to find out a little more about its beginnings." She estimated that 7,500 visitors had taken her tour in the three years since she founded her company, despite an almost complete lack of advertising. (I heard about the tour from a friend who had taken it.) On today's tour we are thirteen from Florida and California and Germany and Switzerland and Japan. One of us appears to be Latino, three are African American, one is Asian, and the rest are white.

I am here because I'm intrigued by the idea of the South Bronx as a packaged historical curiosity, the urban equivalent of Colonial Williamsburg, something to be seen from the window of a passing bus. In a way, today's trip embodies what hip-hop has always promised its listeners: a guided tour of the ghetto. From the comfort of our own living rooms, we have been afforded what appears to be an unfiltered view of inner-city black life, bite-sized excursions through the South Bronx or Harlem or Compton or Atlanta or Houston. At the end of our living-room tour, we turn off our CD player, and, *voilà*, we're back home again, enriched and ennobled by our adventuring.

The Hush Tour feels like the logical next step, a way for rap fans to dip their toes a bit farther into the shallows of black life without fully diving in. Before boarding the bus I spoke curbside with Ian Shaw, a scruffy thirty-something white guy in a knock-off Knicks jersey who had traveled with his father, David, all the way from Birmingham, England, to take the tour. He told me he had loved hip-hop ever since an obsession with Eminem had led him to listen to 50 Cent "and all the black guys." A guided tour of the area from which the culture sprang seemed the perfect opportunity: "I've been fascinated with the Bronx ever since I saw that film *The Warriors*," Shaw told me, alluding to Walter Hill's 1979 fictional movie about rival gangs battling it out in New York's mean streets. "But I'm not game enough to go to those neighborhoods on my own."

Predicting this kind of unease, the Hush Tour organizers asked us to meet in the relatively comfortable environment of midtown Manhattan, from where the bus I'm now sitting in will whisk us north. On the way here this morning, I encountered dozens of reminders of just how prominent a cultural force hip-hop has become. A photograph of a Kanye West acolyte, John Legend, hung in the window of the Gap store. A corner newsstand placed its pile of *XXL* magazines, a hip-hop publication, prominently in front of its other offerings. A deliveryman walked past me wearing a T-shirt that promoted the latest hip-hop-attitude-inflected ad campaign for 7-Up: the front of his shirt read MAKE 7, the back, UP YOURS.

I also passed a billboard promoting the History Channel. In it, a man in a business suit held up a cardboard sign that read, FIND OUT WHAT THE WORLD WAS LIKE BEFORE IT WAS OVERRUN BY BURGER JOINTS AND COFFEE CHAINS. I don't spend much time watching the History Channel, but it is easy to relate to the advertisement's sentiment. Who doesn't want to return to a simpler, more honest time, before the artificiality and compromises of modern life corrupted us all? That is another promise of the Hush Tour. Today, hip-hop is a massive commercial industry, a confusing and complicated jumble of money, power, and culture. The Hush Tour will give a glimpse—if just for a few hours—of hip-hop's pure, authentic earlier days, back when MCs, DJs, graffiti artists, and dancers performed strictly to impress or amuse one another, not in the hopes of wangling a recording contract or securing a sneaker endorsement or getting a music video played on heavy rotation. It will return tourists to a time before the whole world—that is, they—started watching.

It is just that hunt for purity, and the nagging feeling that modern life had driven me away from my authentic core, that led to my love of hip-hop in the first place. According to Kenneth T. Jackson, an urban historian, the suburbs were designed to provide a sanctuary from the corrupting influence of the city, where the family unit could fulfill its role as a "personal bastion against society, a place of refuge, free from outside control," and "a safeguard against the moral slide of society as a whole into sinfulness and greed." But to a teenager, the suburbs felt conformist and deadening, that quest for sanctity curdling into an artificial world where every impulse and thought was preapproved and predigested. Growing up, I became consumed with the idea that I was simulating life rather than actually experiencing it. I dutifully lusted after cheerleaders and went to homecoming dances, but couldn't help feeling that I was performing my adolescence. Every school bell and station wagon seemed a prop in a vast *Truman Show*–ish movie set designed to create the production that was my childhood. Not that the traditional forms of shrink-wrapped rebellion offered much of an alternative: drag racing, shoplifting, vandalism all seemed to be written into the script, prefabricated gestures that suggested individualism rather than embodying it. Just as Ralph Waldo Emerson and Henry David Thoreau looked to the wilderness to escape what they saw as the confining, artificial strictures of their society, so I sensed that there was a world where people lived with a sense of freedom and risk and chaos—of *real life*—that my own childhood seemed engineered to avoid.

None of this is particularly groundbreaking stuff. Libertines and countercultural thinkers have been trying to escape the conformist binds of mass culture since the time of Jean-Jacques Rousseau, who argued in the eighteenth century that European society separated its citizens from their pure, uninhibited state. If I were a little older, I may have become enamored of the punk movement, whose followers tried to discover their natural freedom by flouting middle-class sensibilities and bourgeois optimism. They spent their evenings doing intentionally ugly things: shooting heroin, dragging smashed glass across their chests, clubbing one another with microphone stands. They created intentionally ugly music: punk's most enthusiastic champion, Lester Bangs, approvingly referred to it as "horrible noise," "hideous racket," "utterly annoying," "oppressive," and "the shriek, the caterwaul, the chainsaw gnarlgnashing, the yowl and the whizz that decapitates." They hung out in intentionally ugly bars: the punk club CBGB has been described as having "the most godforsaken bathroom in Christendom." Legs McNeil, the founder of *Punk* magazine, once said that the movement's fundamental ethos was an attempt to be "as offensive as possible." But by the time of my adolescence, even this rebellion had *itself* been packaged and sold to me, in the form of Sex Pistols

T-shirts and Christian Slater films such as *Pump Up the Volume* and *Heathers*. There seemed to be no alternative, no way to break out of the compromise of mass culture and to find pure, unmediated living.

Small wonder, then, that I'd become fascinated by hip-hop's depictions of the South Bronx, which made Dante's *Inferno* read like a benign travel brochure. Forgotten or ignored by politicians and urban planners (to say nothing of college admissions officers and marketers), hip-hop's pioneers faced challenges that I, in my hermetic biosphere of a childhood, could only imagine. Ironically enough, it was the "white-flight" exodus of earlier generations of the middle class, abandoning the city for the perceived racial purity of the suburbs, that had helped create these miserable inner-city conditions. Still, to me, the South Bronx represented a different kind of purity: a purity of authentic suffering and egoless existence.

And most of the people living there were black, which to my mind made their struggle all the more immediate. I was not the first bourgeois white kid to equate skin color with authenticity. Rousseau, Paul Gauguin, and Gustave Flaubert all sought refuge from stodgy European mores, in the "noble savages" of North America, Tahiti, and Egypt, respectively. Even the punks of the late 1970s felt that their own self-conscious counterculture could never be as pure and effortless as that of black Americans. As Iggy Pop once said, "In Detroit, if you were a white kid, your dream would be to be a black thug with a guitar and play like one." The musician Richard Hell once told the *New Musical Express* that "punks are niggers"; the writer Lester Bangs wore a T-shirt proclaiming himself LAST OF THE WHITE NIGGERS; and Patti Smith recorded "Rock and Roll Nigger," with a chorus that celebrated the desire to live "outside of society," concisely summarizing the rebellious appeal of blackness. In 1978, punk godfather Lou Reed satirized the widespread lust for blackness in a song called "I Wanna Be

Black," in which he plaintively sang that he no longer wanted to be "a fucked-up middle-class college student." If anything linked the anything-goes provocation of the punks with my own sheltered childhood, it was this belief that blackness provided the purest form of escape from mainstream society. And if hip-hop couldn't provide me with that same liberation by physically transporting me into that world, it gave me the next best thing: a window seat from which to observe it.

Once we are all settled on the Hush Tour bus, Debra Harris introduces our guide for the afternoon: Rahiem, a member of the iconic rap group Grandmaster Flash and the Furious Five. The Furious Five performed a number of classic songs in the early 1980s, but they are best remembered for 1982's "The Message," a track that sounded more like a radio bulletin from the DMZ than a dance record. Over a sparse, reverb-heavy backing track, Melle Mel, the MC, spat rhymes detailing his struggle to keep from going under in a world where junkies prowled alleys with baseball bats, kids smoked marijuana at school, and women were shoved in front of subway trains. "Don't push me," he warned over and over, "cuz I'm close to the edge."

"The Message" introduced the notion that rap lyrics, which had previously refrained from any subject matter more socially significant than partying, could channel the experience and emotion of inner-city black America. To white audiences, the song's performers offered a maiden tour of black rage that felt like the first authentic view of the horrors of the South Bronx. The song became an instant smash, going gold and winning the Best Single of 1982 award in the *Village Voice*'s influential "Pazz and Jop" critics' poll. "Never in Pazz & Jop history has any record occasioned such blanket ecstasy as Grandmaster Flash & the Furious Five's 'The Message,'" wrote the *Voice*'s Robert Christgau.

But it turns out that, as in any guided tour, what appeared to be raw and authentic was at least partly manufactured. The members of the Furious Five themselves were less than enthusiastic about the song, fearful that an audience weaned on feel-good party rhymes would balk at lyrics that made them feel so bad. The concept, and much of the lyrics, actually came from Edward "Duke Bootee" Fletcher, a member of the Five's backing band. The Five's label chief, Sugar Hill Records' Sylvia Robinson—who in a previous incarnation as half of Mickey & Sylvia was best known as the slinky chanteuse who sang "Love Is Strange"—insisted, over their objections, that the group record the song. What seemed the unfiltered voice of the ghetto was in fact, as Rahiem was to tell me later, "one of the best career decisions that anybody made for us."

It's also not clear that the people of the South Bronx—whose reality "The Message" purported to describe—were any more enthusiastic about the song than the band itself. "People hated that record," Russell Simmons, the cofounder of Def Jam, once told *The New Republic*. "I remember the Junebug, a famous DJ of the time, was playing it up at the Fever, and Ronnie DJ put a pistol to his head and said, 'Take that record off and break it or I'll blow you're fucking head off.' The whole club stopped until he broke that record and put it in the garbage."

Rahiem takes the microphone and tells us that in sixteen days his group will be fêted on VH1's *Hip-Hop Honors* (an annual program that memorializes the culture's most important figures) alongside Big Daddy Kane, Ice-T, LL Cool J, and Salt-n-Pepa. A well-preserved forty-two, Rahiem, with his shaved head, sleepy eyes, and bright red FDNY T-shirt, looks remarkably young to be a legend. Then again, he also seems a bit too legendary to be a tour guide. This, it turns out, is another mission of Hush Tours: to provide a salary and visibility for hip-hop's originators, many of whom have faded into poverty and obscurity while their descendants have gone on to dominate popular culture. "The pioneers are so underrepresented here," Debra Harris told me. "I thought it was a good idea to have them employed and doing something they love."

As our bus rumbles up Madison Avenue, Rahiem alternates between pointing out various sites of interest—the funeral home where the murdered rapper The Notorious B.I.G. was laid to rest in 1997; the Madison Avenue boutiques "where some of your more well-paid hip-hop artists shop"—and giving us a primer on hip-hop's history. He lists the four elements of hip-hop culture—rapping, DJing, graffiti, and breaking—all of which were developed in overlapping social circles throughout the ghettos of New York during the mid to late 1970s. He tells us that the father of hip-hop was DJ Kool Herc. Herc, a Bronx-based Jamaican immigrant previously known as Clive Campbell, noticed that crowds at his house parties tended to respond most strongly to a song's "breaks"—the moment of instrumental payoff when the vocals drop out and the music climaxes—and developed a technique called the "merry-go-round" to link a record's breaks together and create an entire song's worth of euphoric release. The Bronx also produced Afrika Bambaataa, the famous "master of records" who, by creating a collection that extended beyond funk and soul to incorporate a vast array of musical influences, from Kraftwerk to Henry Mancini, helped create hip-hop's open-eared, postmodern sound. Bambaataa also expanded hip-hop's social mission by using the music to convert his Black Spades gang into a peace-loving collective known as the Universal Zulu Nation. He kept peace at his parties by cutting off the music at the first hint of skirmish, chanting "no violence," and refusing to continue until the good vibes were restored. Grandmaster Flash, Rahiem's DJ and the third member of hip-hop's holy trinity, also hailed from the South Bronx. A student at Samuel Gompers Vocational and Technical High School who was christened Joseph Saddler, Flash reinvented his turntables as musical instruments, thus introducing hip-hop's cut-and-paste sample-happy aesthetic.

Together, Herc, Bambaataa, and Flash became borough celebrities, their parties legendary, and their mutual respect and competitive spirit pushing one another to new heights of creativity. The Bronx, once known only for crime and poverty, was beginning to develop its own homegrown culture. The historian Jeff Chang writes that hip-hop helped introduce a new value system to the community, so recently dominated by gangs. "In the Bronx's new hierarchy of cool, the man with the records had replaced the man with the colors. Violence did not suddenly end; how could it? But an enormous amount of creative energy was now ready to be released from the bottom of American society, and the staggering implications of this moment eventually would echo around the world."

Rahiem peppers his lecture with questions, testing us on our knowledge of hip-hop trivia. Most of the passengers respond to his queries with shy silence, like schoolchildren who are either ashamed of not knowing the answers or wary of appearing like know-it-alls, but one tourist shares no such compunction. A tall, loose-bodied white dude who wears a sleeveless Public Enemy shirt and introduces himself as DJ Gummo is quick to respond to Rahiem's quizzes, usually with the correct answer. Rahiem asks where, other than indoor recreation centers, early hip-hop DJs used to perform, and Gummo quickly answers "the parks." When Rahiem asks where they found the electricity to power their turntables, Gummo responds "the light posts."

I understand DJ Gummo's urge to impress. I've met plenty of white rap fans who have a little bit of DJ Gummo in them— indeed, I'm one of them. You can find us at rap concerts, knowingly mouthing the lyrics along to every song or ostentatiously hooting in recognition when some obscure track plays over the sound system. You can see us dropping references to little-known lyrics on our blogs, or hear us peppering our conversation with long-forgotten quotations. We have a tendency to take on the air of Talmudic scholars, bent on internalizing every syllable of text and rattling off every historical milestone. Maybe we're hoping that by sinking so deeply into these details, somewhere in there we'll find some nugget that ennobles our own, relatively mundane existence. Maybe we hope that our demonstrations of hip-hop knowledge will prove to our audiences that we, unlike some white-boys-come-lately, are truly invested in the culture. Maybe we're trying to explore and explode the artistic mystery that so enchants us; perhaps our quest for information is really our urge to analyze, to take apart, to dissect. Or maybe it is simply an urge to connect, a way to get closer to that seemingly pure spirit that always feels just out of our reach.

DJ Gummo, it turns out, has lived much of his life in pursuit of that spirit. He later tells me that as a kid growing up in suburban southern California, he idolized New York City, to the extent that he and his friends formed a group called NYP—the letters stood for "New York Posse"—and stocked their wardrobes with Yankees caps: "We were just a bunch of white kids, wishing we were from New York, singing Boogie Down Productions," the rap group headed by KRS-One, whose song "South Bronx" remains the iconic paean to hip-hop's birthplace. Now a repo man and part-time disc jockey, DJ Gummo, whose real name is Josh McIntosh, is celebrating his thirty-second birthday with this, his first trip to New York. "It's such a big part of my life," he tells me. "You can't be a hip-hop fan without going to New York."

For now, DJ Gummo is content to answer Rahiem's questions with a speed and accuracy that impress even our guide. "Wow,"

Rahiem acknowledges after DJ Gummo's fourth or fifth correct answer. "We've got a ringer in the audience."

DJ Gummo beams.

This is the highlight of the tour so far, watching DJ Gummo soak up the approval of one of his idols. To me, it represents the best of what hip-hop can offer, the opportunity for two people from opposite ends of the country, of different skin color and socioeconomic status, to come together over their mutual fascination with street culture. I get the same buzz when I speak with veterans of hip-hop's early years about the cross-cultural mind meldings that took place back then. This was more than twenty years ago in the hipster confines of lower Manhattan, where MCs, DJs, breakers, and graffiti artists found common cause with the punks, cross-dressers, and new wavers that had taken up residence there. By the early 1980s the punk fascination with hip-hop had turned downtown New York into a multicultural fantasyland, a brief, golden moment that is still remembered as the Edenic high point of hip-hop's innocence.

The punk–hip-hop alliance was the brainchild of a Brooklynite known primarily by his nom de guerre, Fab 5 Freddy (his birth name is Fred Brathwaite), a black graffiti artist and hip-hop enthusiast who first recognized that the young street culture could appeal to people outside its native neighborhoods. "I was reading some early articles about the burgeoning punk movement in England, and about [bands like] the Stooges and the MC5," Fab told me. "There was this pure rebel essence that punk was bringing back to the table. And I was thinking, 'Whoa. This is the same thing that this rap shit is about.' "

If anything, that rap shit was even more offensive to the powers that be than punk could ever hope to be. For instance, who could make for more romantic heroes than graffiti artists, properly known as "writers," who made their names by sneaking into train yards at night, dodging transit cops, and spray-painting their outlaw art across the side of subway cars? They were the bane of square officialdom. In 1972, Mayor John Lindsay referred to graffiti writers as "insecure cowards" and launched a war on vandalism. Lindsay's successor, Edward Koch, created an ill-fated public-relations campaign, surrounded the train yards with guard dogs, and introduced a chemical wash called "the buff" that made the graffiti illegible by smearing the paint into an ugly mess.

Anything that so disgusted New York's authority figures was bound to impress the rebels of downtown Manhattan, and Fab was soon arranging graffiti shows and schmoozing some of the art-punk scene's brightest lights. He appeared in the video for Blondie's 1981 hit "Rapture," a rap-rock hybrid that converted hip-hop's experimental optimism into pop success. He quickly grew to become best friends with Patti Astor, a wild child from Cincinnati who had moved to New York to study acting with Lee Strasberg, and entrenched herself in the underground film scene. She convinced Fab and their mutual friend, Charlie Ahearn, to cast her in the 1982 movie *Wild Style*, a quasi-documentary film that is still one of the most beloved relics of hip-hop's early days. Astor also acted as curator for the Fun Gallery, a seat-of-the-pants art gallery in the heart of the grotty East Village that aimed to appeal to the neighborhood's resident rebels and outsiders. "We were aware of the art world, but we just thought it stunk," Astor says. "People dressed in white outfits rolling around on the floor? I mean, snooze." When she started curating exhibits for the gallery, she turned to the friends she had met through Fab, whose graffiti sounded ideal for a gallery that aimed to become a thorn in the side of the art establishment.

But oddly enough, the Fun Gallery almost immediately became a smash success among the very insiders it had sought to provoke.

OTHER PEOPLE'S PROPERTY

Even the snootiest members of the art world turned out to see— and buy—Astor's artists' latest works. In 1982, *Artforum* ran a full-page photograph of Astor and declared that her gallery was "the bunker where the action truly headquarters." The openings turned into block parties that overflowed into the street and jammed traffic, bringing together hip-hop kids from the South Bronx and East New York, mink-wearing matrons from Summit, New Jersey, downtown club hoppers, rock royalty, and bigwig collectors terrified of missing the Next Big Thing. It was a Xanadu of cross-cultural bridge building. But it also raised uncomfortable questions: Were these patrons there for the art, or the countercultural buzz? Were they true supporters of the culture? Or were they just tourists?

We Hush tourists must give rise to a similarly striking set of questions as our bus pulls up to our first stop, the Graffiti Hall of Fame, a schoolyard where some of the city's best-known graffiti writers return every year to splash their candy-colored signatures across the concrete walls. As we pour onto the playground, Rahiem hands us floppy Kangol hats and cheap plastic gold-colored necklaces, "trinkets to get you in the spirit of old-school hip-hop." DJ Gummo refuses the gewgaws with a terse "no bling," but the rest of us toss on our new accessories, snapping shots of one another in front of the inscrutable Technicolor signatures that grace the city walls behind us. We aren't alone here; a heavyset Latino man stands in the northwest corner, checking out the art, but when he sees all of us, dressed to the nines in cheap, throwback hip-hop gear, he hightails it.

"There was a time when graffiti was outlawed," Rahiem tells us. "But now you can see the work of prominent graffiti artists in galleries all over the world. And they charge a lot of money for it."

Ian and David Shaw, my fellow tourists from Birmingham, approach me. They do not wear their costumes particularly well.

JASON TANZ

Specifically, they don't seem to understand that their necklaces are just cheap drug-store doodads and not believable bling facsimiles. David, in particular, appears quite impressed with his getup, posing straightfaced and serious, his eyes hidden behind half-tinted sunglasses, his Kangol hat twisted resolutely sideways. I hope that I don't look quite so ridiculous—I like to think that I'm carrying myself with a bit more ironic knowingness—but I'm sure that I probably do.

"This is Harlem, right?" Ian asks.

I can understand his confusion. Harlem is the traditional capital city of black America, but as we look around the playground, there's not much to distinguish this particular site from any other city block. It's a pleasant enough street: clean, sunny, and peaceful. Still, I can see in Ian's eyes his excitement at landing in this place, so closely associated in the pop-cultural imagination with crime and violence and chaos and blackness.

"Yeah," I tell him. "Well, Spanish Harlem." Ian beams, then turns to take a photograph of his father in front of the graffiti wall.

After a few more minutes of snapshots, we pile back onto the bus and continue tooling around Harlem. Rahiem takes us past the corner of 106th and Park Avenue, the intersection that provides the name for a popular music-video program on BET, the Black Entertainment Television network. He takes us into the historic Apollo Theater on 125th Street, where, he tells us, he has performed. (One member of our group comments, "It looks so much bigger on TV." "That's what TV's supposed to do," Rahiem responds.) We drive to Rucker Park, a series of basketball courts on 155th Street and Frederick Douglass Boulevard, where, Rahiem tells us, NBA and college players return every summer to play pickup games. He shares with us his memories of watching a game while sitting next to Bill Clinton, Dr. J, and NBA Commissioner

David Stern. "On a day when there's a game going on," Rahiem says, "the streets are mobbed with people, there's police barricades, and you can't just walk in—you need a ticket."

We aren't seeing that kind of action today; instead, three teenagers in oversized jerseys mope around the court, lazily tossing up a ball every few minutes and pretending not to notice us. The Japanese woman in our group gets as close as she can to a kid wearing a Jason Kidd jersey, and snaps his photograph.

Between stops, Rahiem drills us on more trivia. He asks us if we know the name of the first hip-hop single, the first hip-hop artist signed to a major label, and the name of the first all-female group. (The answers, Rahiem says, are the Fatback Band's "King Tim III (Personality Jock)," Kurtis Blow, and the Sequence, respectively.) DJ Gummo gamely tries to play along, but it's clear that he's reaching his limit. When Rahiem asks us to name hip-hop's first ghostwriter, Gummo remains silent.

The answer, it turns out, is Grandmaster Caz (an abbreviation of Casanova), a onetime member of the Cold Crush Brothers whose rhymes were lifted and committed to wax in a little ditty called "Rapper's Delight." Today the song is remembered as hip-hop's warning shot, the first sign that a new street culture was poised to take over modern music; despite its fifteen-minute length, it hit number four on the R&B charts and number thirty-six on the pop charts. But the story behind the song is a bit less heroic. It starts with Sylvia Robinson, the Sugar Hill Records chief, who after taking in a hip-hop performance at a New York club was eager to commit rap to record. She was led to Henry "Big Bank Hank" Jackson, Cold Crush's manager, and propositioned him at the pizza parlor where he worked. He recited some Cold Crush rhymes, was joined by two other aspiring rappers who happened to walk by, and the Sugarhill Gang was born. The next Monday, the slapdash trio showed up at Sugar Hill Studios—Jackson allegedly carrying

Grandmaster Caz's rhyme book, which he had asked to borrow—
and recorded the track in one take. That is how history is made.

The song was a hit, but not everyone was thrilled with hip-hop's
new profile. Grandmaster Caz, understandably upset at hearing his
own name claimed by another rapper in the lyrics of a hit pop song
("I'm the C-A-S-N the O-V-A"), has said that the song "didn't really represent what MCing was or what rap and hip-hop was." "We
said, 'Who the hell is this, coming out with our stuff on records?' "
Afrika Bambaataa told a reporter. It is one of hip-hop's foundational
ironies. The song that first introduced white America to the burgeoning culture of hip-hop, ostensibly an authentic vehicle of black
expression, was itself a corporate-engineered simulation.

Eventually, we land at the restaurant where we are scheduled to
have lunch: a soul-food buffet on Harlem's 125th Street. I quickly
separate myself from Ian and David Shaw—who is still wearing his
hat and chain, possibly under the assumption that he is blending
in—and seek out DJ Gummo. He is sitting at a table with his traveling companion, Darian Wilson, an African American man with
a pierced lip who works "in the mortgage industry" and who has
bonded with Gummo over their shared love of hip-hop.

"Hip-hop made me the nonracist person I am," Gummo tells
me, digging into his chicken. "Coming from an area like Orange
County, there's almost no black people, and the whole hip-hop
thing was almost taboo. I used to go to shows where I was the only
white guy. Now the shows are predominantly Caucasian audiences.
That's a trip. I hate to say it, but that seems to take away the authenticity of it."

This tour, Gummo says, has been giving him all the authenticity he can handle. "I'm like a kid in a candy store here," he says.
"There's just so much history." But soon the conversation turns
to the current state of hip-hop, a less happy subject for Gummo,
who sees rap's current manifestation as a lyrically bankrupt,

mass-marketed, vapid shadow of the free-spirited music that so en-raptured him as a sheltered white kid. "It's shit," he says. "And it's getting worse every year." When Gummo isn't repossessing cars, he DJs events, usually weddings or school dances, but often finds him-self forced to play the popular breed of hip-hop that he so disdains. "It's torture. It hurts to put on a wack song and have to sit there and watch everybody get into it. Like the Ying Yang Twins' 'Wait' [a recent hit that drew some controversy for promising to "beat that pussy up," among other things]. I played that at a backyard birthday party. It was the worst night of my life, musically."

Gummo looks over his shoulder at Rahiem, who is sitting alone at his table, talking into his cell phone. "We should bring Rahiem over here. 'Yo, tell us some stories,' " Gummo says. But rather than approach Rahiem's table, he heads downstairs for another spin around the buffet. While I wait for him to return, I glance across the street and notice a billboard advertising VitaminWater. It depicts the rapper 50 Cent studying a copy of the *Wall Street Journal* while half-naked women stand frozen in mid-shimmy behind him. The head-line of his newspaper reads P&G TO BUY GILLETTE FOR $54 BILLION.

My conversation with DJ Gummo reminds me of a book I read re-cently, *Nation of Rebels*, by Joseph Heath and Andrew Potter, in which the authors describe the fundamental fallacy of "exotic" tourism, and its belief that "[i]f civilization is to blame [for our alienation from life's true meaning], it stands to reason that 'reality' can still be found elsewhere—in uncivilized cultures, esoteric religions or even ancient history." Ironically, the sheer numbers of tourists seeking au-thentically exotic experiences soon makes it impossible for them to find any locale that isn't in some way packaged for their delectation. "As more visitors pile into [an] area," Heath and Potter write, "it be-comes more 'touristy,' less exotic, which ruins it for the people who got there first . . . Thanks to their unceasing efforts at scouring the earth in search of ever more exotic locales, countercultural rebels have functioned for decades as the 'shock troops' of mass tourism."

Heath and Potter could have been writing about what happened to graffiti, which enjoyed a brief moment as New York's hot art trend following the success of Patti Astor's Fun Gallery. So recently dismissed as hooligans and outlaws, graffiti writers were now celebrated in publications such as *Art in America* and *Artforum*. Established collectors such as Dolores Neumann and big-name SoHo and Fifty-seventh Street gallery owners such as Barbara Gladstone, Sidney Janis, and Tony Shafrazi began courting graffiti writers with the possibility of big bucks and art-world immortality. One by one the artists peeled themselves away from Astor's stable. Publicly, Astor remained supportive—"As soon as these guys started stabbing me in the back I knew we were important," she jokes—but her partner, Bill Stelling, says that the vagaries of the art world left him "disillusioned."

There is a scene in the film *Wild Style* in which Fab 5 Freddy's character convinces a graffiti writer to join him at a cocktail party populated by art insiders. The writer is visibly uncomfortable throughout the entire affair—particularly when a glamorous woman invites him into her bedroom to look at her painting by Roy Lichtenstein, and then draws him into bed. That kind of thing, several graffiti artists say, happened all the time.

"Pretty early on, we were under no illusions that these folks were just thrilled with the fact that they were rubbing shoulders with outlaws," says Lady Pink, one of the most prominent writers of the time.

"There was a lot of 'Oh, look! They wear their hats sideways! Isn't that cute?' kind of shit," says Zephyr, another popular artist.

Meanwhile, the East Village sprouted new galleries in the style of the Fun Gallery, but these were of a different breed: less seat-of-the-pants, more self-conscious, and, often, extensions of the very art-world insularity that Stelling and Astor hoped to eviscerate. Rents in the neighborhood, once so affordable, began creeping upward. "There's a new wave of galleries that I would call the second wave, that seems to be a bit more precise about what they want to show," one gallery owner told a reporter. And that "new wave" threatened to price out the old. One night in 1982, Patti Astor wandered out into the street with a bar of soap and scrawled YANKEE GO HOME across the windows of a neighboring gallery.

But the Yankees stayed right where they were, and by the summer of 1985 the writing was on the wall for Astor instead. Staying afloat in the increasingly competitive East Village art world that she had created meant giving up the devil-may-care attitude and adopting a more professional approach—and that seemed to contradict the whole point of the gallery.

The art world's flirtation with graffiti writers did not last much longer, after gallery owners tired of what they deemed the artists' unconventional behavior and disappointing sales. After a couple of years, even graffiti's most prominent advocates jumped ship. "They were young, unreliable, and always broke no matter how much money they made," Sidney Janis told a reporter. In a 1987 *Village Voice* article called "Graffiti R.I.P.: How the Art World Loved 'Em and Left 'Em," Elizabeth Hess wrote that one of the best-known and most talented graffiti artists was working as a wheelchair repairman. "Mention the word 'graffiti' these days and most art dealers look at you as if you've been living under a rock," Hess wrote.

"By 1984, it's over in the United States," Carlo McCormick, a senior editor at *Paper* who had an influential art column in the *East Village Eye* in the early 1980s, says. "The scene fractured and there was a lot of bitterness. People who had been in the same crew didn't want to be in the same room with one another." Some writers fled to the friendlier shores of Europe, where graffiti art proved a more lasting craze, and built enduring careers, but many disappeared. And they could not return to the train yards: after years of fruitless battles, Mayor Ed Koch had finally succeeded in perfecting "the buff," his antigraffiti chemical. Almost as soon as a writer sprayed his tag on a car, it vanished.

The East Village's reign as art district would not last much longer, as the same culture of professionalism and escalating rents that had led to the Fun Gallery's demise soon claimed more victims. By 1987, only a handful of galleries remained. In 1997, when a graduate student named Liza Kirwin began conducting interviews for a doctoral dissertation on the East Village art scene, she was met with horror and embarrassment. "Nobody talks about the East Village any more, nobody," one gallery staffer told her. "People are taking it off their résumés."

"This is it," Rahiem says, with the enthusiasm of, well, of a tour guide who has given this speech hundreds of times, which is what he is. "We are crossing this bridge, and when we get to the other side, we will officially be in the Boogie Down Bronx."

With a build-up like this, to say nothing of the two decades of mythology we've all consumed, my tour mates could be forgiven for expecting our traversal of the Harlem River, which separates Manhattan and the Bronx, to feel like crossing the River Styx and heading into some forbidding netherworld that will forever transform us. But the crossing is, of course, anticlimactic. Now that we're in the Bronx, it doesn't feel remarkably different from any place we've visited in Manhattan. Its boulevards are wide, its sidewalks clean. People of all races walk the streets, doing the same things that normal people do—carrying groceries, walking dogs, pushing strollers. If Rahiem hadn't told us, we wouldn't know we were in a different borough. Just like those thrill-seeking East Village art patrons, we've headed into a new neighborhood expecting to find danger and menace and adventure, and instead find ourselves staring into a world that very closely resembles the one we just left.

"What's the name of that bridge?" DJ Gummo asks, from his perch in the backseat.

"The 155th Street Bridge," Rahiem answers dismissively. In fact, it is technically known as the Macombs Dam Bridge, but DJ Gummo appears to have worn Rahiem down. A few minutes earlier, clearly infused with the romance of New York, Gummo asked whether DJs who don't own their own cars can ever be seen schlepping crates of records onto buses on their way to gigs. But Rahiem quickly deflates this line of questioning: "I know a few DJs who don't have cars. Grandmaster Caz is one of them. He travels by luxury car service." It is, of course, hard to blame Rahiem for his unwillingness to play along. He's already leading a four-hour tour; it seems unfair that he should also be expected to help all of his customers live their hip-hop fantasies of befriending a real live rapper.

Indeed, Rahiem seems to be fading as we course through the Bronx. He answers his cell phone every time it rings, sometimes in the middle of one of his monologues, even if it's just to tell the caller that he'll call back later. His patter becomes an odd combination of ghetto swagger and don't-believe-the-hype myth busting. Just over the Harlem-Bronx border, he gestures to a sun-dappled grassy expanse that, he tells us, is known as Pickle Park: "It's called that for a reason; you don't want to come here at night." He points out the Bronx Criminal Court, "a nice place to visit, if you're not a criminal." (I cannot believe this is true.) He also asks us what our friends told us when we mentioned we were going to tour the South Bronx, encouraging us to poke fun at our preconceptions of the neighborhood. And he suggests that the members of the group come up here on our own after the tour and hang out, pointing out that the real streets are not as dangerous as hip-hop might have led us to believe. He drives us past the site of the Disco Fever, which was once ground zero of the South Bronx's hip-hop scene. Today, the space is occupied by a 99-cent store.

Our last stop is the Bronx Walk of Fame, a series of street signs honoring the borough's most accomplished natives, including Regis Philbin, Jake LaMotta, KRS-One, and Diahann Carroll. We come to a stop outside an attractive apartment building at 1015 Grand Concourse, where Rahiem leads us out of the bus and points up at a sign commemorating his group, Grandmaster Flash and the Furious Five.

"This is where I'm going to come when I can't pay my rent anymore," Rahiem jokes. "I'm going to sleep on this square of pavement underneath this sign."

We stand there, staring up at the sign and dutifully taking photographs, while a few feet away a woman with butterscotch skin and curly hair leans out of the passenger window of her parked car, talking to a friend. She must be amused by our gawking, because she turns to Rahiem to ask where we've all come from. Rahiem shrugs. "All over. Germany. Switzerland. Japan." The woman looks at us, smiles, and waves.

"Welcome!" she says, kindly.

I smile back, like everybody else, and I wave my little white reporter's notepad, and I realize that, as far as this woman is concerned, I'm just another tourist. If there were some way for me to accomplish it without looking insane, I'd tell her that this simply isn't the case. I'd tell her that I'm here as a journalist and dyed-in-the-wool rap fan, not as some fly-by-night visitor. I don't want her to think that I've traveled to the South Bronx for the same reason that those art-world sophisticates patronized graffiti artists—to purchase packaged proximity to blackness. I feel like DJ Gummo must have felt when he spoke with Rahiem, desperate to set myself apart from the other white faces, to prove to her that my interest in hip-hop goes beyond a half-day tour. I'm sure she doesn't see it, but if she'd look into my eyes she'd notice a faintly pleading look, one that says: "I'm not like these people; I live here; I'm one of you guys." But that only lasts a second, because then we have to pile back into the bus and head back into Manhattan.

CHAPTER THREE
Spin Control: A History of Breakdancing in the Suburbs

How can we know the dancer from the dance?
—**William Butler Yeats, "Among School Children"**

The August sunlight is just dying as I enter McCarren Park, a patch of grass in the Greenpoint area of Brooklyn, so it takes me a while to find the handball courts. I've come here at the invitation of King Uprock. King Uprock is in his early forties now, but back in the early 1980s, he danced with a breaking crew called the Dynamic Rockers, world-famous at the time. His given name is Ralph Casanova, which already sounds heroic enough, but everyone started calling him "King Uprock" after he won a heated dance battle in 1980, and he still carries the title with pride. Every week from September through June, King Uprock hosts free dance lessons at an elementary school in Queens, and he also organizes something called the B-Boy Contender Series, a multiround dance tournament. Even though he's got a bit of a paunch these days and may not be quite as flexible as he used to be, when it comes to hip-hop's dance—known as breaking, b-boying, rocking, or, most commonly, breakdancing—King Uprock does not fuck around.

When I tell most people my age that I'm writing about breakdancing, they respond with either a wistful glint or a guilty grin.

OTHER PEOPLE'S PROPERTY

They lean toward me and confess that they spent the summer before junior high school learning how to breakdance. They share their kitschy breakdancing monikers. They shake their heads as they recount the hours they spent in their garages, attempting to master moves such as the headspin and the robot. For a section of the demographic known as Generation X, breakdancing occupies the same space as Rubik's Cubes and Flock of Seagulls CDs: a defining, short-lived fad that disappeared from schoolyards almost as quickly as it arrived.

Although breaking quickly vanished from the popular consciousness, and from the streets of urban and suburban America, a small band of dedicated practitioners have refused to let the dance completely die, and today it is enjoying a resurgence. You can find b-boy clubs in high schools and on college campuses. Repertory groups such as Rennie Harris Puremovement and the Floorlords tour county fairs and performing-arts centers. Every year, the Rock Steady Crew, the most influential and famous of the breaking groups, hosts an anniversary celebration in New York that draws scores of celebrants, and the annual B-Boy Masters Pro-Am in Miami pulls in hundreds more. Amateur dancers log onto Web sites such as bboy.org and mrwiggles.biz to purchase the latest instructional videos. And in the most heavily touristed areas of New York, such as Washington Square Park and Columbus Circle, groups of dancers gamely wring a few bucks from passersby. But breakers are a relatively rare sight today compared to breakdance's heyday, a brief moment when b-boys could be found on practically every street corner, playground, or television set, and in every dance studio. Stumbling upon them in their natural habitat feels a bit like catching a glimpse of a rare endangered bird.

That's why, when King Uprock told me over the telephone that he sponsors a group of breakdancers that meets in McCarren Park every summer weeknight from about seven P.M. to one A.M.,

I asked if I could come check it out. This is my first visit, so I wander around aimlessly for a while until I hear the dull *thwok* of the last remaining handball players, trying to wring a few more minutes of play out of the waning daylight. I follow the sound and there they are, about twenty breakers, most of them between ten and fifteen years of age, but some of them in their midtwenties. King Uprock isn't here yet, so I introduce myself to the forty-something guy with the gymnast's body and flared ears who is stretching in the middle of the loose circle of dancers, and who is, I gather from the fact that he looks about twice as old as everyone else there, the group's leader. He gives me his business card, which states that his name is Richard Santiago; during the day he is an accountant. He dances under the nickname Break Easy, and everyone here refers to him as Papa Rich.

The kids who surround Papa Rich are members (or aspiring members) of his breaking crew, a team of dancers who encourage one another to develop new moves and who challenge rival crews to dance competitions. These challenges, called battles, have historically provided some of breaking's greatest moments. B-boying began spontaneously as a series of steps that black teenagers used to grab attention at packed house parties in the early 1970s. But over the years, it developed into a source of competition, a (mostly) nonviolent outlet for poor black and Latino kids from the inner city to release aggression. Breakers aligned themselves with crews that squared off against one another, and pushed each other to new heights of creativity and skill. A b-boy battle was not an Up With People, feel-good extravaganza but, as a flier for one battle declared, "a competitive, warlike dance, making the opponent look bad." To that end, dancers ended their performances in "freezes": poses often designed to inflict maximum humiliation. The most popular of these was the crotch grab, but others spun into positions of ostentatious languor, as if demonstrating what little effort it took to dispose of their rivals. Still others mimed shitting all over their foes. At times the dancers' disputes resembled those of rival gangs, and post-battle fights were common. Still, the dance provided a generation of kids with relatively productive ways to channel their competitive instincts.

"Back then, we had something to prove," Richie "Fast Break" Williams, who founded a New York crew called Magnificent Force, says. "Everybody wanted to be champion gladiators."

Papa Rich's gladiators are just warming up; someone has turned on a tape of mostly instrumental soul and hip-hop classics, somebody else has unrolled a large square of linoleum, and about a dozen dancers have arranged themselves in a circle around it, taking turns showing off their moves. As they do, Papa Rich points out some of his most talented pupils, whom he calls his "children": E-Rock, a Polish immigrant whose first words in English were the breaking terms "b-boy" and "six-step"; Looney, a ten-year-old whose sophisticated steps seem to belie his age; Eri, a twenty-four-year-old Japanese woman who looks at least ten years younger, thanks to her oversized baseball jersey and sideways-pointing cap. Eri barely stops moving all night, practicing a two-person routine with Rich and trying to master the float, a move that requires balancing on the palm of one hand and using a free arm to spin her body. "She's battle-ready," Rich says approvingly, before admitting that's a hypothetical assessment: there really isn't anyone out there for Eri to battle. "We're in need of a nemesis," he says.

The members of Rich's crew do more than just dance together; they go to movies and hold barbecues and celebrate one another's birthdays. More than one of them tells me that the crew is a surrogate family, a group on whom they can rely for support and love and friendship and attention when their parents aren't around, which they tell me is much of the time. "You feel like everybody's related," says J. J., a sixteen-year-old who just started learning to dance this summer. "Rich is like a big brother."

Still, dancing is this group's focus, possibly its obsession. One teenager tells me, his face all deadpan seriousness, "I talk about it, I think about it, and when I sleep I dream about it." Another shares his discovery that his masturbation schedule was making his body weaker and hurting his moves. "I was like, 'I gotta stop jerking off,' " he says. (That resolution didn't last.)

Rich tells me that breaking provides these dancers with a focus and purpose that they wouldn't have otherwise, as well as positive role models and social influences. This, he tells me, is the true spirit of hip-hop, a culture that encourages the kids whom mainstream society has ignored, that gives them goals to work toward, and that inspires them to develop their skills and discover themselves. Rich speaks about this with an almost religious conviction. "Hip-hop always presents you with a question: When you're presented with a challenge, what are you going to do? Are you going to step up to it?" he explains. "Their own soul is what I'm looking for them to come up with."

All this affection, dedication, and scrappy energy nearly moves me to tears, which would not do much for me, credibility-wise. This is something of a concern, since most of the dancers here, especially the older ones, seem wary of journalists. I've noticed this protective attitude among many of the b-boys I've spoken with, particularly those who were around to witness the dance's original heyday in the early 1980s. A couple of months earlier, when I tried to contact one particularly legendary dancer, he directed me to his manager, who proceeded to ask me whether I had already secured the promise of financial compensation for my work, and how much of that compensation I would be prepared to share with his client. Here at McCarren Park, some of the dancers ask—not unkindly, but guardedly—exactly why I'm writing a book about hip-hop and what my angle is. One woman does not hide her belief that my book will prove to be a major distortion, just like everything else that has ever been written about hip-hop.

But it is hard to blame the dancers for being suspicious or for protecting their financial interests, especially considering what happened to most of them twenty years ago, when breaking first made the jump into mainstream American pop culture and took on a new name, "breakdancing," and new meaning. What started as an expression of inner-city aggression and struggle became a symbol of the go-go Reagan 1980s, illustrating not so much life on the street as life on the Street. Breakers starred in music videos and advertisements, breaking films clogged cineplexes, breaking classes filled dance studios, and breaking gear was hailed as the latest in back-to-school fashion. Gift-buying parents, still recuperating from the wounds they'd suffered while brawling over the last Cabbage Patch Kid, swiped up instructional videos and twenty-dollar breakdancing kits that included folding mats, padded gloves, and "head wax."

And then it disappeared from sight. The pop culture graveyard is filled with short-lived dance fads, and breakdancing was on its way to joining the mashed potato and the hustle around the same time that Prince Charles—perhaps the whitest man who ever lived—was seen busting moves in a November 1984 issue of *People* magazine. Whereas white America might today remember breakdancing as an innocent infatuation, most b-boys look back on that time with bitterness and resentment, as a symbol of what happens when you lose control over your art.

"It was wreckage," remembers Henry Chalfant, a photographer who documented and promoted the work of young graffiti artists and breakers. "Young kids with great expectations had the rug pulled out from under them and didn't know what to do. A lot of them got involved in drug dealing and that kind of thing. The

promise of money and fame just dried up, and that was very em-
bittering. I knew somebody who was part of those early trips to
Europe, taking limousine rides to the airport. I saw him a few years
later and he had gone through hell. He had a drug problem and
had been to jail and the hospital. He told me, 'For five years, it was
an amazing ride. I shook hands with the Queen of England. And
now where am I?' "

This lesson—beware the world's fickle affection—has not been
lost on the current generation of aspiring b-boys in McCarren Park.
"The niggas that I look up to are dead or fucking junkies," says Josh,
a caramel-skinned Latino with huge biceps, a curly ponytail, and
a thin mustache, who tells me that his mother used to b-girl. "You
should write that hip-hop has lost its feeling. We're the only ones
keeping it alive."

"We're like spiritual soldiers here," Tiny, another b-boy, tells
me. "Basically, they forgot that it's about the streets. If you don't
give water to the root, how are you going to have a flower or a
tree? And they all stopped dancing in the street."

One afternoon, I hunker down to remind myself of how I first
learned about breakdancing when I was growing up. I was never a
very coordinated kid, and so I never got deeply into the dance, but
like pretty much everyone in my junior high school, I could boast
one signature move—in my case, a piss-poor rendition of the robot, that jerky series of movements that, when executed with skill,
makes the performer appear like a mechanical man. (I, on the other
hand, looked like I was having some kind of seizure.) Like most
suburbanites, my impressions of breakdancing were formed by
movies—three films, specifically: *Flashdance*, *Beat Street*, and *Breakin'*.
Although I never caught them in the theater, these movies helped

turn b-boying into a suburban dance craze and shaped our understanding of what the dance meant. So in the name of research, I make some popcorn, pick up the DVDs, and settle in for a long, nostalgic afternoon.

Flashdance is first. When it was released in 1983, Malcolm Gladwell was still seventeen years away from popularizing the phrase "tipping point," so breakers didn't yet have a name for the seventy-six-second Rock Steady Crew cameo smuggled into the film. The story of a welder-by-day-exotic-dancer-by-night who successfully auditions her way into a fancy Pittsburgh ballet school, *Flashdance* became an international sensation; the film went on to gross $93 million. Some moviegoers were won over by the hit soundtrack, others were wowed by star Jennifer Beals's ability to remove her bra under her sweater. But a sizable portion of the audience was most energized when Beals's character, inspired by a Rock Steady Crew street performance, threw a Bronx-style backspin into her dance routine. Beals didn't actually perform the spin; Rock Steady's Richie "Crazy Legs" Colon, in wig and leotard, filled in for her. Still, it remains an undeniably inspiring moment, an example of a struggling and ambitious young woman achieving her dreams by following her unique passions. Even more important, it reinterpreted the dance as a working-class tool of career advancement, the very embodiment of the American dream.

By the time of *Flashdance*, breakdancing had already come far from the battle-riddled milieu of its creation. The mainstreaming began in 1981, when a front-page *Village Voice* article introduced b-boying to the world. *20/20* picked up the story, and soon dancers could be seen showing off their talents on every network. From *Ripley's Believe It Or Not!* to *The Merv Griffin Show*, breakdancing was pitched down the center lane of the most middle-of-the-road variety shows, lending the art form an eager-to-please, look-ma-no-hands quality that undercut the air of aggression that had defined it. Staged before a studio audience, broadcast to viewers nationwide, these performances by their very nature deemphasized the competitive aspects of street battling. For instance, under their manager, Michael Holman, the New York City Breakers, a b-boy supergroup culled from crews from around the city, presented polished programs instead of scrappy showdowns. "When I wanted to do shows, it wasn't going to be 'We'll just stand around and throw down,'" Holman says. "There wouldn't be battles. We would have group routines, breaking into single routines, back to groups, back to singles."

Watching *Flashdance* reminds me of the optimism and excitement that once surrounded breakdancing. Just as Jennifer Beals's character successfully breaks into the elite dance academy, so breakers began cropping up in even the fustiest bastions of high society. On January 21, 1984, the well-heeled dance patrons who attended the opening of the San Francisco Ballet's season received a surprise encore when forty-seven black and Latino b-boys took the stage to the strains of Michael Jackson's "Thriller." "My idea was to bring the street onto the stage," explained the codirector, Michael Smulin. That same month, Akiva Talmi, a classical ballet promoter, told *USA Today* that a nationwide breaking tour he was planning would "take it from the streets to Carnegie Hall." Burger King, Pepsi, and Panasonic all sponsored local breaking competitions or featured breakers in television advertisements. The Rock Steady Crew danced for Queen Elizabeth II during a European tour, and even recorded a rap song, "Hey You, the Rock Steady Crew," that climbed the European charts. Breaking, it seemed, had opened the doors of the American elite to a group of rough-necked outsiders who just months earlier were living in some of the poorest areas of the country. *Flashdance* may not have imitated life, but life seemed to be imitating *Flashdance*.

The stage was set for the breakdancing movies that stormed multiplexes during the summer of 1984. The film critic J. Hoberman has described the power of movies to express the nation's subconscious "dream life." "United before the same vision," he writes in his book *The Dream Life*, "enthralled by a common illusion, a populace might well believe itself to be a nation." Hoberman was writing of the films of the 1960s, but he might as well have been referring to *Beat Street* and *Breakin'*, the next movies on my list, which suggested b-boying as a pain-free way of solving the problems of poverty and racism.

These were particularly pressing concerns in the mid-1980s, as the federal government slashed the Lyndon Johnson–era Great Society benefits to the poor. Between 1979 and 1983, the percentage of Americans living below the poverty level jumped from 11.7 percent to 15.2 percent. Almost half of African Americans under the age of eighteen, 46.6 percent, lived below the poverty line in 1984. B-boying appeared to provide the only hint of optimism. Although breaking was not created or perfected with social mobility in mind, in the American imagination it was impossible to separate the dance from its social effects. For a country that was grappling with its moral responsibility to the less fortunate at the same time that it was cutting the government programs to aid them, breakdancing provided a feel-good narrative straight out of Horatio Alger, showing an America where it was still possible to transcend even the most hostile of upbringings through imagination, hard work, and creativity. The breaking boom seemed to offer a rejoinder to those who complained that budget cuts were threatening the future of inner-city minority youth: Let 'em dance.

That's not the message that Steven Hager hoped to convey when he wrote a screenplay entitled *The Perfect Beat*. Hager had covered hip-hop culture for the *Village Voice*, the New York *Daily*

News, and the *SoHo Weekly News*, and fashioned a warts-and-all look at the South Bronx that would force viewers to recognize the difficult lives from which hip-hop had been created. His script depicted a city filled with violent gangs and drug dealers, with characters that freebased cocaine and hung out with prostitutes and burst into flame.

It is hard to imagine how that screenplay turned into *Beat Street*, an upbeat tale about a group of artistic kids struggling—successfully, eventually—against a world that doesn't recognize their talents. Although tragedy visits the characters when one of them dies freakishly at the hands of a rival graffiti writer, the closest the film comes to a political statement occurs during the movie's final scene, when a rapper tells his audience that "the future of the world is in your hands." Harry Belafonte, whose production company bought Hager's screenplay, told the *Chicago Tribune* that he wanted to make a film that "can change the impressions people may have of the South Bronx. I would like people to understand that there is a humanity that exists there that is worth anything anyone would be willing to invest." It is hard to fault his ideals. And the film did strive toward authenticity, featuring performances from the Rock Steady Crew, New York City Breakers, Afrika Bambaataa, DJ Kool Herc, the Treacherous Three, and many other hip-hop icons. Still, Hager tells me, "Harry bought my script, then threw it out the window and replaced it with a limp and bogus story line signifying nothing." Their disagreement foreshadowed the arguments over representations of inner-city violence that would dominate the discussion of hip-hop for most of its life: whether black America was better served with positive images or "truthful" ones.

That *Beat Street* was received as 1984's serious breakdancing movie only goes to show how frivolous the competition was, and it is with foreboding that I turn to *Breakin'*, the third film in the triumverate, an even frothier vision of hip-hop that makes *Beat Street* look like *Boyz N the Hood*. *Breakin'* was rushed through production to beat *Beat Street* to the screen; for many American filmgoers, this was their first vision of hip-hop culture. Their unlikely guides to the ghetto: Menahem Golan and Yoram Globus, two Israeli cousins who ran a quickie movie mill called the Cannon Group.

Golan and Globus had purchased the faltering Cannon in 1979, and returned the company to profitability by producing pulpy flicks such as *Hercules* and *Sahara*, slapdash simulations of Hollywood fare that might bomb in the United States but played well in overseas markets. (Golan once referred to their domestic box office receipts as "gravy.") Eventually their ambitions extended beyond sending cheap knockoffs of American culture overseas; by 1983, they were peddling cheap knockoffs of overseas culture to Americans. In September of that year they released *Revenge of the Ninja,* in which a Japanese ninja faces off against the Mafia in Salt Lake City. The *New York Times* described the film as "a sadistic, bloody, foul-mouthed action movie" where "credibility is checked at the door."

Cannon's breakdancing movie, *Breakin'*, presents a similar mishmash of half-baked cultural cues and by-the-book plot devices. Most notably, *Breakin'* contains little actual breaking. The movie was filmed in Los Angeles, where South Bronx b-boying had begun to merge with the homegrown dances of "locking" and "popping," which combined smooth movement with quick, robotic flourishes. Although the street dances developed separately from b-boying, by the early 1980s East Coast breakers had begun to incorporate West Coast moves into their dance, and vice versa. The characters in *Breakin'* spend much more time popping and locking than they do breaking. But this was not the film's only innacuracy.

"I got the script and I was like, 'Ah, excuse me, we don't talk like this,'" says Timothy "Popin' Pete" Solomon, a member of a Fresno dance crew, the Electric Boogaloos, who appeared in the film. "'We don't talk like this, we don't dress like this, and we certainly don't dance to the music you guys are playing.'"

But verisimilitude was not the point. Produced and directed by Israelis, made for a mere $1.3 million, the film shoehorns the breaking craze into a traditional Hollywood story line. *Breakin'* focuses on Kelly, a struggling white dancer seeking a "whole new life." She finds one after befriending two friendly "street dancers"—one black, one Latino—and forming a dance trio with them. Despite her agent's initial protests that "street dancing belongs in the street" and the efforts of her spurned former teacher to discredit her, Kelly eventually wins over California's stuffy dance establishment with her new, exciting style. The film is a paean to social mobility, the heroes' quests to prove themselves standing in for the all-American urge to compete and succeed in the marketplace, and presents an idealized vision of the country as a place that inevitably rewards such efforts. *Breakin'* ends with the suggestion that filmgoers have participated in uplifting impoverished ghetto residents simply by watching a movie. The closing montage features a rap by a young Ice-T informing filmgoers that "for most city youth" hip-hop is "their only chance to gain recognition," and closing with instructions as to the best way to help young hip-hoppers' dreams come true: "Stop and watch." That equation of passive pop-culture consumption with social action would pervade white America's relationship with hip-hop for the next two decades.

Today, *Breakin'*'s flaws are easy to spot: the corny dialogue, awkward editing, and blatantly unconsummated romance between Kelly and Adolfo "Shabba-Doo" Quiñones, the film's Latino male lead. But none of this kept audiences away. *Breakin'* was the top-grossing film its opening weekend of May 4, and would take in more than $35 million during its box office run. (*Beat Street*, which lost the race to the big screen, took in a disappointing $12.5 million in its first three weeks.) Quiñones was hailed by *Dancemagazine* as "street dance's first matinee idol," an icon whose California home had become a mecca for struggling b-boys and poppers trying to catch a similar break. "Every morning all these street dancers congregate on my front lawn to show me their moves," Quiñones said. "It's like one big recital."

Meanwhile, America's love affair with breakdancing had spun out of the movie theaters and into the unlikeliest of neighborhoods. No longer content to just watch breakers perform, kids in even the whitest, most sheltered communities began mimicking the moves they were seeing on the big screen. *Newsweek* celebrated the dance's takeover of the country with a July 1984 cover story, "Breaking Out," declaring that breaking had "hit the heartland" and profiling aspiring young b-boys and b-girls in places like DeWitt, Michigan, and Houston. In Cleveland, a radio station canceled a breakdancing contest when a crowd of five thousand competitors showed up; the dispersed kids began literally dancing in the streets, clogging traffic for three hours.

In the South Bronx, b-boy maneuvers were learned through an apprenticeship system, but suburban kids without natural mentors could head to the bookstore and pick up, for instance, the best-selling *Breakdancing*, a how-to guide by Mr. Fresh and the Supreme Rockers. With the right book, kids could learn to mimic more than dance steps. William H. Watkins's *Breakdance!* reads like a Baedeker Guide to the South Bronx, instructing readers in how to talk, dress, and act like an authentic inner-city youth. Joking that "this is for your own protection," Watkins's "official breakdance dictionary" included such useful phrases as "Yeah, we need some fresh gear, word" (translation: "Yeah, we need some good performance clothes, that's a fact") and "We were chilling out, checking a def jam" ("We were just hanging around, listening to good music"). Sartorial "essentials" included baggy pants, gold nameplate necklaces, and "def" sunglasses. Aspiring dancers who required more personal instruction could sign up for the new breakdancing classes being offered at dance studios across the country. The aisles of newly built video-rental stores carried instructional videos such as *Let's Break* and K-Tel's *Break Dancing!*

As breaking gained steam, it came to be seen less of an expression of urban minority youth than as an established fact of teen life. A June 18 editorial cartoon in the *Detroit News* depicted two white girls seated in a Norman Rockwellian ice-cream parlor. "I know Scott is a creep," the caption read, "but he just happens to be the best break-dancer in the Livonia school system!" Louisiana's JPSO Hot Rock Express, a team of breakdancers sponsored by the local sheriff's department, entertained the elderly at Metaire Manor, an apartment complex. "I used to be a snob about music—I've studied with the Boston Symphony—but this is enjoyable," a fifty-year-old forensic-scientist-turned-aspiring-b-boy told the *Washington Post*. "It's like Bach." A group of white Detroit-area community college students formed the Cosmic Crew and performed breakdancing routines for children's birthdays and office Christmas parties. "It came originally from African Americans, but that didn't matter," Tim Danczuk, who danced with the Cosmic Crew under the name Trixx, says. "It was just a cool thing to do."

To be sure, breakdancing garnered its share of bourgeois disapproval. Shopkeepers in San Bernadino's Central City Mall proposed a ban on breaking after crowds of onlookers allegedly "intimidated and obstructed shoppers." A high school in Bound Brook, New Jersey, prohibited clothing associated with breakdancing, including untied shoelaces, from being worn in class. And the folksy columnist Bob Greene lamented the presence of breakdancing in the "affluent, upper-middle-class, white-as-Wonder-Bread suburban area" where he grew up.

Still, most of the tongue-clucking was of the those-darn-kids variety. Elvis Presley's debut thirty years earlier may have been met with the apocalyptic fury that greets the blackening of the culture, but breaking was just another youth fad, something that could be dismissed with a pat on the head and a roll of the eyes. "Frankly, I miss the old style of dancing," grumbled the columnist Lewis Grizzard. "There was even a time, all you young buckaroos might like to know, when people actually had partners when they danced." In the *Christian Science Monitor* an op-ed writer worried that her daughter would "go through her teenage years without knowing what it's like to have a boy ask her to dance." And the medical community warned of the dangers of engaging in newfangled contortions in papers with titles such as "Breakdancer's Pulmonary Embolism" and "Differential Diagnosis of Scrotal Pain After Break Dancing."

Breakdancing's newfound respectability befuddled some of its earlier acolytes. When Greg Selkoe, a rebellious Boston-area white kid who was attracted to hip-hop's "outsider edge," started breaking in 1983, he was kicked out of his private school for his aggressive b-boy behavior, including challenging his classmates to dance battles. But at his new school, in the upper-crusty suburb of Brookline, breaking was promoted as wholesome athletic fare; the school even paid a group of area dancers to teach the students some moves. And when he took his cardboard out to Main Street during family summers on Nantucket, Selkoe was no longer an exile. Not only could he pull in fifty dollars a night from appreciative audiences, but he attracted a group of like-minded white boys anxious to show off their steps. Still, they didn't always respond well to Selkoe's credibility-conscious challenges. "I had this whole mentality from when I'd started out," Selkoe says. "I'd do a freeze and grab my balls and the guys would be like, 'What the hell, dude? I don't want to battle you! I'm just trying to do the kick-worm here!'" Before long, Selkoe hung up his dancing shoes: "The fad kind of killed it for me."

After almost five hours of breakdancing movies, I feel a little woozy. If I were a completist, I'd keep going. I'd check out the slapdash *Breakin'* sequel, *Breakin' 2: Electric Boogaloo*, and *Body Rock*, which starred *Falcon Crest*'s Lorenzo Lamas as a breaker named Chilly. But to be honest, I don't have it in me. The breaking movies, with their cut-and-paste story arcs and relentlessly cheery messages, have grown predictable and tiresome. Apparently I'm not the only one who felt this way—both *Breakin' 2* and *Body Rock* quickly disappeared. By the fall of 1984, skeptics had begun to predict that the public's fascination with breakdancing had peaked. In September, *USA Today* quoted a retail-stock analyst who warned that "breakdancing will go away as quickly as it came in."

But not every breakdancing fan was prepared to give up on the dance. To see just how far breaking had come—and how much its meaning had changed—check out a copy of Ronald Reagan's second inaugural celebration, which was televised in January of 1985. The cummerbunded crowd filing into the Convention Center was clearly ready to celebrate, and it's hard to blame them; two months earlier, their candidate had been reelected president with a dominating 525 electoral votes, winning every state but Minnesota and the District of Columbia. The result was not a surprise: depending on who you asked, Reagan was known as the Great Communicator or the Teflon President, a man seemingly able to sell any policy or deflect any criticism with a wave of his hand and an aw-shucks chuckle.

But Reagan was not known for his avant-garde taste in popular culture, and the line-up of the fiftieth inaugural gala shows why. Although the emcee, Frank Sinatra, welcomed "fun seekers from either party" to what he jokingly called "Thriller number two," most of the evening's entertainment was closer in spirit to the corkscrew-haired moppet who belted out the national anthem: patriotic and toothless. Rich Little, an impressionist, delivered his trademark Catskills-on-the-Potomac Reagan routine (sample joke: "People ask me if I'm going to sell jets to Israel this year. I don't think so. What would they want with a bunch of football players?"). Tony Randall, Tom Selleck, and Robert Wagner all made appearances. Even taking into account the presence of Pearl Bailey, the television actor Emmanuel Lewis, and Mr. T—who recalled his previous exploits playing Santa Claus at the White House and asked, "Where else but America can a black man from the ghetto play a white man from the North Pole and get away with it?"—it's hard to imagine a whiter evening of entertainment.

Until, that is, about an hour into the performance, when folksy Hollywood icon Jimmy Stewart introduced the next act. "And now," he said, "to present the excitement of youth, the sights and the sounds of the big city, here are the New York City Breakers." The eight teenagers scrambled onto the stage to the opening strains of the In-credible Bongo Band's "Apache," wearing skin-tight white jump-suits and wide smiles. The crowd gasped and hooted as the dancers whirled and slid across the stage. Occasionally, the camera cut to the avuncular Reagan, grinning his approval of the wholesome display.

Reagan was about as un-hip-hop as a president could be. His vision of America favored the open range over the claustrophobic city, churchgoers instead of club hoppers, brush-clearing cowboys rather than mike-toting rappers. The idea of Reagan as a hip-hop fan seemed so ridiculous that the leftie wag Garry Trudeau wrote a comic musical, *Rap Master Ronnie*, around the premise.

And this is to say nothing of Reagan's policies toward those who did not fit into his vision of an America of Main Streets and town squares. During Reagan's first term, funding for food stamps and Aid to Families with Dependent Children was cut by 13 percent, spending for child nutrition was slashed by 28 percent, and spending on general employment and training programs was cut by 35 percent. The Congressional Budget Office found that Reagan's 1981 budget cuts alone pushed 560,000 people, including 325,000 children, below the poverty line. The black unemployment rate rose to 15.1 percent, double the rate for whites. The president dismissed the ghettos as "pockets of poverty [that] haven't caught up," and conservatives argued that the lingering effects of Great Society–era "patronizing socialism" were to blame for the disparities.

At the same time, Reagan helped the United States rediscover its feel-good self-image. During his first term, the country replaced a half-decade of self-doubt with overemphatic chest-beating, telling itself over and over again just how blessed and special it was. Beered-up sports fans at the 1980 winter Olympics chanted "U.S.A.! U.S.A.!" in bullying staccato as they cheered their athletic avatars on to victory. Sylvester Stallone donned John Rambo's bandanna and championed the unrecognized heroism of the Vietnam War. Extravagance and excess were the watchwords of style, as evidenced by the $25,000 dress that the new first lady wore to the opulent inaugural ball. Americans took a similarly barrel-chested approach to the economy, racking up record levels of spending but saving little. The same could be said of the federal government, which saw the deficit balloon to $208 billion in 1983. The *Washington Post* compared the lessons of the president's first term to those espoused in Norman Vincent Peale's classic best-selling book, *The Power of Positive Thinking*, characterized by the *Post* as "You can will your way out of trouble. If you feel good enough about yourself, in the current pop-psychological phrase, the real state of affairs hardly matters." Small wonder then that Reagan would so approve of the New York City Breakers' display, which seemed to prove—inner-city blight be damned—that it was still possible for even the poorest American to succeed through individual initiative. Breakdancing suggested that we could simply moonwalk across our racial divide, that solving our economic and social problems could be as easy as spinning on your back.

By Reagan's second inaugural gala, however, breakdancing was already well into its death spiral. Breakdancing's last hurrah took place in July of 1984, when the city of Los Angeles hosted the Summer Olympic Games. The event, a patriotic capstone to Ronald Reagan's feel-good first term, was designed to illustrate, as Peter Ueberroth, the event's organizer, put it, the American "spirit of can-do, can-work, can accomplish—you can do things without being on the government dole." As if to underscore this point, the opening ceremonies ended with the choreographed whirlings of two hundred breakdancers, America's demonstration to the world that it knew how to take care of its own. Just as the nation reinterpreted the dark lyrics of Bruce Springsteen's "Born in the U.S.A." as a jingoistic celebration of the homeland, it transformed breakdancing into America's official serenade of the free market.

That rosy glow followed most Americans into the voting booths in November, when they overwhelmingly reelected Reagan to his second term. The so-called fairness issue—concern over the impact that Reagan's policies had on the poor, emphasized by the Democrats to great effect during the 1982 midterm elections— proved less effective this time around, as voters internalized the message that individual initiative, and not government programs, held the keys to success in the United States. "A lot of people who are poor are poor through no fault of their own," one Reagan-supporting housewife from Mequon, Wisconsin, told the *Washington Post* just before the 1984 election. "But unfortunately, Mondale's going to give my money to everybody, whether they're down and out because they're lazy or because they're not."

Breakdancers' good fortunes would prove more short-lived than Reagan's. With the benefit of hindsight, it seems obvious that breakdancing was destined to be a short-lived fad, a craze that would enthrall white Americans for a summer or two before they moved on, leaving b-boys holding the cardboard. Once the thrill of emulation wore off—or, more commonly, once the promise of being able to move like a black person proved frustratingly difficult to achieve—there was little to sustain breakdancing as a cultural force. "It was like anything when you're a kid. It was popular and people just started doing it, and then it went away," says Matt Zimmerman, who spent one teenage summer in an all-white breaking group in working-class Philadelphia (he grew up to work in New York University's information-technology department). "And it wasn't like we were into hip-hop or black culture or anything after that. I never thought of it like that. It was really just this isolated thing." By the dawn of 1985, most breaking crews, suddenly unable to support themselves with paying gigs, had quickly and quietly disbanded. Some of the dancers who months earlier had performed before packed crowds and even on national television now found themselves without a source of income, and turned in desperation to drugs and crime, the very dangers that breaking had once helped them avoid. "They took breaking away from us," a dancer named Freeze from the L.A. Breakers has said. "Gang banging and drug dealing moved in."

At around the same time, a new vision of American blackness mugged its way into the nation's living rooms. *The Cosby Show* starred Bill Cosby as obstetrician Cliff Huxtable, Phylicia Ayers-Allen (later Rashad) as his lawyer wife, and four charming children as their well-behaved if occasionally exasperating brood. Departing from the national dialogue surrounding the black underclass, the Cosby clan inhabited a well-appointed Brooklyn brownstone. Previous black sitcom characters such as George Jefferson and Fred Sanford derived much of their putdown-based humor from "the dozens," an African American comic tradition that emphasized creative taunting. The Huxtables eschewed such archetypically "black" forms of comedy. Indeed, their blackness was barely acknowledged. "This new series is not about a black middle-class family," the *Christian Science Monitor* noted approvingly. "It concerns itself with a middle-class family of 'yuppies' who happen to be black."

Some complained that *The Cosby Show*'s vision of blackness painted an overly rosy view of race relations; the *Village Voice* argued that Bill Cosby "no longer qualifies as black enough to be an Uncle Tom." But others said that the program offered a much-needed glimpse into a growing demographic: in 1986, the percentage of black people earning more than $35,000 a year rose to 21.2 percent, up from 15.7 percent sixteen years before. Critics adored the show, viewers made it by far the most popular half hour on television, and William Raspberry, an African American columnist, hailed its efforts to help "white America understand that blackness isn't necessarily a pathological condition."

The Cosby Show lasted the rest of the decade, finally ending its run in 1992, and forever altered American conceptions of blackness. Yet even its legacy remained mixed: a 1992 University of Massachusetts study, financed by Bill Cosby himself, found that many whites pointed to the fictional Huxtables as evidence that programs such as affirmative action were no longer necessary to promote black achievement. One of the researchers, Justin Lewis, summed up the attitude of his white interviewees: "If blacks aren't making it, that's their fault. Look at all those other black families that are making it."

To see who is making it in the mid-2000s, take a look at New Canaan, Connecticut, a bedroom community on the edge of the New York border. It is the kind of neighborhood that prides itself on the number of activities it can offer its offspring as they go through the self-improvement regimen known as contemporary childhood. Perched near the top of *Money* magazine's "Best Places to Live" list—its inhabitants enjoyed the country's third-highest mean income in 2005, at more than $150,000—its kids can take riding lessons at New Canaan Mounted Troop, a thirteen-acre horse farm, join the local lacrosse league, or sign up for New Canaan High School's sailing squad, literary magazine, or paddle tennis club.

I have traveled deep into commuter country, seventy minutes and one transfer by Metro-North train from New York City, because twenty years after it disappeared from suburbs like this one, breakdancing has been making a comeback in New Canaan. At weddings and bar mitzvahs, the town's white kids have been taking to the floor, celebrating with backspins and kick-worms. "You go to sixteen parties and you see all the kids dancing on the floor," one New Canaanite mother tells me. "It's just a thing that these kids—ten, eleven, twelve years old—want to do."

Fortunately for the children of New Canaan, they have the opportunity to learn their moves from a real live b-boy. Once a week, Chellamar Bernard, the twenty-five-year-old son of Haitan immigrants, commutes from Brooklyn to teach breaking classes at the New Canaan Academy of Tap, founded in 2001. Elaine Young, the academy's founder, got the idea to introduce b-boy classes in 2004 when she decided that her male students might prefer a more muscular alternative to the ballet, jazz, tap, lyrical, and modern dance lessons she already offered, all of which are taught by women. "It's really something that the boys are interested in learning," Young says. "These guys are ready for a male role model."

At four P.M., as soon as the first students scramble through the studio's French doors, Bernard begins barking orders at them. "Let's take three laps!" he shouts, and the children run around the room in a loose circle. "Criss-cross! Reverse! Back to the center! Space yourselves out! Jumping jacks! Go! Stop! We can do this together, right?" Bernard is not smiling and neither are the kids, who stare at themselves in the wall-length mirror with thin-lipped grimaces of determination and exertion, eager to prove to Bernard that they can control their awkward young bodies. Bernard stands about six feet tall, has a wispy goatee and huge arms, and is the only black person in the room. He starts every class with twenty minutes of stretches and conditioning before teaching any steps. He ends by having the students make a circle and encouraging them to take turns improvising in the center, a re-creation of the classic "cipher," in which b-boys try to one-up one another with their moves. One by one the kids take their turn, jerkily testing their six-steps. As they finish, they look imploringly at Bernard, seeking some sign of approval, which he doles out in consistent but modest doses, like a tough but fair football coach.

Bernard has become an instantly popular figure to the boys of New Canaan, but it is impossible to know how much of his appeal can be attributed to the undeniably spectacular dance that he so excels at, how much to his mature charisma, how much to his position as male authority figure, and how much to ethnic novelty. "My son and I play tennis here every day from five to six, and one night we walked in and he saw Chellamar, and my son was like, 'Whoa, Mom!'" a woman in a white mock turtleneck tells Young, as she watches her son approvingly through the studio's French door. "I'm so glad you brought him out here. There's not much rhythm in New Canaan."

"The first time I met him, I expected someone—I don't know how to put this—maybe louder or more aggressive," Young tells me, her voice betraying an accent that comes from spending the first twenty years of her life in London. "But he has a gentle, calming side to him. He's not in your face. The first time I met him, I felt like I'd known him for years."

Like the dancers I visited in August in McCarren Park, Bernard has a tendency to speak of hip-hop as a metaphysical force, particularly when he reminisces about his experiences learning how to break as a student at LaGuardia High School, a well-known performing arts school in Manhattan. "We b-boyed on the streets of New York a few times, just randomly," he says. "We'd go into the train stations and see live musicians playing, and it would just hit us. We'd start performing with the musicians and the crowds would build. Afterwards, the musician would be like, 'Thanks,' and try to share the money with us, and we were like, 'No.' We didn't intend to do it. We didn't want to steal the spotlight. The energy was just right."

Bernard is trying to inculcate his students with an understanding of breaking that goes beyond dance moves. Once a month he offers his students a history lesson instead of dance instruction, part of his attempt to lure his students into a greater understanding of hip-hop culture, and of the pressures and anxieties that helped to create and sustain it. Two weeks ago they watched *The Freshest Kids*, a 2002 documentary that is generally regarded by b-boys as the most accurate attempt to disentangle breaking's complicated history. "The intensity of b-boying and the intensity of our situation in the ghetto, all that piled into one," Pop Master Fabel, a dancer with the Rock Steady Crew, says during the film. "It's a lot deeper than, 'Well, this is fun.'"

But fun, of course, is exactly what these students are after. It is what their parents hope the kids are having when they are dropped off here every week. Fun is what shows on the kids' beaming faces as they run out of class, eager to show off their new moves. Fun is what provides the connection between these students' New Canaan and Bernard's Brooklyn. If breakdancing were not fun,

Bernard would not be here. This is the challenge that Bernard faces. If breakdancing's history tells us nothing else, it is that fun can create cross-cultural linkages, but whether or not those linkages can then be used to transmit anything more meaningful, more difficult, more challenging, less *fun* . . . that's another question.

And so Bernard does not tell his students everything. He does not tell them, for instance, why he's favoring his right side, even though he is left-handed. Three months ago, he tells me, three off-duty police officers surrounded him outside his father's house in Queens, announced that he fit the description of a crime suspect, and proceeded to tackle and beat him up. Bernard ended up with a shattered shoulder and a three-evening prison stint for resisting arrest. He has a scar on his shoulder where doctors performed arthroscopic surgery.

Bernard harbors no illusions. On the train ride back to Brooklyn, he says that he can't imagine even his most dedicated students will ever trek into New York to test their skills against city-bred b-boys. "In no way, shape, or form am I in New Canaan trying to breed the world's next great breaking crew," he says. But he hopes that his lessons can begin to expose his students to a world outside their own, give them hints of a life that they will never experience for themselves, show them that for some kids b-boying is more than just another entry in a roster of after-school activities, something to fill the slot between basketball practice and Greek lessons. But he has to do it in a way that will not make them uncomfortable. "What I'm doing is still safe here," he tells me. "It's not in the streets. They don't understand that kind of atmosphere. I have to make it so that Mommy's happy and they're happy. It's still safe for them."

It is a compromise, Bernard says, that he has learned to live with. "That's what it is to be a teacher, to switch it up for your students, to take the material and find a way to get it across to them.

What I've really seen in Brooklyn, what I've really seen in Harlem, what I've really seen in the Bronx and Boston, that's not going to come out, because I've trained myself to understand that you have to know what language you're speaking." Just then, the train conductor walks by to collect our tickets. Bernard hands his over, and settles into his seat for the long trip back home at the end of the night.

CHAPTER FOUR

Crossover: Hip-Pop Hits the Airwaves

—Where is succor?
—In the new music.

—Donald Barthelme, "The New Music"

It's a cloudy mid-September day, and I am depressed. I'm driving through downtown Green Bay, Wisconsin, a small collection of municipal office buildings and dreary mom-and-pop shops, and even on a Tuesday morning the streets are deserted. It rained last night, and a few stray drops still cling to my windshield. The morning haze is only beginning to lift; there is a muggy, heavy quality to the air that fills the city with a lazy silence. I drive slowly past near-empty businesses: the Centerfold Lounge Gentleman's Club and Ralph's Antiques and Smitty's Automart and Coaches Corner Club and Grill, bearing a billboard that advertises its $3.99 pig roast. If I had to pick a soundtrack to match this scenery, I'd probably choose a lonely, mournful cello solo.

So it's jarring to tune the radio to WLYD, better known as Wild 99.7, and find myself lambasted by the kind of music that sounds like it's being pumped out of a packed South Beach nightclub. Wild 99.7 is Green Bay's hip-hop station, and its offerings are relentlessly up-tempo, a nonstop adrenaline rush of stuttering drums and explosive synthesizer stabs that blur the line between music and sound effect. Over this backdrop, a series of black voices provide a stream of exhortation, heavy breathing, and braggadocio. The rapper mogul Jermaine Dupri pleads for a stripper's attention; Houston's Slim Thug informs me that his necklace costs more than my house; and Ebony Eyez offers what seems a reasonable exchange of services: If she allows me to bend her over, can she stick her ass in my face?

This is not a familiar question for most Green Bay residents, who tend to be more comfortable with queries like "Would you like your chili served over rice or noodles?" or "How 'bout them Packers?" Particularly the latter: Green Bay's football team provides the city with not only two nicknames ("Titletown" and "Packerville") but also pretty much its entire identity. The blue-collar, tradition-soaked team—the country's third oldest, initially owned by a meatpacking facility—exemplifies Green Bay's deadpan humility and get-'er-done ruggedness. It is the perfect icon for this town of paper mills and Catholic churches, where people tend to think you're showing off if you drive a BMW. "Time passes you by here," a twenty-year-old real estate agent told me. "A lot of people are very opposed to change."

Nevertheless, Green Bay is changing, as several residents are quick to tell me. For instance, in 1990 the city had only 453 black residents. In 2000 there were about 1,400. But this fact has not exactly turned Green Bay, population 101,000, into a melting pot; it remains almost 86 percent white, 11 percentage points higher than the United States as a whole, and only 1.4 percent black, more than 10 points lower than the rest of the country.

So when WLYD began playing hip-hop instead of soft rock in 2002, its listeners were incredulous. Many thought the move was a joke or a stunt to draw attention to the station before it switched formats again. "For this community, it was kind of a blow," says Jason

OTHER PEOPLE'S PROPERTY

Hillery, who served as WLYD's program director for three years. "Like, 'Wow, I can't believe that this music is actually here.' "

I can understand that shock. I remember, when I was in high school in the early 1990s, switching on my car radio to find that the local pop station had changed formats and now played hip-hop and R&B. The disc jockeys began peppering their patter with flashes of Ebonics, like "word" and "a'ight." Pop-rap groups such as Marky Mark and the Funky Bunch and MC Hammer soon provided the soundtrack for my drives around the city, exhorting me to "feel it, feel it!" and warning me that I "can't touch this," pumping me up as I headed to the bowling alley or my after-school job at the bookstore. It was as if someone had turned a dial a few degrees while I slept, subtly making the entire city and culture of Tacoma just a little bit blacker. For better or worse, that's probably how the citizens of Green Bay feel. Or the citizens of Springfield, Missouri, or Colorado Springs, Colorado, or both Portlands (Maine and Oregon)—all melanin-challenged locales that today host their own hip-hop stations.

The same could be said of the country as a whole. Although hip-hop songs have occasionally popped up on radio playlists since the mid-1980s, they have grown to dominate the Top 40; in 2005, the hip-hop acts 50 Cent, Black Eyed Peas, Bow Wow, The Game, Kanye West, Lil Jon, Missy Elliott, and Will Smith contributed thirteen of the country's thirty most-played songs. This takeover of the *Billboard* charts would have been unthinkable during hip-hop's early years, when the music was, with few exceptions, avoided by radio programmers of all stripes, who viewed it as a passing fad or, worse, an openly hostile social trend. "Radio stayed away from hip-hop for a very, very long time," says Raphael George, who compiles the hip-hop and R&B charts for *Billboard*. "In its early stages, hip-hop was seen as revolutionary, anti-establishment, countercultural."

It was also seen as black, which did not help matters any. Although music by black artists had been a staple of pop music stations since the 1960s, by the mid-1980s, the music industry was in the middle of a racial retrenchment. A 1987 piece in the *New York Times* announced that the industry "proceeds as if music by and for blacks is alien to the tastes of the nonblack majority." (The article also quoted a study by the NAACP which found that "no other industry in America so openly classifies its operations on a racial basis.") The pop charts, so recently integrated, became the domain of mostly white artists and audiences; black artists, even established ones such as Luther Vandross and the Gap Band, had a hard time getting heard on radio stations not specifically targeted to black audiences.

Now black music is once again the soundtrack to pop America, a fact that seems to reflect not just our musical tastes but a change in the way we think of ourselves as a country. In his classic collection of essays, *Mystery Train*, Greil Marcus wrote about the ambition of the pop musician: "[A]t its best it is an impulse to wholeness, an attempt not to deny diversity, or to hide from it, but to discover what it is that diverse people can authentically share. It is a desire of the artist to remake America on his or her own terms." It is that promise of a remade America—a new America, a hip-hop America, a *black* America—that so energizes the celebrations of hip-hop's pop success. "The explosion of rap music scared the hell out of complacent radio producers and the public at large," says Quincy McCoy, a former disc jockey and author of *No Static*, a guide for radio programmers. "Now it's become an essential part of the mainstream. It's great. I never thought it would happen."

"You can call hip-hop 'ethnic music,'" says Dusty Hayes, the program director for KXBT, a hip-hop station in Austin. "That's not true. It is the Top Forty music of today." This promise of a redefined America may be what so terrifies hip-hop's enemies. Beneath the shocked claims of trampled morality (for instance, Dan Quayle's position that Tupac Shakur's *2pacalypse Now* "has no place in our society") it is hard not to hear something else: the fear of a black planet, or at the very least a blacker nation.

The optimistic read of hip-hop's pop dominance holds that a pure, undeniable shot of ghetto authenticity has penetrated the heart of the mainstream. In his 2001 autobiography, *Life and Def*, Russell Simmons shared his crossover strategy: "If you never com promise, your core audience will come with you as you grow. Then you build on their loyalty and bring in other people. That's how a great band becomes a hugely popular one . . . You have to know your core and noncore audiences and understand how to reach both without alienating either."

But not everyone is thrilled with hip-hop's transformation from pop-radio pariah to Top 40 staple. In the late 1980s and early 1990s, hip-hop purists charged pop phenomena such as Tone-Loc and Kris Kross with peddling pale imitations of a less compromising musical form, homogenizing rap to make it more appealing to a broad audience. Rappers themselves have often drawn distinctions between "real" and "pop" hip-hop, implying that acts that find a spot on Top 40 radio have compromised their art—and, in some cases, their black identities—to reach mainstream listeners. In 1989, KRS-One distinguished between "commercial pap" and "that raw ghetto sound." Even some of rap's most beloved pop artists have balked at their own success. De La Soul's debut LP, 1989's *3 Feet High and Rising*, sampled the Turtles, contained lyrics that herald the coming of the "D.A.I.S.Y. age"—an acronym for "Da Inner Sound, Y'All"—and seemed to presage a hippie–hip-hop nexus. But the group's follow-up, the self-loathing *De La Soul Is Dead*, depicted a smashed pot of daisies on the cover and darker lyrics (for instance, "can't stand the pop music"). They named their third album, 1993's *Buhloone Mind State*, after their governing philosophy: the group may "blow up" (become successful), but it would never water down its songs or image in an attempt to "go pop." Ice Cube put it more succinctly in his 1990 song "Turn Off the Radio": "Fuck Top Forty."

At the core of these complaints is the fear that authentic, individual voices are automatically threatened by the homogenizing specter of pop radio, a fear that is almost as old, and as ingrained, as pop culture itself. Perhaps no one put it better than Theodor Adorno, the German-born philosopher whose best-known works assailed what he termed "the culture industry." In his 1941 essay "On Popular Music," Adorno argued that the "fundamental characteristic of popular music" was "standardization," and deemed the very idea of mass entertainment "wholly antagonistic to the ideal of individuality in a free, liberal society." In 1947's *Dialectic of Enlightenment*, he and his coauthor, Max Horkheimer, warned that mass culture always promoted "obedience to the social hierarchy," offering not true enlightenment or change, but only "mass deception." (This critique will sound familiar to fans of Elvis Costello, who once musically excoriated the "lot of fools" who program radio stations for trying to "anaesthetize the way that you feel.")

So which is it? Is hip-hop changing pop radio, or is pop radio changing hip-hop? I have come to Green Bay to see how pop radio's twin roles—top-down standardization machine and bottom-up country-redefining Trojan horse—meet and hash out an uneasy compromise. Pop radio weighs our transgressive fantasies against our plodding realities, and provides a unique snapshot of our national character. It tells us just who, and in this case how black, we allow ourselves to be.

I spent more hours of my youth than I would care to admit watching reruns of the sitcom *WKRP in Cincinatti*, and if I learned nothing else in that time (and I surely did not), I discovered that radio is a free-wheeling, iconoclastic business, full of incorrigible free spirits with outsized personalities who play whatever they hell they want while their egghead station managers stammer nervously in the background. This impression was only reinforced when I first learned about pop radio's real rebel icons: The fifties' Alan "Moondog" Freed, the doomed visionary who coined the term "rock and roll" and helped turn black soul music into a generation-defining cultural force; and the sixties' and seventies' Bobby "Wolfman Jack" Smith, the mad genius who broadcast his rock-infused samizdat from a pirate station across the Mexican border, tempting his audience with the forbidden allure of black sexuality. That tradition of insolence continues to dominate the public face of radio, from Howard Stern's FCC baiting to the envelope-pushing banter of morning "zoo crews."

But the behind-the-scenes reality is that—surprise!—radio is a cold, heartless business dominated by number crunchers, paid consultants, and market researchers. Rival stations, desperate to protect themselves from competitors, lash out against one another in bizarre and brutal ways: poaching one another's talent; referring to their competitors on the air as "coke-sniffing DJs"; or threatening to sexually abuse their children. Station managers, afraid of losing a sliver of listenership or advertising sales by appearing either too timid or too adventurous, seek experts and data to confirm their music and marketing decisions. The situation has grown so bad that even the National Association of Broadcasters–sponsored textbook *Radio: The Book* complains that "too often, research plays 100% of the role in decision making."

And so it turns out that hip-hop invaded Green Bay's airwaves not simply because some rap-music fan thought it was a good idea, but as a strategy perpetrated by Midwest Communications, Inc., the company that owns WLYD, in order to protect its flagship station, WIXX. WIXX is known as a "heritage Top 40," which means it is a long-established station. In 2001, a rival began siphoning away younger listeners by adding more hip-hop music to its playlist. So executives at Midwest Communications decided to launch WLYD, previously an underperforming "adult contemporary," as a rap station, thereby winning over most of the hip-hop fans from the rival Top 40 station and destroying its ratings. The dominance of WIXX was sealed.

"It totally took the hipness out of the other radio station," Jeff McCarthy, Midwest Communications' vice president, tells me. "They never reacted, and as a result they disappeared. We took them down."

In addition to WLYD and WIXX, Midwest Communications, Inc., owns a country, a sports-talk, and a news station, whose studios are all arranged along a long hallway in an office building that looks and feels like a junior high school. WLYD's studio, the tiniest of all, is tucked into a corner at the very end of the hall. I'm a bit astonished to see it. The last time I stepped into a radio studio was in 1995, when I hosted a late-night jazz program on my college station. I remember the gig as one of near-constant frenzy, of scrambling to cue up CDs and records and cartridges and forgetting to repeat the call letters every fifteen minutes and not realizing that I was playing John Coltrane's "A Love Supreme" at the wrong speed. By contrast, the WLYD studio is as serene as a dojo. Gone are all those befuddling switches and dials and DATs and cartridges. Gone, for that matter, are all the records and CDs. Instead, a lone computer hulks HAL-like in the corner, silently and automatically running through the day's song list, which WLYD staffers entered in last night. There is a live human being here, Randy "Haze" Jones, but he is not hustling around the studio cueing up the next record; he's calmly surfing the Internet and managing his fantasy football team.

Jones had no idea about Midwest Communications' corporate strategy when he turned on WLYD in 2002; he just couldn't believe that he was hearing hip-hop in Green Bay. As a senior in high school, Jones, a gregarious African American with a do-rag and wide grin, moved to Green Bay from Compton—the Los Angeles neighborhood infamous for birthing N.W.A., Compton's Most Wanted, and a slew of other gangsta rap groups—to live with his uncle and stay out of trouble. "Somebody came running to me saying, 'Oh my god, turn on the radio! There's hip-hop on the radio!' And I'm like, 'Yeah, right. I haven't heard hip-hop here since I left L.A.' I was really surprised. Everybody was talking about it." Two weeks later, he grabbed a friend and applied for a job as a late-night disc jockey.

That friend was Devon "D-Dawg" Ashmann, a chubby blond white kid from the nearby farming community of Seymour. Ashmann is another hip-hop true believer who grew up listening to rap's raw beats. "There's nothing but farms and cows there," Ashmann tells me. "Hip-hop really stuck out." The two got a late-night slot, hosting a program together under the name "Deez Nuts." Now, Ashmann is a morning-drive cohost. Jones serves as assistant program director. He is one of WLYD's two black employees, referred to by his coworkers as "the icon of hip-hop in this city."

Yet even Jones has a hard time programming a station that retains hip-hop's spirit while appealing to Green Bay's conservative tastes. "You've got to cater to both the Top Forty side and the hip-hop side, and that's the problem I think we've been having," Jones says. "Our ratings go up and down, because we don't know exactly how much to give them. Should we give them crunk, or should we go the pop route? We don't want to become WIXX, but we don't want to drive people away."

Those are the kinds of challenges that WLYD's staff has had to face since the station began, and the brunt of that responsibility rests with Nate Mitchell, the station's program manager. Mitchell is a skinny, friendly white guy in his midthirties with a blond mustache, wood-bead necklace, and a huge reservoir of nervous energy, most of which is focused on his attempts to create a hip-hop station that Green Bay will accept, which he calls "one of the most difficult things I've ever had to do." Fortunately, he tells me, he has a strategy: "We're trying to take the 'ghetto' out of it." This means that he steers clear of playing too much music that projects any aura of inner-city danger or forbidding blackness. This is also why his on-air talent doesn't refer to the music it plays as hip-hop, preferring terms such as "Green Bay's party station" that don't carry the same racial connotations. Even the station's catchphrase—"your station, your music"—sounds like a straightforward appeal: Hey, it's okay, white people. Don't be scared. This music belongs to you.

It would be hard to imagine a less intimidating person to deliver that message than Amy Alexander. She is rail-thin, her hair is as bright yellow as the sun would be if it weren't behind a thick layer of cloud cover, and her eyes are the kind of piercing blue that people try to replicate with colored contact lenses. She has a NASCAR tattoo on her left shoulderblade (which she sort of regrets) and a pronounced midwestern accent. She does not particularly like hip-hop music. But four months ago, Mitchell hired her to cohost WLYD's morning show, which is now called "The Wild Wake-Up Show with D-Dawg and Amy Alexander."

"My Ebonics are not all up to snuff," Alexander admits. "I don't consider myself hip-hop. But I'm here to represent the people that like the music but don't necessarily have hip-hop in them."

Hip-hop is the first form of black music that has relied on people who look like Amy Alexander to get played on the radio. Up until the late 1970s, black musicians proved their mettle on black-appeal stations before "crossing over" to pop stations—a tactic that soon became an entrenched record-company strategy. Motown's founder, Berry Gordy, who determined that 70 percent of a record's sales had to come from white listeners in order for it to be a hit, depended on the support of black disc jockeys and programmers to build an audience before he attempted to tackle the pop charts. In 1971, an in-house study conducted by CBS Records found that 30 percent of the Top 40 consisted of songs that had crossed over from soul stations, and concluded that successfully getting music played on a black station "is perhaps the most effective way of getting a record to a Top 40 playlist."

That was before disco. I don't particularly like disco, but I can't imagine hating it as much as so many Americans did in the late 1970s: 50,000 White Sox fans once filled Chicago's Comiskey Park for a "Disco Demolition Night" promotion, during which a pile of records was destroyed in the infield; the crowd was so infused with bloodlust that it erupted into a riot and the second game of the scheduled double-header had to be canceled. The antidisco agitators may have objected to the music genre's ad nauseum dominance of popular culture, but radio programmers interpreted the "disco sucks" movement to mean that white Americans no longer wanted to listen to any R&B-tinged music. "The disco backlash didn't necessarily hit a lot of disco," says Sean Ross, a vice president of music and programming for Edison Media Research, a firm that conducts research for radio stations. "It kept the majority of black music off Top Forty in a big way for the next couple of years."

All of which helps explain why, with a few exceptions, black-appeal radio stations—the same ones that helped introduce jazz, rock, and soul to the nation—largely shunned hip-hop when it was created in the late 1970s and early 1980s, fearing the music would prove to be just another fad, like disco. "We resisted it," says Donnie Simpson, a nationally renowned morning host at WPGC in Washington, D.C., and a former host of BET's *Video Soul*. "I remember thinking, 'This is something that will last nine months.'"

An even bigger concern was that black stations, dependent on the middle-aged, middle-class black audience most likely to attract advertisers, would alienate their target demographic if they played too much hip-hop. "It's just difficult for listeners over twenty-five to accept [rap] in a large dose," a programming director at WGCI, a leading black station, told *Billboard*. "If I play two rap records in a row, they're gone. I'm not going after twelve-plus, I'm going after twenty-five to thirty-four, and with that in mind, I just can't play more rap."

Bill Stephney, the former president of Def Jam who started out in the label's promotions department in the mid-1980s, saw more than economic pressures at play. "The stations that were completely vehement [in their refusal to play hip-hop] were the black-owned black-music stations. There's a station down in Louisiana. I talked to the owner, who was a black man. He was the first guy to coin the phrase 'jungle music,'" says Stephney. "It's because of what the music represented to that particular generation, the post–civil rights, *Jeffersons*, moving-on-up generation. We were so segregated by fact and by law that anything that didn't present black people in what they felt was the best light was categorically rejected. And hip-hop probably wound up at the top of that list."

The rapper Ice-T rephrased this argument more starkly in 1988, at the twelfth annual Black Radio Exclusive conference: "The bourgeois people in black radio don't want to be black."

With the traditional avenues of advancement shut off to them, hip-hop artists and labels began focusing on a different target. Since they couldn't depend on black radio audiences to prove their music's commercial appeal, label heads began to target pop stations directly. Top 40 stations may have been wary to play controversial black music, but they didn't carry the economic or social baggage of their black-radio counterparts. Their relationships with their advertisers were more stable, and they had no specific ax to grind with the younger generation of black musicians. It was just a matter of finding the right song, one that could appeal to rock audiences as much as it did rap audiences. "Historically, black artists go to R&B stations, and white artists go to rock stations," Stephney says. "Hip-hop changed that dynamic."

But it didn't do so quickly or easily. It wasn't until 1986 that Stephney oversaw the release of the song that would launch hip-hop's crossover campaign, "Walk This Way," a duet between Run-DMC and Aerosmith. Almost since its first album in 1984, Run-DMC—the duo, based in Hollis, Queens, of Joseph "Run" Simmons and Darryl "DMC" McDaniels, backed by DJ Jason "Jam Master Jay" Mizell—won accolades from rap fans for their stripped-down, booming sound, a stark contrast to the disco-based tracks that had remained hip-hop's stock in trade (and that Run-DMC casually dismissed as "old school"). They had also consistently dabbled in the intersection of rock and rap. Their 1984 song "Rock Box" featured an honest-to-goodness heavy-metal guitar solo. The following year, the *King of Rock* album included song titles such as "Can You Rock It like This" and "Rock the House" and lyrics that compared the group to the Beatles.

But "Walk This Way," an update of Aerosmith's 1975 metal rave-up, went further. Run-DMC had casually rapped over the guitar riff from Aerosmith's song for years, but it was Rick Rubin, a white, Long Island–bred rock fan who cofounded Def Jam and produced Run-DMC's *Raising Hell*, who convinced them to record a complete remake. Apart from the black voices and amplified beat, there is little to distinguish Run-DMC's 1986 version from Aerosmith's original. The lyrics are decidedly un-hip-hop, probably because they were written by two white guys from Boston, Aerosmith's Steve Tyler and Joe Perry. (The song's story line is unclear, but its motifs—postprom virginity shedding; horny cheerleaders; "sleazy" schoolgirls—come straight from the heavy-metal school of bad-boy wish fulfillment.)

The song was the perfect vehicle to sneak rap on to pop-radio playlists. Top 40 disc jockeys, always aware of their white listeners' fickle dial-twirling digits, credited the song to "Aerosmith, featuring Run-DMC." The *Los Angeles Times* praised the fact that the song "aimed more at disarming listeners than challenging them." Indeed, white audiences seemed even more comfortable with the song than black ones: "Walk This Way" spent fifteen weeks on Billboard's Top 100, topping out at number four. It only reached number eight on the R&B charts.

"At least in Detroit, I don't recall that record being played in the black community as much," says Jay Dixon, who worked at that city's WJLB when "Walk This Way" was released, and who now serves as an in-house consultant for Cox Radio. "We knew it was Run-DMC, and we respected it. We didn't think they were selling out. But from a real 'street' perspective, that wasn't our core music."

Apparently, Run-DMC didn't think so either. "Walk This Way" has become such an iconic statement of rap-rock alliance that it comes as a surprise to read, in Ronin Ro's biography, *Raising Hell*, that the group itself despised the song, and that the seemingly mutual admiration between Run-DMC and Aerosmith was a grand illusion. According to Ro, Run-DMC hated the very idea of remaking "Walk This Way." They cried as they transcribed the lyrics, which they considered "hillbilly bullshit." They worried that Rubin was taking "that rap-rock shit too far" and was "trying to ruin us." They felt that they were selling out and that their black audience would never forgive them. And they resented and despised the members of Aerosmith.

But all of that animosity would remain backstage; to its audience, "Walk This Way" welcomed in a new era of explicitly white-friendly hip-hop. The stage was set for the Beastie Boys, who not only rapped about topics that middle-class white kids could understand, or rapped over samples that middle-class white kids could recognize, including Led Zeppelin's "When the Levee Breaks," War's "Low Rider," and the theme song to *Mr. Ed*, but were in fact (upper-)middle-class white kids themselves. Michael "Mike D" Diamond, Adam "Ad-Rock" Horovitz, and Adam "MCA" Yauch grew up as snot-nosed New York kids, the sons of prominent art dealers, the playwright Israel Horovitz, and an architect, respectively. Like so many New Yorkers in the early 1980s, they arrived at rap through punk rock. The group was initially formed as a punk band, a ragtag combo that specialized in sloppy emulations of their hardcore heroes: Black Flag, Bad Brains, Minor Threat. They got turned on to hip-hop when the first wave of MCs began trickling into the punk-rock venues of downtown Manhattan and were eventually inspired to record their own rap track: "Cooky Puss," a prank phone call to a Carvel ice cream store set to a beat. The song won them some airplay on college radio stations, and before long they hooked up with Rick Rubin. In 1984 they released their first single, "Rock Hard," making them Def Jam's first white act.

The Beasties so blurred the line between rock and rap that it became impossible to tell the difference. The group's first major unveiling occurred when they opened for Madonna during her 1985 "Virgin Tour" and their modus operandi—hotel-room trashing, beer chucking, audience provoking, woman taunting—seemed pulled from the pages of the Led Zeppelin biography *Hammer of the Gods*. A television ad referred to the Beastie Boys' music as "American rock 'n' roll," *Newsweek* hailed the group as "one of rock's hottest new acts," and radio listeners who heard their first, and most successful, pop single, "Fight for Your Right" could be forgiven for thinking that the Beastie Boys weren't a rap group at all, but a bunch of particularly atonal metalheads. Over a slashing guitar, the three MCs chanted lyrics that spoke directly to the concerns of rebellious suburban teenagers, railing against parents who forbade pornographic magazines, smoking, and long hair. The song spent eighteen weeks on the Hot 100, and would help their debut LP, *Licensed to Ill*, become the first rap album to hit number one on the *Billboard* pop charts and the first to sell more than 5 million copies.

Not that the Beastie Boys weren't popular among rap's core audience. Coming so early in hip-hop's development, the group avoided much of the suspicion and animosity that later white rappers would face. As Def Jam artists, the group was associated with hip-hop royalty such as Rick Rubin, Russell Simmons, LL Cool J, and Run-DMC. And rappers such as Chuck D appreciated that the Beastie Boys were honest about their background and interests: "[A]s long as they talked about white boys and beer and stuff like that, who could knock their topics?" he later told a reporter. The Beastie Boys also proved their mettle by performing regularly in front of black audiences: opening for Kurtis Blow, rapping at the Bronx nightclub Disco Fever, and touring with Run-DMC, LL Cool J, and Whodini. *Licensed to Ill* reached number two on the "urban" charts (a euphemistic reference to what was once called the "black" charts), although hip-hop audiences tended to gravitate to different songs than the ones on pop radio. "Hold It Now, Hit It" reached number fifty-five on the urban charts but never made the *Billboard* Hot 100. Meanwhile, "Fight for Your Right" and "Brass Monkey," the two singles that did crack the Hot 100, never made it onto the urban charts.

But despite their hip-hop credentials and their popularity with both black and white audiences, the Beastie Boys were quickly defined by the bratty rock stance of "Fight for Your Right." The group itself would denounce the Rick Rubin–produced song, particularly its "big rock drums" and its "real Top Forty cheesy rock sound," and would later distance itself from its rowdy frat-boy image. Nevertheless, "Fight for Your Right" remains the Beastie

Boys' most famous song, and it helped turn *Licensed to Ill* into one of the best-selling hip-hop albums of all time; twenty years later, it still sells well over 100,000 copies a year, according to Nielsen SoundScan.

"Walk This Way" and "Fight for Your Right" were so successful that they unleashed a string of rap-rock hybrid followers. The Fat Boys released "Wipeout," a joint effort with the Beach Boys, and rap updates of Chubby Checker's "The Twist" and the Kingsmen's "Louie Louie"; all three landed in the *Billboard* Hot 100. Tone-Loc's "Wild Thing," which sampled Van Halen's "Jamie's Cryin'," spent twenty-five weeks on the pop charts, topping out at number two. DJ Jazzy Jeff & the Fresh Prince, two middle-class kids from Philadelphia, explained the come-one-come-all appeal of their music: "You don't have to be from a certain background or age or color or place to understand my music," Will "Fresh Prince" Smith, then nineteen, told the *New York Times* after his *He's the DJ, I'm the Rapper* sold more than 1.3 million copies.

The implication of Smith's statement, that hip-hop acted as a multiethnic, melting-pot bridge builder, is belied by its subtextual counterpoint: you *did* have to be from a "certain background" to appreciate some of hip-hop's rougher offerings. And if you only listened to pop radio in the 1980s, you would never have heard some of rap's most beloved, respected, and important musicians, including Eric B and Rakim, Boogie Down Productions, Public Enemy, Schoolly D, Too $hort, Big Daddy Kane, N.W.A., Ultramagnetic MCs, Jungle Brothers, Kool G Rap, EPMD, Queen Latifah, and Geto Boys—none of whom had a song on the *Billboard* Hot 100 during that decade.

About eighteen months before my trip to Green Bay, in March 2004, presidential candidate John Kerry, speaking at an MTV forum, described hip-hop as "important," adding, "There's a lot of anger. A lot of social energy in it. . . . It's a reflection of the street and it's a reflection of life."

It's probably safe to say that Senator Kerry wasn't listening to WLYD, because if he had been he wouldn't have heard much anger or social energy, to say nothing of the stereotypical rap topics of guns, gangs, and drugs. Instead, the songs on WLYD's playlist tend to emphasize a topic familiar to pop-music listeners of all ages: sex. A typical hour of programming features "Badd" by the Ying Yang Twins, in which the group analyzes the merits of a stripper's performance, and "Your Body" by Pretty Ricky, whose musical seduction includes an offer to give listeners "a taste of the salami." WLYD's playlist also includes "Outta Control," a joint venture between 50 Cent and Mobb Deep. Mobb Deep, a pair of MCs from New York's Queensbridge housing projects, has made albums since 1995 and has earned a cult following for its unrelentingly grim soundscapes and depressingly violent lyrics. But "Outta Control" depicts the two rappers trolling the floor of a dance club "like a scene from soft porn," and looking for women to impregnate. As of September 2005 the song sits at number five on *Billboard*'s rap charts.

This sort of thing frustrates Randy Jones, WLYD's Compton-bred assistant program director. "There is some real serious hip-hop out there, but all people see is the pop stuff, the bubblegum," he says. "Stuff like Nas or Common or Talib Kweli"—rappers who are known for their political lyrics—"we can't play that. They're speaking a message, and people don't want to hear that. They want to go about their everyday lives and hear about dancing and going to a club and having a little fun. If people want to hear a message, they'll turn on the news."

Even some of the most popular hip-hop artists won't find their more political statements broadcast over WLYD's airwaves. Kanye West's "Gold Digger," about a money-grubbing female, lands itself in heavy rotation, but if Green Bay listeners want to hear his "Crack Music," in which he accuses Ronald Reagan of putting an end to the Black Panthers, they'll have to buy his album. In the weeks after Hurricane Katrina, West caused a stir when he adlibbed during a live televised fundraiser that "George Bush doesn't care about black people." But WLYD's listeners won't hear that speech. Instead, Ben LuMaye, the station's imaging director, has put together a short promotional segment called a "sweep" that features West's stirring words when he accepted a recent award: "Right now, it's my time and my moment. I plan to celebrate, and scream, and pop champagne every chance I get, cuz I'm in the building, baby!" It's not altogether surprising that the station would favor this speech over West's political statement; LuMaye has a signed photo of President Bush in his office, in which the president thanks him for his "early commitment and dedication as a Charter Member of the campaign in Wisconsin."

As a matter of fact, if the only exposure you had to African Americans came from listening to stations like WLYD, you might conclude that they are the wealthiest people in the United States. Just as WLYD's DJs create an artificial environment in which its white listeners can feel comfortable, they have also created an artificial world in which every black person is a living embodiment of the American dream. Between the lyrics extolling their enormous cars and electronic accessories and jeweled necklaces and plated teeth and hot tubs and champagne—to say nothing of the expensive-sounding women draped over everything—hip-hop appears to have succeeded where generations of social policy have failed, enriching the country's poorest inhabitants beyond anyone's wildest imaginings. The roster of pop-rappers is filled with devoted capitalists, whether it's Jay-Z boasting of his executive position as president of Def Jam, or Boyz N Da Hood equating crack pushing with entrepreneurialism or Cassidy proudly proclaiming himself a "hustla" with the enthusiasm of someone applying for a job at a marketing firm.

Jason Hillery, Nate Mitchell's predecessor as Wild 99.7's program director, tells me that it is precisely hip-hop's gaudy ostentation and can-do spirit that makes the music so attractive to Green Bay's blue-collar listeners. A lot of them, he tells me, don't have as much money as they might like, or feel held down by their boss, or frustrated with their station in life. Those people may derive some comfort in listening to stories of others who have overcome adversity. (As he tells me this, I'm reminded of that cranky philosopher, Theodor Adorno, who wrote that popular entertainment served to make the members of its audience better workers, since it helped them "escape the mechanized work process so that they can cope with it again." It's easy to imagine WLYD's listeners grabbing a quick shot of Ying Yang Twins to help them face another day of office drudgery.) "That's what hip-hop's all about," Hillery tells me. "It's having nice things, going out with the hottest women, and drinking the most expensive booze."

It was not always like this, even on pop radio. For a brief period in the early 1990s, programmers, inspired by the success of *Yo! MTV Raps* and still hoping to define the white hip-hop audience, allowed bleak depictions of inner-city lives onto their airwaves. Ice Cube's "It Was a Good Day," a sarcastic paean to a day in which none of his friends were killed or arrested, hit number fifteen on the Hot 100 in 1993. Dr. Dre, Geto Boys, Snoop Doggy Dogg, and the Wu-Tang Clan, street-approved groups who merged their pop sensibilities with something like social critique, all made it onto the list as well. These are the groups that John Kerry was likely thinking of when, ten years later, he described hip-hop as a voice of urban anger and pain. But when I ask Hillery about this, he shoots me the look of a teenager forced to explain to his grandmother how cell-phone text-messaging works. "Hip-hop used to be very much about bucking the system," he says. "Now, it's about a culture of people who have made it, who have overcome the odds and done what everybody over the years said they couldn't do. They made a ton of money and they rule the world. And they're celebrating it."

But not everyone is celebrating. In 2005, David "Davey D" Cook, a Bay Area hip-hop radio personality, told two thousand attendees at the National Conference for Media Reform in St. Louis that corporate-owned radio stations use the music to distract their listeners from the serious issues facing their community. Pop hip-hop, he argued, isn't just vapid; it is a tool of the powers that be, who "spend a lot of time studying and figuring out ways to seduce and attract and lull a lot of the people who aren't in this room to sleep and make it seem like what they present is something that is all good, and therefore there's no problem. Until one day we wake up and find out that there's a lot of things we don't know about, there's a lot of laws that have been passed, there's a lot of things that are missing that are very important to our lives, but by then, the train has left the station."

It is my last night in Green Bay, and I am drunk. I blame Nate Mitchell. He's the one who invited me to a dimly lit, wood-paneled bar called the Stein, located about a block from the radio station. We've been talking about the dissertation that Mitchell is in the middle of writing, on his way to earning a Ph.D. in literature from the University of Iowa. About an hour ago, one of the regulars here—and everybody here seems to be a regular—declared that it was time to play a drinking game; the bartender produced five dice, and we've been rolling for rounds of peppermint schnapps ever since. A few shots in, Mitchell excuses himself to use the bathroom, and when he leaves, the burly contractor sitting next to me leans over and mutters conspiratorially: "Nate's going after the wrong crowd with that station. Who's going to pay to advertise to a bunch of poor black guys?"

I am glad that Mitchell is not here to hear this, because I think that his head might explode. After all the de-ghettofying, all the friendly on-air banter and sanitized playlists and welcoming catch-phrases, some people here just can't seem to outgrow the notion that only black people listen to hip-hop. But my drinking partner is correct in one regard: advertisers *won't* give much business to WLYD if they think the station only attracts poor black listeners.

And that's why WLYD does not call itself an "urban" station. When Mitchell reports his station's playlist to the national trade publications, he does so as a "CHR rhythmic," "CHR" standing for "contemporary hit radio," a term that means Top 40. To the un-trained ear, this can be a pretty subtle distinction. If you were in an empty room with your eyes closed, you would probably not be able to tell whether you were listening to a CHR rhythmic or urban sta-tion. You would probably hear a lot of the same artists singing a lot of the same songs. In fact, the only fundamental difference between the two formats is their audiences. Urban stations target black lis-teners, whereas CHR rhythmic stations target a more ethnically mixed—usually, a whiter—crowd.

The rhythmic CHR format, also known as "churban," was created in the mid-1980s, when a smattering of new stations began playing the kind of postdisco music that had previously been the exclusive bailiwick of black radio. The tactic was designed to win over black and white listeners without the stations having to iden-tify themselves as "urban," and therefore "black." The strategy drew scorn from some black programmers, who argued that the churban stations were taking the black stations' strengths, their mu-sic and listeners, and none of their drawbacks, the suspicion that some advertisers felt toward stations that aligned themselves too closely with black audiences. By the early 1990s, after hip-hop proved to be as popular in the suburbs as the inner city, more pop stations reinvented themselves as churbans, this time incorporating more rap into their song selections. But they did not adjust their format designation, the category under which they reported their playlists, ever fearful that advertisers would see "urban" stations as appealing solely to black listeners.

Rick Cummings, president of the radio division of Emmis Communications, served as program director of Los Angeles' hugely popular churban station Power 106 in the early 1990s. The station was one of the first to use the CHR rhythmic designation. "When we first put Power 106 on the air, *Radio and Records* insisted that we report as an urban station," Cummings explains. "And we said, 'We're not going to report if that's our only choice.'" Power 106, he says, was designed to appeal to a mix of Latino, Asian, African American, and suburban kids. Even though the station played much the same music as its urban counterparts, labeling the station "urban" would be an inaccurate description of its target audience. Of course, there were financial reasons for the decision as well. "I think we fight it better than most companies, but there has always been a discount: advertising aimed at the African American community is not as pricey as advertising considered to be quote-unquote 'mass appeal.' That doesn't make it right, but that's reality."

Some black radio professionals saw a race-based double standard. "Two stations could play the exact same things, one could be urban and one could be CHR," says Kevin Ross, a radio programmer and publisher of *Radio Facts* magazine, an urban-radio trade publication. "But the minute you say anything 'black'—like, 'we're proud to be part of the black community'—that made you black. So what a lot of the CHR stations did was, realizing how popular the 'black' thing was, they hired nonblack people to emulate black culture. As long as you had some white announcers—most black stations don't have white announcers—and as long as you don't say the word 'black' or have any news-oriented programming on the weekend, you can play the exact same music and not be called 'urban.' "

In 2006, 109 stations reported to *Radio and Records* as "rhythmic CHR" stations, and 96 reported as "urban." "Right now," says Edison Media Research's Sean Ross, "there are only four markets in the country that don't have some station playing hip-hop. But only half of those admit to being hip-hop or R&B stations. The rest call themselves Top 40."

If I were to return to Green Bay eight months later, in May 2006, and drive through the city's downtown, I probably wouldn't be as startled by the music being broadcast on 99.7 as I was before. I wouldn't hear Jermaine Dupri or Slim Thug or Ebony Eyez. Instead, I'd hear the likes of such soothing artists as Chicago, Journey, Sheryl Crow, and James Taylor. The station's call letters are no longer WLYD, its fans no longer call it Wild 99.7, and it no longer claims to be "Green Bay's party station." Almost four years after hip-hop was introduced to Green Bay's airwaves, Midwest Communications has ended the experiment. The station that has replaced WLYD is "The Bay," WZBY. Jeff McCarthy, Midwest Communications' vice president, explains the station's philosophy to me when I call him to check up: "If you took the year 1986, and you went twenty years back and twenty years forward, that's the station." I have no idea what that means, but I get an idea from checking out the new station's Web site, and see that all of the eight artists pictured there are white.

Wild 99.7's demise was a long time coming. Two weeks after my visit, WLYD's managers, still trying to placate wary advertisers, got rid of much of the staff. Program Director Nate Mitchell left to finish his dissertation. Randy "Haze" Jones was fired, as was

Devon "D-Dawg" Ashmann. The only employees that survived the cuts were the imaging director Ben LuMaye, who became the station's program director, and Amy Alexander, the blonde, NASCAR-tattooed morning cohost. The playlist was tweaked to include even more accessible, pop-friendly hip hop: less Dr. Dre and Young Jeezy; more Robin Thicke, a white R&B crooner who is the son of a former sitcom star, Alan Thicke. When I found out about the firings, I called Jones and Ashmann. When I originally met Ashmann in Green Bay, he told me that he hoped to spend the rest of his life at the station: "I can't picture myself doing anything else. I think it was meant to be." When I called him after his firing, he was nonplussed: "They said they just wanted to take the station in another direction," he said. "Radio's a bizarre business." Jones didn't call me back.

Even after the changes, though, advertisers remained skittish. According to Ben LuMaye, if the station had had salespeople who were more comfortable with hip-hop, it would still be on the air today. "There's no reason that we shouldn't have been able to sell this station to every retailer in the mall," he says. "The sales staff would tell me, 'The clients had legitimate complaints. They told me they didn't want that kind of clientele in their store.' And [the salespeople] would have no response to it. They wouldn't say, 'Wait a minute. We've got a ton of twenty-four-to-thirty-five-year-old females with money that want to spend it.' "

If pop radio can tell us, as Greil Marcus wrote, "what it is that diverse people can authentically share," then what are we to make of all this? After all the market research and the program directors and the fickle listeners and the nervous advertisers and the format wars, how much are we really sharing? At least in Green Bay, the answer is: nothing. The community is too small, too white, too conservative to allow hip-hop to flourish, no matter how diluted. Most American cities have been able to reach some synthesis, however unsatisfactory, of the pop dream of making music that belongs to all of America and the hip-hop dream of making music that reflects the unfiltered emotions of black people. But in Green Bay, Jeff McCarthy tells me, those twin missions just weren't able to fight their way to a compromise: If WLYD played too much pop-rap, it lost the more serious rap fans. If it played more serious rap, it lost pop listeners. "The mainstream wasn't large enough, and the hard-core wasn't large enough," he says, "and it's very difficult to mix the two."

CHAPTER FIVE
Great White Hopes: Wegroes
Shed Their Skin

How else except by becoming a Negro could a white man hope to
learn the truth?

—John Howard Griffin, *Black like Me*

Tha Pumpsta remembers the day he realized that he wanted to be
black. This was when he was in high school, around the turn of the
twenty-first century, before he was Tha Pumpsta. Back then he was
just Jeremy Parker, a white kid who never much fit in, growing up
in Cobb County, a well-heeled suburb of Atlanta. Parker was already a hip-hop fan; he had tricked out his 1989 Ford Tempo with
custom twelve-inch subwoofers, the better to blast music by southern hip-hop groups like Luther Campbell and Three 6 Mafia as he
tooled through the quiet streets of Newt Gingrich country.

"I was always a loud kid," Tha Pumpsta tells me. "I was always
getting into trouble. I'd get in my car and be like, 'Fuck you, bitch!'
and I'd turn on the rap music and pull a wheelie out of the parking
lot. I was a fucking bad-ass redneck kid who listened to hip-hop."

But it was when he attended Freaknik, Atlanta's now-defunct
annual citywide block party, which drew revelers from black colleges
across the country, that he saw what he wanted to become. "That is
the most amazing time I ever had in my life," he says. "I've never

been so excited and impressed and scared at the same time. These people were blasting music out of their cars and dancing and I just enjoyed that. Maybe I envied it in some weird way or wanted to identify with it. More than I wanted to go back to Cobb County and identify with what was fuckin' going on there."

Now Tha Pumpsta is twenty-five years old. When I meet him at one P.M. one rainy fall afternoon, he is wearing his eyelids at half-mast and a white tank top with wide blue stripes that give him the appearance of a lifeguard from the 1950s. His right biceps sports a tattoo, a florid commemoration to his recently departed dog Patches, whom he discusses with great emotion but without removing the smirk from his face. We're at a diner a few blocks from Tha Pumpsta's apartment in Williamsburg, Brooklyn. This is a working-class Latino, Hassidic, Italian, and Polish neighborhood, but it is best known as a haven for hipsters, the kind of folks who turned the trucker hat into an ironic fashion statement. This restaurant is a perfect example of the area's shabby, tongue-in-chic aesthetic; it appears to be a rundown greasy spoon, until you walk through the doors and learn that the daily specials include a leek-and-gruyère frittata and steamed skate.

Tha Pumpsta admits that his whole life is drenched in this kind of irony. Even his nickname is something of a joke; he thought of the name one day as part of a free-associative rhyme, and it bears no significance beyond its comical misspelling and its vague air of sexual menace. He plays me some hip-hop-inflected dance music that he's recently recorded, futuro-retro bleeps and sirens over synth-pop drums, lyrics warning of a "sonic boom in my hotel room," and I can't decide whether or not to chuckle. But when I ask him about the hip-hop dance parties that he hosts, which he calls "Kill Whitie!," and a statement that he made to the press a few weeks ago in which he said that he hoped his events would help to "kill the whiteness inside," he tells me that he is completely sincere.

"For so long we've been told that racism doesn't exist, that it's over," he says. "Kill Whitie! addresses those issues that need to be addressed. This is a new generation and we're trying to dispel stereotypes. We're trying to change. But at the same time, it's not a conscious thing; it's a dance party."

In my trips to Green Bay and New Canaan, I saw the ways in which hip-hop culture is adapted, how white Americans reinterpret its meaning to fit the images they want to hold of their country and themselves. But Tha Pumpsta represents an opposing impulse: he is using hip-hop to reinterpret *himself*. To put it crudely, he is not listening to hip-hop in an attempt to make it whiter; he is listening to hip-hop in an attempt to make himself blacker. Like DJ Gummo, he wants to vault the line between observation and participation, between watching black people and becoming them.

It would be easy to dismiss Tha Pumpsta as a wigger, a contraction of "white" or "wannabe" and "nigger." The term denotes a white kid with an unhealthy, usually skin-deep fascination with hip-hop culture. Everyone knows a wigger when they see one. They're those guys who wander through strip malls in packs, laughing too loudly and wearing jeans that pool around their ankles. They look to black culture for ways to masculinize their appearance, and to scare the hell out of square adults. Everybody, it seems, hates wiggers: white racists consider them race traitors, a risk to the so-called purity of Anglo-America through their adoption of black personae. Antiracists shake their heads at their reductive and often offensive interpretations of blackness. Hip-hop fans deride them as insincere drive-by tourists whose interest in the culture will last only as long as their desire to annoy their parents. They are chided as both insecure and cocky, self-loathing and self-aggrandizing. They are the people at whom baby boomers of all stripes shake their heads and wonder, "What's becoming of this generation?"

I am going to discuss wiggerism in the next chapter, but that seems an unfair label with which to brand people like Tha Pumpsta. I suggest "Wegroes"—a new word that is a contraction of "white" and "Negro"—as a better fit. "Negro" may be an outdated, even offensive term, referring as it does to a previous era's struggles and prejudices. But it also carries with it an air of respectability, dignity, old-school nobility, the sense of a bygone quest for equality, and an almost quaint belief in the possibility of finding common ground between well-intentioned people of all races. It is this last belief that separates Wegroes from wiggers. Wiggers are fascinated by the way in which African Americans are different from white people; Wegroes hope to emphasize the ways in which we are similar. Wiggers listen to rap to bolster their self-image; Wegroes do so in a sincere, if often flawed, attempt to acknowledge, and hopefully move beyond, the historic responsibilities of their race. Wiggers seek countercultural flash; Wegroes are drawn by the promise of transcending their racial identities.

These are abstract terms. There is probably no such thing as a wigger or Wegro. Every white rap fan encompasses elements of both. So Tha Pumpsta, for instance, can find a wiggerish fascination with what he sees as liberated, sexual black bodies at Freaknik. But he also is commited to the Wegro belief that hip-hop can help further the struggle for black equality. As an adolescent, Tha Pumpsta's love of rap music blossomed into an unironic interest in the civil rights movement. "I couldn't fathom segregated life," he remembers. "A colored water fountain? I couldn't imagine that. It seemed so absurd to me." He read books by Martin Luther King Jr. and Malcolm X. In high school, he printed and sold five hundred T-shirts that depicted two interlocking hands, one black and one white, over the statement ENDING RACISM STARTS WITH YOU.

It was this color-blind optimism, Tha Pumpsta says, that brought him to Williamsburg in 2000. Back then, to hear him tell it, although the area was in the midst of a massive gentrification wave, when he played his records at local bars and clubs his events were packed with ethnically diverse residents. Tha Pumpsta says that he made an effort to integrate himself into the existing community, unlike his fellow gentrifiers, who were content to hang out at coffee shops designed to appeal to the upscale newcomers. He came up with the name "Kill Whitie!" in ironic protest, a way of distinguishing himself from his pigment-mates. "It was beautiful," he says. "I can't explain it, but it made sense."

In one way or another, almost every white hip-hop fan is infected by Wegroism. At its best, Wegroism can lead to a serious and significant critique of race and culture. William Upski Wimsatt is one of hip-hop's best-known Wegroes: he wrote *Bomb the Suburbs*, a manifesto celebrating the revolutionary power of hip-hop and attempting to define white people's proper (and limited) role in the culture. Danny Hoch is a Wegro: as a writer and actor, he has created a number of one-man shows and a movie, *Whiteboyz*, that ably dissect his fascination with hip-hop. The journalist Bakari Kitwana has profiled dozens of Wegroes and sees in them "the dawning of a new reality of race in America."

But there are times when Wegroism can also feel a little, well, creepy. Take Warren Beatty's 1998 film *Bulworth*, in which a depressed and self-loathing politician finds his passion reignited by hip-hop. Suddenly he's speaking—or, rather painfully, rapping—truth to power, waxing cynical about his own money-grubbing campaign whistlestops, and critiquing the news media's myopia. He rediscovers his connection to the common man, collects policy advice from his poor black constituents, and reclaims the mantle of civil rights that he had abandoned on his journey through the Washington power elite. On the surface, *Bulworth* seems a textbook example of Wegro enlightenment. But by the end of the film, you can't help but wonder whether Bulworth's efforts don't do more for his own self-image than for the people he purports to help. The movie culminates in what might be the ultimate Wegro fantasy: a character played by Halle Berry assures Beatty's character that he need not feel uneasy for being white, refers to him as "my nigga," and makes out with him, after which he is assassinated in a montage that suggests the murder of Martin Luther King Jr.

The fundamental tenet of Wegroism—that white Americans can use popular culture to shed their whiteness—is almost as old as American popular culture itself. During the 1920s, when white New Yorkers routinely traveled north of 125th Street to partake of the cultural offerings of the Harlem Renaissance, the writer and critic Carl Van Vechten became one of the most vocal white proponents of African American culture, befriending such prominent black figures as Langston Hughes and James Weldon Johnson, and commissioning a portrait, called *A Prediction*, that showed him with black skin. The Jewish jazz saxophonist and clarinetist Mezz Mezzrow so immersed himself in black culture that, he writes in his autobiography, he "not only loved those colored boys, but I was one of them—I felt closer to them than I felt to the whites, and I even got the same treatment they got." Jerry Leiber and Mike Stoller, Jewish songwriters who penned such early rock hits as "Hound Dog" and "Love Potion No. 9," used to argue about who was blackest. "I felt black," Leiber told *Rolling Stone* in 1990. "I *was*, as far as I was concerned."

Not all Wegroes used their race-transcending powers to noble ends. Throughout the nineteenth century, white minstrels smeared on blackface and presented a bastardized form of black folk music to white audiences. Today, minstrel shows are regarded primarily—and fairly—as a national shame, an embarrassing stretch of pop-culture history during which whites entertained themselves with the most insulting caricatures of black life. But in his influential study *Love & Theft*, Eric Lott, a professor of American Studies at the University of Virginia, argues that at least part of the minstrels' appeal stemmed from a more noble and curious source: white Americans' desire to play with and subvert the seemingly iron-clad rules of race. Lott sees in minstrel-show audiences an American working class drawn to emulate that which is forbidden to them, to colonize that which they cannot be, to both scorn and adore that which their own history and society keeps so separate from them. Lott describes minstrel shows as a complicated and contradictory hodgepodge of racial confusion, envy, curiosity, and fear, "a simultaneous drawing up and crossing of racial boundaries. Minstrel performers often attempted to repress through ridicule the real interest in black cultural practices they nonetheless betrayed—minstrelsy's mixed erotic economy of celebration and exploitation." That mischanneled desire to cross racial boundaries may also explain why blackface performers boasted repeatedly of their special knowledge of American blackness. They described themselves as "original Negroes" and "the very pinks of negro singers." One performer, Ben Cotton, described sitting in with black musicians on Mississippi riverboats, singing along to their banjo-backed melodies as he perfected his act: "I was the first white man they had seen who sang as they did; but we were brothers for the time being and perfectly happy."

White audiences' appetite for racial transformation has proved nearly inexhaustible. Some of the United States' most important cultural milestones consist of white people pretending, quite literally, to be black. D. W. Griffith's *Birth of a Nation*, the first blockbuster feature-length film, famously employed white actors in blackface portraying characters who drove home Griffith's outrageously racist thesis: that black men constituted a threat to white American purity. The lead character of Al Jolson's *Jazz Singer*, the first "talkie," found redemption in greasepaint, blacking up for a performance of the song "Mammy" that convinced his suspicious mother of the nobility of his stage career. NBC Radio's *Amos 'n' Andy*, in which two white men named Charles Correll and Freeman Gosden dramatized the comic exploits of two black men, proved the potential of broadcasting networks when the show became a national panic in 1929. Audiences were captivated by the ability of two white men to play African Americans so convincingly. The historian Melvin Patrick Ely describes a performance in San Francisco during which Correll and Gosden removed their blackface but continued their performance. The vision of black personalities and voices streaming out of white bodies drove the crowd to "near abandon."

Of course, the success of these performances was not due solely, or even mostly, to the noble desire to break down racial barriers. Blackface performers repeatedly portrayed black people as malapropism-prone, stupid, lazy, carefree buffoons—as fundamentally less than human. In her book *Racechanges*, the Indiana University English professor Susan Gubar argued that blackface actors, through their depictions of African Americans as inferior, helped white audiences rationalize the unequal society from which they benefited, as if these seemingly subhuman blacks somehow deserved their treatment: "Thus, what blackface entertainers attempted to annihilate was white responsibility for a past injurious to African Americans, the 'symbolic debt' they owed the dead."

Minstrelsy may be a thing of the past, but the cognitive dissonance that many white people feel about their privileged positions remains. In his 1965 essay "White Man's Guilt," James Baldwin poked fun at whites who engage in "stammering, terrified dialogues" with "the black conscience, the black man in America. The nature of this stammering can be reduced to a plea. Do not blame me. I was not there. I did not do it." It is precisely this self-consciousness—this attempt to separate oneself from the collective wrongdoings of our past—that causes some to view even the best-intentioned Wegroes with suspicion: one can't help but feel that there's something self-serving in their attempts to commune and identify with black life. Rather than assuaging their guilt by portraying African Americans as inferior, as earlier minstrels did, Wegroes appear to be trying to excuse themselves from their "symbolic debt" by defining themselves as somehow apart from their whiteness, and by adopting the culture of the oppressed. Bernard Wolfe, who cowrote Mezzrow's autobiography, felt that the desire to emulate blackness could not be separated from the desire to punish it, writing in an afterword, "I began to wonder whether Negrophilia and Negrophobia were, as linear, one-way logic would suggest, polar opposites, or whether to get at the devious psychology of the thing you wouldn't have to see the two mindsets dialectically."

That helps explain why not everyone has been thrilled by Tha Pumpsta's Kill Whitie! parties. The problems began in late August 2005, when the *Washington Post* published an article that described one of his Williamsburg soirées. The writer, Michelle Garcia, described the event as a "melanin-lacking hip-hop party" where a white DJ played rap music to entertain a largely white crowd, who used the music as an excuse to grind up against one another and found in the event "a safe environment to be freaky." But her main complaint stemmed from the name of Tha Pumpsta's event, and the sight of a group of smug Caucasians chanting "Kill whitie!" as they downed pricey drinks. Although Garcia quoted Tha Pumpsta's argument that his dance parties represented a good-faith effort to "kill the whiteness inside," she compared him to Elvis Presley, that infamous expropriator, derided the party's attendees as "young white hipsters believing they can shed white privilege by parodying the black hip-hop life," and mentioned a flier for one of the parties that offered free admission to anyone who brought fried chicken. "[S]ome," Garcia wrote, "think he might be mocking black people."

For his part, Tha Pumpsta describes the article as "complete and blatant misinformation." He argues that his party was deliberately misunderstood by a journalist intent on exploiting racial tensions at an event that was designed to destroy them. He points out that the article contains not one word about Kill Whitie!'s co-organizer, Shannon Funchess, who is black. He says that he never intended for his fried-chicken gimmick to be seen as a racial slight. ("I'm fucking southern, you know what I mean? That's what I grew up on.") He argues that Garcia misrepresented the ethnic makeup of the crowd as "all-white." And most important, he says, she misinterpreted his love of hip-hop and his sincere efforts to transcend racial boundaries as ironic shtick. "All we ever tried to do was dispel racial stereotypes," he says. "We have genuine love for this music, and we just feel torn apart."

"Tearing apart" is exactly what most rap fans felt like doing to Tha Pumpsta after reading the *Washington Post* piece. Scores of hip-hop bloggers posted the article, usually over some disparaging response. "This type of party is a clear display of how comfortable and lackadaisical these so-called hipsters are," one comment read. "They should step back and see how lucky they are to even be able to walk the streets of Williamsburg, before shaking the delicate foundation of tolerance that New Yorkers developed over this last decade." Not all critiques were quite so genteel. "Kill anybody at these parties for the good of humanity," read one.

Tha Pumpsta responded as self-described persecuted rebel-artists have throughout hip-hop's history: with middle finger raised. He posted comebacks to his many critics, arguing that the *Washington Post* would never understand Kill Whitie! because "they're the whitie we're trying to kill." And he prepared for his next Kill Whitie! party, to be held three days after the article's publication, at a Brooklyn club called Savalas. "I had three security guards because all these people were threatening to kill me," he says. "I was like, 'I'm fucking throwing this party. And if I die? Then fucking so be it.'" (In the end, he said, few protestors bothered to show up, and those who did merely waved a couple of signs and yelled for a few minutes.) Yet Tha Pumpsta's travails had not ended. Days later, he learned that an upcoming show at the Frying Pan, a high-profile floating dance party on a boat in Manhattan's Hudson River, had been canceled because of the controversy. Tha Pumpsta countered by rebooking the party at another venue. BANNED IN NYC! his fliers boasted, above photos of fat-rumped black women.

The contradictions inherent in Tha Pumpsta's Kill Whitie! parties remind me of a fifteen-year-old photograph that lies in a cardboard box somewhere in my parents' basement. During the summer of 1990, when I was sixteen years old, I spent two weeks attending a Jewish summer camp in Saratoga, California. I have many fond memories—lining up at the canteen to buy ice-cream sandwiches, singing folk songs around a campfire, venturing into San Francisco to catch a performance of Les Misérables—but the photograph is the only tangible memento I have kept from that time. In it, about thirty of us beam into the camera, our skin pink from so many days spent frolicking outdoors. Front and center, white plastic letters spell out our session's defining catchphrase against a black felt board: FIGHT THE POWER.

That phrase came courtesy of Public Enemy, a rap group that brilliantly introduced a new form of mass entertainment: radical racial politics backed by blistering beats. Rappers had dabbled in social protest ever since Grandmaster Flash and the Furious Five's "The Message" proved its commercial viability. Everything from Run-DMC's "Hard Times" to the Treacherous Three's "Xmas Rap" took on the challenges facing impoverished inner-city residents. Ice-T, Schoolly D, and KRS-One's bleak documentation of ghetto ultraviolence (which would later blossom into the subgenre of gangsta rap) carried an implicit political message bemoaning the abandonment of the inner cities. But for the most part, even the most strident of mideighties hip-hop artists took positions that were easy for white liberals to endorse: poverty is bad; gang violence results in tragedy; drug addiction destroys lives; more should be done to deal with inner-city unemployment; police officers shouldn't assume that every black man is a criminal.

But Public Enemy—a collection of outsized personalities, revolutionary rhetoric, and hyperkinetic sampling—upped the ante. The group resembled a radical collective more than a music act: it featured its own "minister of information," the beret-clad Professor Griff; a "media assassin" in the form of Harry Allen, whose role was to provide counterpropaganda to "the hype" published in the mainstream press; and even its own army, a band of bodyguards called the S1Ws (for "security of the first world"), who marched across the stage bearing stoic expressions and fake Uzis. The cover for Public Enemy's first album, 1987's *Yo! Bum Rush the Show*, showed the group huddled around their frontman, Chuck D, in a basement, seemingly preparing for armed insurrection, over the repeated slogan "the government's responsible." The group's logo depicted the silhouette of a (presumably black) man caught in a gun sight's crosshairs.

But it was not until their sophomore effort in 1988, *It Takes a Nation of Millions to Hold Us Back*, that the group perfected the combination of agitating beats and agitprop that would become their trademark. *Nation of Millions* kicked off with a sample of a Malcolm X speech and continued with lyrics that extolled Louis Farrakhan, the controversial leader of the Nation of Islam; derided the media as racist; bemoaned the fact that drug dealers were selling their wares to "the brother man" instead of "the other man"; and asserted that J. Edgar Hoover arranged the assassinations of Martin Luther King Jr. and Malcolm X. Flavor Flav, ostensibly the act's comic relief, cackled unnervingly, like a court jester facing the apocalypse. The music was no easier to digest, composed of squealing air-raid sirens, stutter-step drum claps, and unrelenting aggression. The producer, Hank Shocklee, has said that his goal was to be "music's worst nightmare."

Instead, the resulting combination of white noise and black rage proved to be a Wegro's wet dream. What better way to express your distance from whiteness than listening to music that seemed to threaten the very foundation of the square white establishment? If you were able to listen to—and actually *enjoy*—this stuff, then how white could you really be? Far from scandalized by the music's exhortations to embrace racial pride and Marcus Garvey–esque self-determination, young white Americans pumped their fists to Chuck D's basso profundo, the muscled militarism of the S1Ws, and the righteous thrashings of the uncompromising production. While some self-proclaimed guardians of civil discourse shook their heads, enough would-be down white boys shook their asses to make the album the latest in Def Jam's series of pop breakthroughs. In a flashback to "The Message," *Nation of Millions* won, by a huge margin, the *Village Voice*'s year-end Pazz and Jop Award for best album. The *Washington Post* seconded Public Enemy's claim to be "the Black Panthers of Rap," applauded the group for "rekindling the spirit of the '60s black power movement in a young audience," and quoted Chuck D's description of his music as "a wake-up call for the nation." The *New York Times* praised *Nation of Millions* for "jam[ming] urban tension and black anger into the foreground." The group's first post-*Nation* single, "Fight the Power"—the theme song of Spike Lee's *Do the Right Thing*, a bleak portrait of the intractability of racial conflict—became, said *The New Republic*, "the biggest college hit of 1989." Public Enemy may have foreseen a nation of millions attempting to hold them back, but they uncovered a nation of millions of white kids who preferred to egg them on.

Of course, I was one of those kids, poring wide-eyed over the lyrics to every song, memorizing every word and every beat, held in thrall by the sheer power and anger that just barely held all that music together. If I just studied hard enough, I thought, I could understand the world, a world that to my adolescent eyes and ears seemed—this time for sure—to be inches away from tearing itself apart. Every time I picked up the newspaper or turned on the news, I was waylayed by another bulletin, another hint of what seemed to be shaping up to become a full-scale race war: the trial of the subway vigilante, Bernard Goetz; the murder of a black boy by Italian Americans in Howard Beach; the accusations (later dismissed) of a black teenager, Tawana Brawley, that she had been gang-raped by six white men; the famous Central Park jogger case, in which a group of black and Latino men were convicted of raping and beating a woman (the convictions were later overturned); Jesse Jackson's infamous "Hymietown" remark. I am sure that some music fans saw Chuck D's angry black man as the newest version of Ozzy Osbourne's bat-eating satanist or David Bowie's ambisexual alien, a marquee attraction signifying nothing beyond his sure-to-shock histrionics. But I saw something else: a mainline directly into the bubbling current of pure, unfiltered, urban blackness, blackness that I could tap into and wallow in until my own soul—if not my skin—took on some of its pigment.

The reality, of course, was a little bit more complicated. The group's members—like those of Run-DMC, De La Soul, and EPMD—actually hailed from the suburbs, not the inner city. Chuck D points out that Roosevelt, Long Island, where he grew up, was in fact a 90 percent black town, that the old resonances of the city-versus-suburb dichotomy did not apply in this case: "The difference was, trees and houses as opposed to buildings with people on top of each other. . . . In some areas of black suburbia, it was nothing but a horizontal project." Still, Chuck says, he made a point of spending as little time in New York City as possible.

"We were these working- to middle-class black kids from sub-urban environments that were relatively safe," Bill Stephney, Public Enemy's original producer, tells me. "I think we'd be lying if we didn't cop to romanticizing things." And although Public Enemy's urgency seemed to burst out of every pore, it took Rick Rubin, Def Jam's white cofounder, to convince the group to pursue a recording career, eventually overcoming both Chuck D's and Russell Simmons's indifference. But none of this mattered. Public Enemy deftly blurred the line between activism and entertainment, creating unignorable art with the passion, urgency, anger, and anti-authoritarian attitude of punk legends such as the Clash and the Sex Pistols.

The Sex Pistols would prove to be a near-perfect analog of Public Enemy. That influential rock band flamed out after only two years, when the contradictions between their nihilistic message and their chart-topping popularity became too confusing for even them to bear. Their lead singer, Johnny Rotten, closed his final concert, in January 1978, with a question, "Ever get the feeling that you've been cheated?" which nicely undercut the band's false promise: that rock musicians could liberate listeners from their most fundamental political and existential dilemmas.

Public Enemy would find it similarly difficult to negotiate its twin roles as professional provocateurs and civil rights spokespeople. When I ask Chuck D whether he thought that *Nation of Millions* was truly revolutionary, he laughs. "We had a recording contract and we were making a record. I mean, come on, now," he says. "If there was anyone out there saying that we should have been revolutionaries, then clearly they were nothing but armchair fanatics." And yet there were plenty of armchair fanatics out there, including many Wegroes, who saw Public Enemy as their own personal revolution and applauded more loudly every time the group took a more combative stance.

Those expectations helped to undo the group's momentum. In May 1989—about fourteen months before I had my photo taken at my Jewish summer camp—a reporter from the *Washington Times* wrote that Professor Griff had told him that Jews were responsible for "the majority of wickedness that goes on across the globe." Public Enemy continued to release music, including two more albums, 1990's *Fear of a Black Planet* and 1991's *Apocalypse '91 . . . The Enemy Strikes Black*, and a slew of songs—including "Can't Truss It," "911 Is a Joke," "By the Time I Get to Arizona," and "Welcome to the Terrordome"—that further demonstrated the musical and commercial power of political rap. But the group eventually lost its relevance as the revolution its music prophesied remained on record, never quite invading the real world.

A few months after meeting with Tha Pumpsta, I am lolling about on the couch, flipping channels, when I stumble across a classic video, "The Gas Face," from one of Public Enemy's successors: 3rd Bass. The song, released in 1989, remains a pretty good example of the politically aware, race-conscious hip-hop that was beginning to come into fashion at that time. Its lyrics critique Eurocentric standards of beauty, South African president P. W. Botha, and expressions that reinforce subliminal racism, such as "bad guys wear black." The video features a predatory white record-label chief, white devils celebrating their plan to instill ignorance throughout the world, and a magnified dictionary definition of the word "black," an implicit criticism of the negative connotations—"dirty, soiled"—associated with blackness.

You can see where this is going: 3rd Bass's two MCs are white. MC Serch, the group's lead rhymer, looks like the kind of kid I met at Jewish summer camp: tubby, with thick glasses and a thinly concealed urge to be the center of attention. He bounces across the set, showing off hip-hop moves that, even more than fifteen years later, look strange coming from a white guy. He turns around to display the name of his group, shaved into the back of his high-top fade haircut. Pete Nice, Serch's more subdued partner, relaxes in a throne, occasionally waggling his cane at the camera. Almost every other performer in the video, from guest rapper Zev Love X to the group's DJ, Richie Rich, is black. I have to tip my hat: *these* guys are Wegroes.

3rd Bass made an even more unusual sight around the time that their album was first released. Public Enemy's success had led to a barrage of political groups, and by the early 1990s radical hip-hop had become a full-blown fad. The members of the group X-Clan wore giant rings in their noses and Africa medallions around their necks while they rapped odes to Nat Turner. Paris, who referred to himself as "P-Dog the militant," endorsed sticking up "the whole damn government." Brand Nubian, whose members subscribed to the beliefs of the Five Percent movement, an offshoot of the Nation of Islam, argued that black people were victims of an ongoing race war and warned, "Beware, devil man."

It was enough to disconcert even hip-hop's prodigal white sons, the Beastie Boys, who, burned out from their *Licensed to Ill*–era frat-boy antics, had decamped to Los Angeles, put out a brilliant but underwhelmingly received second album, and were working on a comeback. "Originally, *Check Your Head* [their comeback album] wasn't going to have any hip-hop on it," Adam "MCA" Yauch told a reporter. "The climate was kind of weird in hip-hop at that time. We felt a little bit alienated. It wasn't like we were saying, 'Oh, we shouldn't play hip-hop right now,' but we were kind of thinking, Let's just play our instruments for a while. . . . Public Enemy's music was this totally different tone, really angry about the history of what's gone on with black people in America. So, I think it just changed the whole climate of hip-hop. A lot of the

hip-hop coming out was really angry." ("We were the whole antithesis of what the Beastie Boys were about," Chuck D says of his
one-time label mates, whom he credits with preparing white America for Public Enemy's emergence. "It's almost like the anti–Beastie
Boys coming out of the Beastie Boys.") The Beasties eventually re-
lented and did record a number of hip-hop tracks, but the resulting
album found a much more grateful audience among white rock
fans than among traditional rap listeners.

But 3rd Bass suggested that you didn't have to be black to be
black nationalists. MC Serch—born Michael Berrin, the Jewish son
of a stockbroker in Far Rockaway, Queens—was a Wegro whose in-
vestment in black life would have made Carl Van Vechten jealous.
Berrin spent so much time on the black side of his hometown that
the local community of Five Percenters gave him his nickname, a
reference to his constant search for information. His partner, Peter
Nash, identified with hip-hop culture more strongly than he did
with his similarly pigmented classmates at Columbia University.
"These kids come from places like Kansas and their parents have
money so they think they can come here and run shit," he told a reporter. "They had no respect for people in the community."

"I didn't think I was white," Serch says. "I thought I was
something else. I honestly believed, in my heart of hearts, I was not
white."

Nobody could accuse 3rd Bass of not having enough respect
for hip-hop culture. If anything, they sometimes seemed to possess
too much. In October of 1989 they released *The Cactus Album*, a
series of songs and skits that tackled the kind of politically charged
material that was becoming rap's lingua franca. The two rappers
kicked off the album with "Sons of 3rd Bass," a thinly veiled assault on the Beastie Boys, whom 3rd Bass charged with stealing
black music. A brief appearance by Russell Simmons helped ce-
ment the group's credibility, as the Def Jam chief compared them

to classic hip-hop acts like the Funky 4+1 and the Furious Five. "Product of the Environment" recalled the two MCs' struggles growing up in outer-borough New York, and closed with a plea to end black-on-black violence and "uplift the race." The performance impressed the African American journalist Playthell Benjamin, who wrote a cover article for the *Village Voice* in which he concluded that the two rappers were "the real deal." But other writers remained less convinced; the *Washington Post*'s music reviewer later dismissed Serch's Wegro efforts with 3rd Bass in three words: "Trying too hard."

Still, that's much better than not trying hard enough, the charge leveled against Vanilla Ice, the next notable white rapper and still one of hip-hop's favorite doofus-villains. Following hot on the heels of superstar MC Hammer—who would prove that hip-hop at its least lyrically complex could sell 10 million records—Vanilla Ice's "Ice Ice Baby" became the first rap single to top *Billboard*'s pop chart in November of 1990, and almost immediately came under attack for its dopey lyrics, uncreative sampling, and chorus that bore a striking similarity to a chant from a black-fraternity step show. With his Aryan good looks—he was once described as "Dolph Lundgren meets James Dean"—Vanilla Ice seemed to embody every hip-hop fan's worst fear: the second coming of Elvis, who would open the door for a slew of white rappers with no connection to or respect for the conditions and populations that created the art form. Not surprisingly, 3rd Bass were some of Vanilla Ice's loudest critics. The video for their most popular song, "Pop Goes the Weasel," showed the two beating up a Vanilla Ice look-alike (actually hardcore legend Henry Rollins), while the lyrics accused a certain nameless someone of skating on "thin ice" and compared him to a Ku Klux Klansman.

To the cries of cultural theft, Vanilla Ice argued that his life experiences qualified him to be considered black enough to rap. He claimed that he hailed from the streets of Miami, that he had attended the same high school as 2 Live Crew's Luther Campbell, and that he had been stabbed several times. After this biography was proved to be a fabrication—Vanilla Ice had actually enjoyed a fairly well-off adolescence in suburban Dallas—and his Christian name, Robert Van Winkle, was discovered, Vanilla Ice was well on his way to spending the rest of his life as a punchline.

The backlash against Vanilla Ice's unforgivable whiteness only further cemented hip-hop's reputation as music by and for black people. But that did not prevent the emergence of the first bumper crop of white rappers in the early 1990s, who faced down the inherent contradiction by defining themselves as essentially other-than-white. House of Pain's Everlast and Danny Boy rapped that they should be considered "Celtic rebels" rather than "blue-eyed devils," pointed to their "Irish intellect" as the source of their funky skills, used shamrocks and bagpipes as symbols of their ethnic pride, and promoted hard-drinking, free-brawling stereotypes that linked them to the roughneckism ascendant in hip-hop at the time. Another white act, Trenton's Italian American Tony D, announced that he was "here to keep rap raw," as opposed to other white rappers whom he deemed sell-outs (for instance, Serch, whom he called a "devil" and a "snake"). Chilly Tee (a.k.a. Travis Knight, the son of Nike founder Phil Knight) declared that he was "born to the establishment but fighting the system" and thanked his family for supporting him while he was "stuck in the struggle."

Of course, plenty of white rappers were content to aim for pop-chart success rather than serious street credibility. But hip-hop had become so consistently and blatantly associated with blackness—and openly edgy about the risk of white appropriation—that even the blandest act felt compelled to feint toward Wegro-ness. Marky Mark, a chiseled Bostonian, surrounded himself with a multicultural Funky Bunch and peppered his CDs with the obligatory tales of inner-city neglect ("Wildside," "The American Dream") and color-blindness

("Music for the People," "Gonna Have a Good Time"). Even Jesse Jaymes, whose lyrical content can be pretty much gleaned from his song titles—they include "$55 Motel" and "Shake It (like a White Girl)"—alluded to his skills on the basketball court, the trademark proving ground of black masculinity.

But no one went as far as Young Black Teenagers, a group of four white guys and one Puerto Rican from the New York area who insisted that their enthusiasm for hip-hop qualified them to be considered black. The group's members—Kamron, ATA, Firstborn, DJ Skribble, and Tommy Never—loudly and repeatedly identified themselves as black. Their first single was titled "Proud to Be Black." On a song called "Daddy Kalled Me Niga Cause I Likeded to Rhyme," they bemoaned the fact that their families objected to their blackness. They even criticized others whom they deemed insufficiently black, whom they judged as trying to "be part of a fad or a trend" rather than expressing their genuine selves. The group proposed that race was not a product of color or ancestry, but a state of mind. "We're taught that all Afro-Americans are black and all Caucasians are white," Kamron told the *Chicago Tribune*'s Greg Kot. "That's a generalization. People should start to individualize."

Young Black Teenagers was produced by the Bomb Squad, the same men who produced Public Enemy's albums. Indeed, the name was producer Hank Shocklee's idea. "Calling them Young Black Teenagers, basically it was America's worst nightmare: white kids representing and being infatuated by and embracing black culture. That was the whole idea," he says.

So Shocklee was shocked to find that most of the objections to the name and lyrics came not from mainstream America but from the hip-hop community. Even the group's bona fides—and an album cameo from Chuck D—weren't enough to convince many people, black or white, of the group's ability to transcend racial categories. Black listeners who heard the song "Proud to be Black" on the radio called to compliment the disc jockey—until they learned of the group's ethnicity; then they demanded it be taken off the air. Concertgoers began to boo when the act took the stage. Young Black Teenagers put out two albums—the always-provocative Shocklee says that their label, MCA, rejected his proposed title for the second: *The Niggaz You Love to Hate*—and found some success with the relatively uncontroversial single "Tap the Bottle," an ode to alcohol. Eventually, though, the constant race-based kerfuffle overwhelmed the group, which disbanded. Their DJ, Skribble, went on to work on a variety of MTV programs, but his bandmates quickly faded into obscurity. The hip-hop community had delivered its verdict on Wegroes: It was one thing for them to listen to rap or identify with black culture. But they could not shed their skin. Not even hip-hop could bestow what X-Clan's Brother J called his "deep, deep blackness."

This was a verdict I eventually came to accept in college, leading me to hang up my Malcolm X hat and retreat into my whiteness. It is a lesson that Carl Van Vechten, that white supporter of the Harlem Renaissance, learned the hard way. In 1926 he published a novel with the title *Nigger Heaven*, a slang term for the balconies of movie theaters. Although the book was a loving testament to black culture and became a best-seller among curious whites, many members of the African American community that Van Vechten so worshipped were horrified. W. E. B. DuBois called it "a blow in the face" and "an affront to the hospitality of black folk." At a book review meeting at the 135th Street branch of the New York Public Library, angry Harlem residents dismissed the book as "an insult to the race." Although Van Vechten's friends, including Langston Hughes and James Weldon Johnson, defended the novel, Van Vechten was never welcome in Harlem again.

At the end of my lunch with Tha Pumpsta, it sounded as if he was starting to come to terms with this lesson as well. He admitted to me that the fried-chicken discount was probably a mistake, that there are some jokes that white people simply cannot and should not make. He understood why some folks took umbrage at his cavalier use of such a loaded (and misspelled) phrase as "Kill Whitie!" a name he said he might discontinue. At the very least, his ramshackle and largely stream-of-conscious identification with black culture and language left him on the defensive. "It would be the furthest thing for me to try and instigate anything racist," he said. "I have the most sincere of intentions."

If Tha Pumpsta needs any tips on how to express his sincerity, he may want to ask for the advice of the white rappers AR-15, who just may be the ultimate Wegroes. AR-15 is a police rifle model, but the group's two members have reinterpreted the term—"flipped" it, in the parlance—to stand for "Anti Racist 15." The "15" refers to the fifteen antiracist principles that the MCs have devised to inform their music and their lives (including "study legacies of resistance," "respect leadership of color," and "create antiracist culture"). On the group's Web site, ar15entertainment.com, they refer to themselves as a combination of the Beastie Boys and Public Enemy, and their lyrics make MC Serch's look like Vanilla Ice's. "If they take you in the morning," they rap in the first track of their EP, *Whiteness in the Crosshairs*, "they will be coming for us at night." "I'm here to get down, just like John Brown!" they sing in another, a reference to the famed white abolitionist.

Jeb Middlebrook, AR-15's front man, raps under the nickname Jus Rhyme, but he used to use the handle Privilege. The name was a self-critical reference to the concept of white privilege. Today, Middlebrook, himself the son of an optometrist and an occupational therapist, says that all whites are inescapably tainted by privilege, but he did not believe this in 2001, when, as a sophomore at Macalester

College in St. Paul, Minnesota, he became obsessed with the idea of escaping it. "Macalester is a private school, very wealthy," Middle-brook tells me. "Our cafeteria was an international food court. We ate on pastel dishes and drank soda out of high-stem crystal glasses. I looked at that, and it all hit me at once: all this stuff is based on death. Wealth is created by someone else not having it or being exploited, so all I could see when I saw that was blood and bones. Who is los-ing out for me to sit here and eat this? It hit me so hard. I read some-where that the truest test of any nation is how it treats the person at the bottom. And I said, 'Who is that in America? Black folks, women, gay folks, and homeless people.' And I said, 'I'm none of that, and I can't be most of that. But I can be homeless.'" Almost immediately, he dropped out of school and flew to San Diego where his friend, and now co-MC, Trevor Wysling, met him at the airport holding a sign that read HIP HOP: HARMING INSTITUTIONAL PRIVILEGE, HOMELESS ON PURPOSE.

After he concluded that he couldn't outrun his privilege by choosing to be homeless, a decision that most homeless people do not have the privilege of making, Middlebrook returned to Min-neapolis, where he finished his undergraduate education at the University of Minnesota. He chuckles when he tells me he flew to California to become homeless, because he figured being destitute would be more comfortable there. "I flew to San Diego using my bank account," he says. "Talk about privilege!" As an undergradu-ate in Minneapolis, he organized the Hip-Hop Co-Op, a coalition of musicians and activists whose proceeds went toward local racial-justice organizations. He also performed his pointed rap songs at political demonstrations; at one rally, held in the rotunda of the Minnesota State Capitol building to protest an anti-welfare bill, he rapped, "I'd rather be right than white, is that all right?" The ques-tion, he tells me, is rhetorical. "You've got to own up to it," he says. "You're white. What are you going to do with that?"

Middlebrook and Wysling have since had the opportunity to ask that question in front of a variety of different audiences; they have toured public high schools in Michigan, leading discussion groups about white privilege and racial justice, and have appeared at the Seventh Annual White Privilege Conference. This is intense stuff, and Middlebrook is an intense guy. When I meet him in Minneapolis, he is dressed head to toe in black and white clothing: black baggy jeans, white bandana, and a black baseball cap, which he later swaps for a white one. He greets me with an expansive hug and a slightly crazed look in his eye. His friends joke that he always looks as if he is about to stab someone.

But maybe you have to be this intense to avoid the inevitable pitfalls of Wegroism. "I feel like the problem with a lot of other white rappers is that it's all about individual success," Wysling says. "Like, 'If I can exist around black people and they accept me, then that's enough. I won.' "

Middlebrook nods. "And I would just ask, 'Is it?' "

Whether or not it is enough, it is certainly something that the members of AR-15 appear to have achieved. During a joint radio interview at the University of Minnesota's student radio station, a local rapper, Truth Maze, is so impressed with the group's passion that he gives them his T-shirt, on which is reproduced a famous quote from Malcolm X: "You been had, you been took, hoodwinked, bamboozled, led astray, run amuck."

"Man, I love y'all, man, straight up," he tells them. "There's nothing around like what you guys are doing. This is a good time. We need you. I really appreciate you."

But not everyone is so appreciative. That same weekend, AR-15 puts on a performance at Minneapolis's Varsity Theater. The group is opening for a popular local band—always a thankless task—and the house is still half empty when Middlebrook and Wysling take the stage. Nevertheless, as their set begins, the two rappers are filled with the fervor that I've come to recognize as their default setting. "We'll just try to fill in this area right here," Middlebrook announces, waving his hand in a circle toward the front of the stage. A few young women who look like freshmen gigglingly oblige, but they are alone. The rest of the crowd stands, unconvinced, around the edges of the room. And not much changes throughout the course of the performance. Despite the billowing smoke machine, despite the stirring beats, despite the group's undeniable passion, it appears that lyrics like "Our lives are our principles" and "We're all guilty of something!" don't have quite the rousing effect the group hoped it might.

I can't say that I'm very surprised. Don't get me wrong, I like AR-15. I like their music. I like their energy. Most of all, I like their message. I like the way they attempt to come to terms with their whiteness, instead of trying to escape it. I respect their refusal to let themselves off the hook, their insistence on admitting their own limitations, their acknowledgment that they will never be able to release themselves from the responsibilities and privileges of whiteness. But I worry that those qualities are precisely what will keep them from becoming popular performers. It's much easier to appreciate the fantasy of abandoning whiteness than it is to come to terms with its impossibility.

At least, that's the conclusion that I come to when I finally attend one of Tha Pumpsta's Kill Whitie! parties. He has invited me to attend so I can see for myself how the *Washington Post* mischaracterized the racial makeup of his audience. The party is held at Rock Star Bar, another Williamsburg haunt, and as I squeeze through the doors I see plenty of attractive twenty-somethings in knee-high tube socks and eighties-throwback T-shirts, some of whom do indeed happen to be black and Latino, but all of whom seem to share the same economic class, cultural values, fashion sense, and attitudes of irony and experimentation. Tha Pumpsta takes the stage at about eleven P.M., wearing an old T-shirt that says PUSHING IRON and that wouldn't look out of place in a twenty-year-old jazzercise video. He rips through a number of songs with his band, the Durty Nanas, live versions of the tracks that appear on his electronic rave-up CD, *Alphabitize the Nation*. As he belts out his over-the-top and disjointed lyrics—"Ain't got no underwear on"; "This be old-school"; "I'm gonna freak you til the moonlight comes"; "Look at them girls, they got them coochie-cutters on"—I have to admit that his presence is electric, as if the Doors' Jim Morrison and 2 Live Crew's Luther Campbell had merged into one body (well, Morrison's body). The crowd seems to agree, rubbing up against one another in a frenzy, euphorically throwing their arms in the air. I stay around through the conclusion of his set, and then I stay for another hour or so, while the DJ plays old, sex-drenched southern hip-hop albums—the same records that Tha Pumpsta used to listen to in his 1989 Ford Tempo. The crowd is still abuzz when I collect myself, eardrums throbbing, and spill out of the Rock Star Bar's hermetic wonderland. Back on the streets of Williamsburg, all is silent and empty, a completely different universe from the one I have just exited. Except for the muffled sound of the beat, you'd never know that anything was going on in there.

CHAPTER SIX
Wiggaz4Life: White Gangstas in the Bubble

Anybody can be a muthafuckin' nigga.

—Dr. Dre, quoted in Mark Blackwell,
"Niggaz4Dinner," *Spin*, September 1991

I am going to go out on a limb and assume that you have not picked up *First Hit's Free*, the debut album from a rapper named Johnny Crack. If you had, you would have heard Johnny's high-pitched, vaguely frantic voice detailing various aspects of his self-professed gangsta outlook. You would have heard him describe his "ice lifestyle," full of Cristal champagne and "bling bling bling." You would have heard him recount his many sexual exploits, including the fact that—and I am sorry to be the one to have to tell you this—he has had sex with your mother. You would have heard him share his theories of interpersonal communication—"If you want to talk to me, yo, you better give me money"—and his threats to "leave your brains mangled all over the fucking place" should you choose to disregard them. You also would have heard his testament to his own entrepreneurial skills as a salesman of crack cocaine, as well as his admission that he occasionally samples his product. And finally, you would have heard about his latest purchase: "I got a new gat, going rat-tat-tat." You would have heard all of this during the first full song, "Back Like Cooked Crack," after which you would have had the chance to listen to these same themes developed ad nauseum over the course of the album's remaining twenty-seven tracks.

None of this much distinguishes Johnny Crack from the hundreds of rappers who work within the musical tradition known as "gangsta rap," that infamous subgenre of hip-hop dedicated to telling grim narratives of inner-city criminal life. Gangsta rap has provided hip-hop with some of its most legendary figures, including, just for instance, The Notorious B.I.G., Tupac Shakur, Dr. Dre, Ice-T, Ice Cube, and Snoop Doggy Dogg. It has provided hip-hop with a mission: empowering a segment of the population that has few other options, and doing battle against those—from police departments to the Parents Music Resource Center to Bill O'Reilly—who would silence or marginalize them. And gangsta rap has also provided hip-hop with a series of tropes—excessive firepower; drug deals; street soldiering; pimping; disrespectful dalliances with alluring-but-untrustworthy women; flamboyant, frequently ill-gotten wealth; sexual superheroism; entrepreneurialism; and the long odds for survival faced by ghetto youth—that have proved so popular that the word "gangsta" has passed beyond cliché to become virtually meaningless. Today, almost every prominent rapper incorporates some gangsta themes into his music.

But there is one aspect of Johnny Crack's oeuvre that sets him apart from his gangsta-rapping peers: he is white. Furthermore, he does not live in South Central Los Angeles or Harlem or Bedford-Stuyvesant or any of his genre's other favored crime-riddled locales. Instead, he hails from Leaside, a suburb of Toronto so safe and insulated that its residents refer to it as "the bubble." And in contrast to his forebears, Johnny Crack happily admits that in real life he is no gangsta. Contrary to his recorded claims, he does not sell crack, nor does he own a gun, apart from the rifle that he uses to occasionally hunt deer. And while he would love to sport some bling, his current job—landscaping during the summer, operating a snowplow during the winter—does not pay him enough.

These factors have conspired to win Johnny Crack a loud and virulent group of online enemies. The popular hip-hop Web site sohh.com has hosted something called the "official Johnny Crack hate thread," in which respondents post the feelings of deep despair that their awareness of Johnny Crack has given them. ("This can't be life," reads one representative message.) Other critics voice less existential but no less pointed rage. People claiming to be Los Angeles Crip members and white supremacists may not be able to agree on much, but they can come together in their hatred of Johnny Crack. "I want to murder u guys, 4real," one post on Johnny's messageboard reads. "If I see any of you wiggers in Tupelo, Mississippi I will personally hang you!" reads another.

Wiggers tend to draw this kind of response. In a better world, the word "wigger" would have derived from "ear wigger," a term used by confidence men in the 1940s to denote an eavesdropper. "Ear wigging" is not a bad description of what some white rap fans hope to accomplish: tapping undetected into a secret communication, gaining unmediated insight into the realities of black life. Even some rappers apparently felt this way about their white audiences. Ice Cube once told bell hooks, "I do records for black kids, and white kids are basically eavesdropping on my records."

But, of course, the term's origins are not quite so innocent or idealistic. "Wigger" entered the common parlance in the late 1980s following a brawl in a Syracuse, New York, high school, when a group of white kids determined that some of their white classmates identified too closely with the school's black students. In February 1990, the word was invoked again in a series of similar dust-ups at Detroit's Cabrini High School. And in 1993, a group of high school students from Morocco, Indiana, received national attention when their hip-hop-inflected style of speech and dress won them the "wigger" appellation, as well as death threats from their classmates.

But if "wigger" began as a term to deride those who came in overly close contact with blacks, today it has grown to mean someone with only cursory contact, who looks instead to a stereotypical, mass-distributed version of the black experience as a source of rage, energy, and identity. There may be no cultural archetype more freely and gleefully lambasted than the wigger. At the movies, teen comedies such as *Can't Hardly Wait* and *Mean Girls* paint wiggers as insecure nerds clinging to black masculinity as a means of appropriating some of the machismo they so lack. The satiric Web site *The Onion* used to feature a fake "guest columnist," Herbert "H-Dog" Kornfeld, who peppered his tales of life in the accounts receivable department at Midstate Office Supply with thugged-out proclamations such as "I gots to represent at tha muthafuckin' company picnic" and "Accountz reeceevin' ain't for no candy-ass temps." A quick Google search of the term "wigger" turns up an endless stream of vitriol. Wiggaz.com, which bills itself as "your online source for wiggers, wiggaz, white rappers, and suburban thugs," features pages of photographs of wiggers in the wild, complete with field notes. ("With his trust fund proceeds in hand, this wigger has set himself apart in the suburbs with the acquision of a sweet ride and rims to match.") Elsewhere, someone has written an online petition to "put an end to the wigger race." "If you are a wigger reading this," the petition reads, "pull up your pants, get a life and stop acting like a retard. If you are a normal person, please sign, and hopefully we can rid ourselves of this disease." When I come across the petition, eighty-two respondents have signed it.

In the face of all this scorn, it is worth remembering that wiggers are not the first band of white ne'er-do-wells to fetishize the trappings of blackness. Indeed, some of the counterculture's most beloved forefathers had wiggerish tendencies. Take Jack Kerouac,

whose jazz-inflected prose derived, at least in part, from an obsession with black Americans, and his belief that they were uniquely
equipped to escape a life of bourgeois drudgery. In *On the Road*, he
wrote of "wishing I were a Negro, feeling that the best the white
world had offered was not enough ecstasy for me, not enough life,
joy, kicks, darkness, music, not enough night."

Perhaps the best description of the wigger, however, comes
from Norman Mailer, whose infamous 1957 essay "The White
Negro" inadvertently showed how adoration could slip seamlessly
into exoticism and condescension: "Knowing in the cells of his existence that life was war, nothing but war, the Negro (all exceptions
admitted) could rarely afford the sophisticated inhibitions of civilization, and so he kept for his survival the art of the primitive, he
lived in the enormous present, he subsisted for his Saturday night
kicks, relinquishing the pleasures of the mind for the more obligatory pleasures of the body, and in his music he gave voice to the
character and quality of his existence, to his rage and the infinite
variations of joy, lust, languor, growl, cramp, pinch, scream and despair of his orgasm."

Mailer's understanding of black culture—as inherently more
criminal, physical, unthinking, brutish, emotional, sexual, and free
than square, uptight whiteness—may stem from a position of deep
admiration. And it certainly does seem an accurate depiction of what
some white people have always seen in blackness. But praising black
people for "liv[ing] in the enormous present" is like praising Jews for
their money-handling abilities. Under the guise of a compliment, it
limits the scope of a black person's expertise, implying that his value
only derives from his difference—from his countercultural cachet.
Black people who are intellectually engaged, middle-class, self-
sustaining, or otherwise not convinced that all of life is "nothing
but war" are relegated to the status of unremarkable exceptions.

It is this belief that defines wiggerism. In contrast to Wegroes, who hope that hip-hop can provide them some escape from the legacy of whiteness, wiggers turn to gangsta rap for its dazzling and terrifying exteriors: all that slang and fashion and scowling. One feels that there is something other than an urge toward racial communion at work here: instead we have white kids embracing what they see as the exceptional qualities of blackness—machismo, authenticity, and the notion that every action can have life-or-death consequences—to fill voids in their own lives, without considering or assuming the suffering that lies beneath it. One white kid summarized everything that offends people about wiggers in 1992, when he told the *Washington Post* that, despite his fascination with African American culture, he had no desire to actually *be* black. "I'm happy being white emulating black," he said. "You can just enjoy it and be part of it without dealing with the downside. You can be black without having the racism they deal with." In other words, wiggers interpret blackness as an easily mimicked series of verbal and physical cues, what Greg Tate calls "the tragic-magical displays of virility exhibited by America's ultimate outsider, the Black male."

And the more tragic, the better! Just as Mailer's hipster found himself drawn to blacks' purported love of "Saturday evening kicks," wiggers tend to celebrate the most extreme examples of antisocial behavior. This is where gangsta rap comes in. Even if you don't think that the music necessarily perverts young minds, you can still worry that white suburbanites who subsist on a steady diet of this stuff may develop some odd ideas about what it means to be black. Wiggers, like Mailer's White Negroes, value black expression only to the degree that it helps them voice some vague rejection of white American society. Blacks are attractive only because they are so exciting and scary and alien, so very different from you and me.

★ ★ ★

When I first meet Johnny Crack and his friends, they appear to have these tragic-magical displays down to a science. They are leaning up against a well-appointed Leaside home, passing joints around and sipping on bottles of beer, which they keep chilled in a snowbank. It takes a few minutes for me to tell them apart, in part because it's hard to see their faces beneath their oversized baseball caps and floppy parka-hoods, and also because they insist on referring to one another only by their hip-hop nicknames. Scott Camball, for instance, is universally known as Heve C; "Heve" is pronounced "heavy," which is a bit ironic since he looks as if a strong headwind would topple him. Mark Tarnovetsky goes by 20 Bagz. Pye Dog won't share his given name with me, in part because his own parents aren't aware of his secret identity. Johnny Crack's real name is John Nesbitt, a name he tells me he hates. First of all, "John" sounds more like a toilet or someone who pays for a prostitute. And then there's "Nesbitt," which is no good because people stress the second syllable, saying things like "how's it going Nes*bitt*?" in a way that implies the word "bitch." That's why, he tells me, he wants to officially change his last name to Ness, which I have to admit sounds cooler, even if it does belong to the most famous anti-gangster of all time.

Together, these guys, along with a seemingly endless supply of friends, part-time rhymers, and hangers-on, make up L-Side Entertainment. L-Side Entertainment could kindly be called a fledgling record label. But it would be more accurate to call it a bunch of white guys in their young twenties who occasionally record rap songs, which they self-publish and sell over the Internet. L-Side Entertainment was officially born at a party at Heve C's house in the spring of 2003, when Johnny Crack had been drinking too much beer and smoking a bit too much marijuana, and began freestyling into the internal microphone of one of Heve's computers. These days they try to record about three songs a week, which is all part of Johnny Crack's plans to ramp up production and "make millions." When they aren't rapping, they're usually still hanging out together, smoking weed, watching movies, playing video games. If Leaside is a bubble, the L-Siders have created a bubble within a bubble, a closed society where everyone speaks in Ebonics, listens to gangsta rap, and dresses the same.

And in which, it must be said, everyone is white. Although Johnny Crack proudly tells me that he used to attend an integrated high school and still has plenty of black friends, there are no black members of L-Side Entertainment. There used to be one but somewhere along the line he must have grown tired of their antics. Today, the only L-Side member with regular exposure to the black community is Heve C, who in addition to creating most of L-Side's music and managing its Web site has ventured into sales, hooking up with disc jockeys in New York who give him a percentage for selling their mixtapes on the streets of Toronto. This does not always go over so well with his largely black clientele. Heve says that he gets the feeling that some of his customers resent him, that they feel like white people are taking over even this now, even something so outrageous and painful and funny and offensive and *black* as gangsta rap. "I'm not as welcomed as I probably would be if I was black," he says. "But I think you can do whatever you want, you know? The world is yours. I don't think they should be getting mad if there's more white people getting into the business."

You can probably imagine for yourself how the L-Siders are dressed. The wigger uniform is pretty familiar by now: oversized sports jerseys and jeans that cling to their lower waists so that their rear pockets fall below the backs of their knees. Johnny Crack's clothes fit so loosely, and he is so skinny, that, should he decide to do a quick round of deep knee-bends, his pants would scarcely ripple. At twenty years of age and five and a half feet, he doesn't look as though he could withstand much in the way of physical assault. Should his many foes follow up on their threats to fly up to Toronto and attack him, Johnny Crack may be in trouble.

Johnny Crack may look harmless enough, but many folks here in Toronto worry that people like him are at least partly responsible for the cloud of violence that has descended upon the city. In 2005, Toronto saw an increase in gang activity, and the number of deaths due to handgun shootings nearly doubled, to fifty. This has proved to be a rattling data point for a city that has canonized its laid-back multiculturalism and low crime rates with the insufferable nickname "Toronto the Good." In their hunt for causes and villains, some civic leaders have turned their sights on hip-hop, which they say glamorizes criminal behavior and antisocial attitudes. "If I had a chance," the president of the Black Business and Professional Association told the *Christian Science Monitor*, "I'd get rid of the black entertainment culture tomorrow." He may not be the only one who feels this way: a member of the Detroit group Blakkattakk recently accused the Canadian government of targeting rappers when they tried to cross the border.

Perhaps this is why, when I am out in public with the members of L-Side, I can't help but notice that heads tend to turn our way. Sometimes these heads are turned in suspicion, as when Johnny Crack plunks himself down in a Chinese restaurant and immediately orders a double vodka with orange juice and a Molson. Sometimes they are turned in annoyance, as when, just a few minutes later, the couple sitting behind us gets visibly fed up with Johnny's repeated and high-decibel use of the adjective "fuckin'." But most frequently they are turned with a look that combines amusement and embarrassment and derision, like people who happen to catch someone with his fly undone.

The members of L-Side have been dressing and talking and acting like this for a while, and they've gotten used to being laughed at.

Johnny Crack, for one, has decided to welcome the derision; after years of unironically embracing gangsta rap, he has turned to self-parody. His music, he tells me, is "comedy rap," poking fun at those *other* wiggers out there who *really* want to be gangstas, instead of just pretending, as he does. This is a pretty subtle distinction, and Johnny confesses to me that his biggest challenge is in convincing people that he is not, in fact, serious. To that end, he's recording ever-more bizarre and offensive rhymes, such as his charming recent track about being born "a little crack baby." He summarizes his business plan thusly: "It's just going to get funnier and funnier and then it's going to blow up."

When Johnny Crack tells me this, I ask him how he knows that his favorite gangsta rappers aren't just joking as well. Maybe some of them, too, are playing with personae, making fun of stereotypes even as they embody them. (I stole this idea from, among others, Henry Louis Gates Jr., a scholar of black culture who has argued that the most outrageous rappers often operate within the African American tradition of "signifying," using irony and exaggeration to create a double-meaning, often missed by clueless white listeners.) I expect this question to completely blow Johnny Crack's mind, and I'm impressed with the blasé manner in which he brushes it off. "The big ones, I think they're probably all fake, but who knows?" he answers.

But not every member of Johnny Crack's posse is quite so cavalier. 20 Bagz—who, with his dusting of facial hair and piercing blue eyes, looks like Kurt Cobain with cornrows—takes his hip-hop very seriously. Although Johnny Crack and Heve C tell me they listen to gangsta rap because it entertains them or excites them or pumps them up, 20 Bagz, a supporting player in the L-Side empire, says that he finds the rappers honorable: "They are going through a crisis over there and no one even listens or knows about it. Kids just wear their pants sagging, but they don't know that shit is real, and people go to jail forever over some bullshit." He has had a chance to learn all of this firsthand through his three stints in prison and his brief experience as a drug-dealer and his struggle with cocaine addiction. "I've seen things that you would never want to see," he says, staring so intensely at me that I can't help but believe him.

These different approaches have led to a considerable amount of tension within the L-Side family, which flares up during even the most innocuous conversation. Take, for instance, this exchange, which occurred after 20 Bagz began answering a question about how L-Side was formed:

> **Johnny Crack**: I don't get any credit? Me and Heve were drunk one night and we started recording freestyles.
>
> **20 Bagz**: No, I mean before all that, how we got into rap before we even knew you.
>
> **Johnny Crack**: This is not rap. That's where you're getting it twisted. This is humor rap.
>
> **Heve C**: You were serious about it at the start, though.
>
> **Johnny Crack**: No, I was not at all. I fucking freestyled while I was drunk. How is that serious?
>
> **20 Bagz**: But then how do you explain how the last song we did was amazing? And that was trying, and it was good, and it was not a joke, though.
>
> **Johnny Crack**: It *is* a joke, though. It's funny because it's all gangsta and it's a bunch of white kids.
>
> **20 Bagz**: But I think it can make money.
>
> **Johnny Crack**: Yeah, being funny. If it's not funny, it's not going to go anywhere.

What these guys are really debating is the degree to which words correspond to their meanings, how much distance exists between using words like "gat" or "crack" or "gangsta" and endorsing or embodying what they represent. This is a question that penetrates to the heart of gangsta rap. One of the first examples of the form is Schoolly D's 1985 track, "P.S.K. What Does It Mean?" The technical answer to Schoolly D's musical question is "Park Side Killers," a Philadelphia street gang of which Schoolly D was a member. But the broader question—what does the song itself, a cold-eyed celebration of prostitution, drug dealing, and gun-brandishing, mean?—is harder to answer.

This question became particularly pointed in 1989, following the release of N.W.A.'s album *Straight Outta Compton*, and particularly the song "F____ tha Police." Some cultural critics held that reciting or listening to the song was virtually indistinguishable from actually taking a gun and killing a police officer. The track, which protested racial profiling and culminated with the simulated imprisonment of an offending officer, quickly won the attention of the FBI, whose assistant director for the Office of Public Affairs sent a letter to N.W.A.'s record label warning that the group "encourages violence against and disrespect for the law officer." *Focus on the Family Citizen*, the newsletter of the self-appointed cultural watchdog Reverend James C. Dobson, ran an article on N.W.A. and urged its readers to "alert local police to the dangers they [the police] may face." Officers arrested two teenagers in Omaha for reciting the song's lyrics, arguing that they constituted a call to arms. When the group broke its word and performed the song at a concert in Detroit, police rushed the stage and the band fled the scene. The distinction between art and crime, between word and deed, appeared to collapse entirely.

N.W.A. didn't clarify matters much when they responded that they were merely "underground street reporters" giving voice to the true emotions of the black underclass. By any account, the conditions of N.W.A.'s hometown of Compton, beset by the influx of crack cocaine and the exodus of job prospects, bore little resemblance to what most American families would recognize as reality. By 1989, the state of California was home to an estimated eighty thousand gang members; police officers were comparing the landscape of South Central to that of the Vietnam conflict; and the U.S. Army was sending doctors to hospitals in Watts so they could train surgeons in a war-zone-like setting. N.W.A. purported to speak the truths that most Americans could scarcely imagine; for evidence of the verisimilitude of their lyrics they showed off their publicity bios, which listed details of their past criminal acts, including car theft, drug sales, robbery, and breaking and entering.

If such performances were inseparable from gang activity, then it was no wonder that so many suburban parents freaked out when they heard their own children listening to N.W.A. or the scad of rap groups that soon followed their example, all of them bunched under the rubric "gangsta rap" (even though some artists preferred the term "reality rap"). The music's spreading popularity seemed to predict the gangs' growing power, power that seemed to be seeping out of inner-city confines and into the safest and most hermetically sealed neighborhoods. In 1988, a graphic artist named Karen Toshima was caught in gang crossfire and killed in the upscale Los Angeles suburb of Westwood, and one year later the *Boston Globe* reported that gang members were making forays into smaller cities such as Randolph and, in the words of one detective, "selling crack everywhere they go." Gangsta rap was so explicit in its linkage of word and deed that it was seen as the aural equivalent of a gateway drug, a first step that led inexorably to a life of street crime. One Los Angeles Police Department sergeant was stunned when his own son was busted for spraying graffiti, and kicked himself, in the pages of the *Los Angeles Times*, for missing the many warning signs. "My son took to using words that I knew were used by gang members," he wrote, bemoaning his mistaken assumption that "listening to rap music had no more significance than previous generations' listening to their own music, which their parents, too, had found objectionable."

"The music is enticing," warned the manager of the Orange County Department of Education's Operation Safe Schools program. "I guarantee you a lot of kids are being seduced."

But if the flap over gangsta rap began as a public policy debate, it soon turned into something else: a site for generational warfare. You didn't have to believe that gangsta rap would turn your son into a drug dealer or be one of the Moral Majoritarians, who were seeking artillery to launch their nascent culture war, to take issue with the litany of the music's offenses, which went way beyond the inappropriate skirt lengths and curfew scoffing that once represented the height of authority flouting. Even lefty-boomer parents found themselves in the uncomfortably square position of begging their kids to turn off that damn racket. It wasn't the obscenity per se, nor even the aggressive instrumentation that they found so troubling as much as the worldview. According to the mythos of the 1960s, pop music was meant to be a source of youthful optimism and idealism; this stuff was the absolute opposite. Jerry Adler, a *Newsweek* columnist, summed up an entire generation's objections to rap in a 1990 cover essay when he asked, "Whatever happened to the idea that rock and roll would make us free?"

Oh, hey, yeah, whatever *did* happen to that idea? Actually, in the years just before gangsta rap's explosion, it appeared to be making something of a rebound. In 1987, two short years before *Straight Outta Compton* broke, a slew of aged hippie heroes—the Grateful Dead, George Harrison, and Robbie Robertson—all released well-received comeback albums. A television special commemorated the twentieth anniversary of the "summer of love" and the Beatles' *Sgt. Pepper's Lonely Hearts Club Band* with gauzy, congratulatory flashbacks. The *Washington Post* announced, "Sixteen-year-olds are wearing tie-dyed T-shirts, sporting the peace symbol and flocking to concerts by the Grateful Dead; the sixties, suddenly and inexplicably, are In." A psychologist told the *New York Times* that many of his adolescent patients wished they had been born twenty years earlier, so that they could have experienced the sixties.

This sixties revival may have provided some cheery nostalgia to suddenly oldish boomers, but to me, an adolescent, it felt like bullying: This is what *we* accomplished; what have *you* done? As a child reared on tales of the powerful and moving sixties—when music mattered and children had the power to truly threaten the foundations of square society—I felt that my own youth culture could not help but pale by comparison. Not that I didn't try to tap into the rebellious spirit of Woodstock. I learned how to play a few Bob Dylan songs on my father's acoustic guitar. I went to see Oliver Stone's *JFK*, and debated the merits of various conspiracy theories. I headed to the planetarium, lay on my back, watched lasers dance on the ceiling to the strains of the Doors' "People Are Strange," and tried desperately to feel like I was experiencing something larger than myself. In college I eagerly attended political marches and rallies on the campus green, cheering my similarly earnest fellow students as they grabbed the battery-powered megaphones and shouted their support of any number of noble causes. But at no point did I ever get the sense that I was changing the world, as all those television shows and magazine articles told me a previous generation had felt. Instead, I felt that I was imitating someone else's childhood fantasy. Eventually this despair turned into resentment. I grew sick to death of boomer culture, particularly the way it sanctimoniously linked its musical tastes and pre-AIDS sexual freedoms and drug experimentation with moral superiority. I was frustrated at the way former hippies and hippie sympathizers used their youth movement as a cudgel, a way to compare their moment of generational euphoria with all that came before and after and find the others lacking. I was annoyed that I couldn't feel the same sense of optimism, for the simple fact that so much of that optimism proved ill-founded.

And so I ran headfirst into the muscled, tattooed arms of gangsta rap. In 1991, Nirvana started a song with a sarcastically off-key rendition of the hippie anthem "Get Together," but to me, the violence and anger of gangsta rap provided a more biting critique of boomer optimism and self-satisfaction. It certainly seemed to annoy the older generation more than Nirvana ever could. Sixties veterans from Tipper Gore to Bill Clinton called out rappers for special scorn. Some depicted their battles against gangsta rap as a continuation of the social causes they had championed three decades earlier. C. DeLores Tucker, who famously partnered with a conservative, Bill Bennett, to pressure record labels to drop gangsta-rap acts, compared her efforts to her experiences in the civil rights movement: "We'll be demonstrating and going to jail, just like we did in the sixties, to show those in power that we're not going to have it." Schools banned clothing associated with the music, particularly the ubiquitous baggy pants, not because they were bellwethers of actual gang activity but because they carried a vague sense of menace and annoyance. A *St. Petersburg Times* opinion piece, bemoaning the loss of Cleaver-family values, wrote that the younger generation's "backward baseball caps turn me off. Beaver, however, a well-adjusted child, wears his baseball cap forward." After a couple of years of this, it became hard to remember what gangsta rap initially represented: the voice of a neglected black America. Instead, the debate spiraled into the purely symbolic, and gangsta rap became the latest vehicle to express generic youth rebellion.

All of this was good for business. As gangsta rap became a generational flashpoint, the music itself proved more and more irresistible. Records with a parental advisory label, which the Recording

Industry Association of America adopted under pressure in 1990, routinely outsold the "clean" versions, which had been scrubbed free of profanity to avoid the sticker. 2 Live Crew, a marginally successful rap group, sold over a million copies of its *As Nasty As They Wanna Be* album, in spite of an effort to ban its sale in Florida that turned the group into a First Amendment cause celebre. And on June 21, 1991, *USA Today* reported that N.W.A.'s full-length follow-up to *Straight Outta Compton, Efil4zaggin*, was the country's top-selling pop album, a feat that only four other rap acts—the Beastie Boys, MC Hammer, Tone-Loc, and Vanilla Ice—had accomplished. Even more surprising was the album's cross-genre appeal, selling to customers that had previously avoided rap in favor of heavy-metal acts such as Guns N' Roses.

But *Efil4zaggin* was a different kind of gangsta rap than that of the first N.W.A. album, more cinematic freak-show than underground news report. Where *Straight Outta Compton* evoked rage, *Efil4zaggin* ratcheted up the terror. The between-song skits played out like pictureless snuff films, with the band's members killing a prostitute and cackling over the sound of machine-gun fire and shrieking civilians. Songs such as "One Less Bitch" and "Appetite for Destruction" painted the rappers as criminally insane rapists, torturers, and murder junkies. And beneath it all throbbed the drum-beat repetition of the infamous n-word. According to *ego trip's Book of Rap Lists, Straight Outta Compton* contained 42 uses of the word "nigga," and *Efil4zaggin* 249. By the end of the album, the word acted more as numbing mantra than provocative slur, an amalgamation of syllables carrying no more inherent meaning than the letters that spelled it.

There are not many albums that still sound shocking fifteen years later, but *Efil4zaggin* is one of them. In a way this is quite an accomplishment. You would think that after so much time and so many followers, the tales of cold-blooded murder and nihilistic glee would lose some of their *frisson*. N.W.A. inspired a deluge of gangsta rappers who mimicked not only the group's musical approach, the West Coast combination of slithery funk and coolly malevolent lyrics, but its philosophical approach as well. Just as N.W.A. claimed to be street reporters, so did their adherents describe their songs as musical representations of their actual lives and emotions. When South Central Los Angeles erupted in flames following the verdict in the 1992 Rodney King trial, gangsta rappers had a four-word message for a confused and terrified world: We told you so. "When rap came out of L.A., what you heard initially was my voice yelling about South Central," Ice-T told *Rolling Stone*. "People thought, 'That shit's crazy,' and ignored it. Then N.W.A. came out and yelled, Ice Cube yelled about it. People said, 'Oh, that's just kids making a buck.' They didn't realize how many niggas with attitude there are out on the street. Now you see them."

This emphasis on verisimilitude has helped to turn rappers' offstage lives into an integral part of the performance. Gangsta rappers are judged not just on their microphone abilities, lyricism, or beats but also on the degree to which their performances are deemed to be honest, representative of their true experiences, fantasies, hopes, dreams. After N.W.A.'s breakup in 1991, Eazy-E's strongest argument against his successful former bandmate Dr. Dre was to accuse him of being a "studio gangsta"—someone who faked his street credentials.

But how can the rap fan determine the real from the fake, the original from the copy, real life from performance? There is an old hip-hop adage, "Real recognizes real," shorthand for the notion that true, authentic gangstas or hip-hop heads have an inherent ability to separate the genuine expressions of urban angst from the pretenders. Perhaps that is so. But what about the rest of us?

This question has grown ever more complicated in the years since N.W.A., as the line between life and performance has grown ever blurrier. Label chief Irv Gotti borrowed his name, fashion sense, and management philosophies from Mafia dons, many of whom lifted their own personae from the pulpy pages of *The Godfather*. The lead rapper of a group called the Geto Boys named himself after a cartoonish film antihero, Tony "Scarface" Montana. His bandmate Bushwick Bill botched a suicide attempt and got shot in the eye; the group's subsequent album cover showed the three MCs at Bushwick Bill's hospital bed after the incident, scowling into the camera. The rappers 50 Cent and the Game nursed ill feelings toward each other that exploded into gunfire outside a Manhattan radio studio, which won them both bushels of press—suspiciously close to both artists' album release dates. Tupac Shakur was gunned down in Las Vegas; Michael Eric Dyson, a professor of humanities and cultural commentator, argued that his downfall stemmed in part from his hip-hop role playing: "Perhaps more than any other rapper, Tupac tried to live the life he rapped about, which had spectacular results in the studio but disastrous results in the world." The Notorious B.I.G. repeatedly performed his own death on album, eventually providing the soundtrack to his own demise when his album *Life After Death*, which included the song "You're Nobody ('Til Somebody Kills You)," was released just after his murder.

How much of this is "keeping it real" and how much play-acting? How much is mere signifying—carrying stereotypes to their breaking points—and how much sincerity? How can anyone "keep it real" when reality itself is so infused with fantasy? How can we tell which lives are based on performance, and which performances are based on life? Or is there even a difference?

★ ★ ★

It's no surprise that the birthplace of the musical genre that raises all these questions would be Los Angeles. I lived in Los Angeles until 1980, when I was five years old. Then my parents—horrified at the air-kissy, let's-lunch-at-Spago, Bret Easton Ellis artificiality of the place—hightailed it to the rootsy Pacific Northwest. This may be why friends have told me that I have an "authenticity fetish": I appear to have inherited my family's distrust of Southern California as a place of plastic insincerity where everyone is acting, seemingly waiting for his big break.

I may hold some extra antipathy for Los Angeles because I also happened to come of age alongside *Beverly Hills 90210*, a truly distasteful program that chronicled the misadventures of a group of self-satisfied, rich white kids who went to high school in Beverly Hills. Every week, characters named Brenda and Dylan would drive sports cars and squint sexily at one another and nurse unrequited crushes and battle such after-school-special challenges as pregnancy scares and alcoholism. The show was baldly unrealistic, and it was impossible for me to watch it without gritting my teeth and shaking my fist at those spoiled Californians, so smug and beautiful and fake. Still, my friends and I watched (and cursed) it regularly, and I can't say that we didn't in some way model our own relationships and fashions and squints on the hyperreal versions we saw on TV every week.

But if you look at a page from the Beverly Hills High School yearbook from around that time, you won't see *Beverly Hills 90210* stars Jason Priestley or Shannen Doherty or Luke Perry gleaming back at you. Instead you'll see a gaggle of well-scrubbed teenagers decked out in the latest gangsta fashions—oversized flannel shirts, Chicago White Sox ball caps—glowering into the camera. They are assembled in self-proclaimed "crews"—"West Side" and "Players," for instance—and their photos are supplemented with a list of their handles: Boog-Dog and Madskills and Crack. Even as my classmates and I were pretending to be Beverly Hills high school students, it turns out that those same students were pretending to be extras in a gangsta-rap video.

The yearbook photo comes courtesy of Luke Buffum, Beverly Hills High class of '94, who tells me that his classmates' emulation didn't end with wardrobes or nicknames. It carried over into the parking lot, where the hottest cars weren't Porsches or Ferraris, but low-riders, often equipped with custom rims, hydraulic switches, and illegally tinted windows. Buffum describes a typical weekend: "You would go to these parties, the streets would be lined with cars as far as the eye can see. You'd roll up, and whatever you were listening to, it had to be hard-core serious, and it had to be gangsta rap. People would be rolling down their windows halfway and yelling 'Drive-by, nigga!' at each other. Then you'd go into the party. It was like a rap video, except it was all white kids. You'd have guys in security jackets who would pat you down for weapons, and then you'd roll in and the first thing you would see would be an open refrigerator filled with forty [-ounce malt liquor] bottles, just like Snoop Doggy Dogg's 'Gin and Juice' video.

"At ten-thirty, all of a sudden the entire place would be surrounded by blue lights. The police would roll in like thirty cars. Everyone would start screaming, throwing their marijuana in chandeliers. Then the police would bust in the door and everyone would pour out of the house, screaming 'It's the pigs!' It was a huge adrenaline rush."

I hate to admit how familiar this all sounds. As Buffum talks, my mind flashes back to a college party where all of the white guests greeted police with a terrified cry of "Five-oh!"—rap-speak for "cop"—as if our plastic cups of Natural Light beer represented as severe an affront to the system as the gun-toting narratives we'd grown so familiar with. Still, my friends and I never pushed the role-playing quite as far as Buffum's classmates. "We were at this party," Buffum continues, "and there were these guys all standing in a group. They started talking junk, and all of a sudden one guy pulls out a gun. He's holding it sideways, just like a gangsta, and he puts it in this other guy's chest. All of a sudden everybody starts freaking out. I started to run, but I was curious, so I stood behind a wall, where I could still see what was going on. This kid with a gun in his chest is taunting the other guy: 'You won't pull the trigger! You're scared!' And the guy pulls the trigger. I almost passed out. But the thing is, the guy doesn't fall down. It was a cap gun. The guy with the cap gun starts running and laughing, and everybody else had already run off, so they thought someone really got shot. It created a movie right there. I think the whole thing was set up to get people excited, but to this day, I don't know for sure."

Johnny Crack flings open the door to his recording studio—actually Heve C's garage, nestled among a row of well-appointed town houses—and asks whether anyone has any chronic. I assume this question is a formality. "Chronic" is street slang for a particularly potent strain of marijuana, and its overpowering smokey-sweet scent wallops me as we enter the garage. I squint through the haze to make out the details of the room, a testament to all things male. Free weights litter the perimeter; a seventy-five-pound Everlast punching bag sways gently in the center. Ripped-out magazine pages decorate the walls, almost every one of which portrays some heavily tattooed rapper glowering menacingly into the camera. (The others feature taut-skinned black women in various stages of undress and repose.) A fake stop sign near the door reads STOP SNITCHING, a street motto discouraging cooperation with the police. The recording equipment, two cheap desktop computers, sits in one corner of the room, next to a miniature synthesizer and a Numark turntable.

We are here to record Johnny Crack's latest song. One indication of Johnny's newfound professionalism is that he has begun writing his rhymes in advance, as opposed to stepping in front of the microphone and spewing (or, to be generous, "freestyling") the first words that pop into his head. He tells me that it takes him about thirty minutes to write his lyrics, and another thirty minutes to record and produce a song.

Once he can get down to the business of recording, that is, which proves inordinately difficult. Heve C's recording studio also serves as an all-purpose crash pad, and a seemingly endless supply of friends cycles through the garage throughout the evening. They take quick bong hits and huddle around the computer to listen to the latest music that Heve C has come up with. The general consensus: pretty sick, although some of the beats need to be "a little more gangsterized" before they're ready to be rhymed over. (Nobody can tell me exactly what this means.) Johnny Crack pulls out his latest rhyme, and everyone gathers around as he tries out his new lyrics. The recitation doesn't come off flawlessly—Johnny cracks up when he gets to a line about shooting his housecat—but for the most part, everyone agrees that Johnny has kept things pretty gully.

"That's a sick flow, man," says one member of the entourage, sipping from a jug of Granite Brewery Ale. "I've never heard that flow from you before, fast and then slow." Johnny beams.

When I step out of the studio, opening the door of the garage and walking into the town house's basement, I have to blink a couple of times to take in the sudden change in atmosphere. It is as if someone has turned on a lightswitch in the middle of a pitch-black room. The weed smoke and beats and photos of black bodies are all gone. I am outside the L-Side gangsta bubble, back in the Leaside suburbia bubble. I climb a staircase that leads to the living room. Heve C's mother is there; she owns this house. Her name is Pat and she teaches organizational behavior at York University's business school. She shakes my hand and offers me a seat on a couch near the eight-foot-tall Christmas tree that glows in the center of the room. She warns me away from the cat, Onyx, who is named for a Pokémon character and not, it turns out, for the early-nineties hardcore rap act responsible for songs such as "Blac Vagina Finda."

Pat parks her Mazda Protegé on the street, something she's had to do ever since she converted her garage into a studio for her son and his friends to use. Her car's windows have been smashed a couple of times, but this, she tells me, is a minor price to pay to know that her son is safe. It turns out that before Heve C began pursuing a career as a hip-hop producer, he, like 20 Bagz, had dabbled in drug dealing. Pat knew nothing about it until she learned that her son had been arrested for possession; she put up six thousand dollars to pay for a lawyer good enough to get Heve C's sentence reduced.

Pat's generosity has won the L-Siders' undying devotion. I have heard four different people tell Heve C that seriously, dude, his mom is awesome. They refer to her as "our Suge Knight," a reference to the terrifying chief of Death Row Records, who has been rumored of doing everything from dangling Vanilla Ice over the side of a building to playing a role in the killing of The Notorious B.I.G.

Even so, Pat is not exactly a big fan of rap music, much of which she says she finds misogynist and racist and homophobic and dreadful. She tells me that her neighbors are terrified of her son (whom she still calls Scott) and his friends, not realizing that they are playacting. Still, now that all of the L-Siders have backed away from the drug dealing and the threats of violence— now that their fascination with black gangstas is back in the realm of fantasy—she says she's happy to provide them with a place to make their music.

"I think what they're doing down there is fine now," she says. "They've distanced themselves enough from the culture. Now they're making fun of it."

Back in the basement, Johnny Crack is still getting ready to unleash his new rhyme, but the garage never gets quiet enough for him to rap; fresh bodies continue to move through the studio, contributing to a constant dull buzz of conversation. Most of the talk consists of place-holding catchphrases, with the increasingly drunk and stoned Leasiders continually telling one another how "gangsta," "gully," and "crack" they are. At one point, a tall, clean-cut guy in a trim leather jacket and dark sweater approaches me.

"We usually dress more gangsta," he apologizes, "but we're going out tonight."

"Honestly, Ryan is fucking gangsta," Johnny says, pointing at the guy. "He will fucking fight."

"No doubt, nigga," Ryan says, twisting his fingers into a W and flinging them next to his face, Tupac Shakur's famed "westside" sign that indicated his fealty to the West Coast.

But all conversation ends when Pye Dog swaggers through the studio doors. The only other member of L-Side with a full-length album to his name, Pye Dog, a burly clown with immaculately gelled hair, lumbers up to me as soon as he sees my microphone and begins shouting impromptu rhymes with such energy that it becomes impossible for anyone else to speak. "I got it all in my head! I got bitches on the bedspread! he shouts. "Yo son, I got ten fingers and they can all pull the trigger!" This goes on for a good five minutes. Eventually, I turn off my recorder. I get the sense he could go on like this indefinitely, rearranging the same snippets of imagery and verbiage—bitches, crack, guns—over and over again. There's nothing shocking about this kind of language anymore. The words no longer connote the threat of actual violence, or sexual prowess. They certainly don't seem to represent the social conditions of the inner city. At this late date, in a place like this, coming out of a guy like Pye Dog, they are simply boring. They are a mass of meaningless tropes and verbal tics, signifying absolutely nothing.

CHAPTER SEVEN
White-on-White Rhyme: *8 Mile*, Nerdcore, and Mooks

White rappers, if they grew up in the suburbs, should play off it, like, "Hi! I'm white."

—**Eminem, quoted in Anthony Bozza,**
Whatever You Say I Am: The Life and Times of Eminem

Let me count the reasons why MC Frontalot should not, if history is a reliable guide, be a successful rapper. First off, he is white. And I don't mean that he "happens to be" white, that his skin color is in some way incongruent with the rest of his personality, in the way that MC Serch or Paul Wall—a popular rapper from Houston with diamond-encrusted teeth and a deep immersion in that city's hip-hop community—happen to be white. MC Frontalot is *white*. His high-pitched voice has that telltale nasal hum common to white rappers, and he tends to overenunciate his words, hitting the *ng*'s and *r*'s hard, rather than smoothly gliding over them like most of the other artists in his genre. He may be the only MC ever to express a deep and abiding love for musical theater; as a member of a theater troupe called Emerald Rain Productions, he cowrote *Young Zombies in Love*, a satirical (non-hip-hop) musical that won an award at the New York Fringe Festival in 1994. His six-foot-one frame is gangly and gawky. When he cracks a joke or reflects on some ridiculous aspect of his rap career, which he often does, his mouth spreads into an eager, goofy grin, and when he laughs, it is a collection of sharp, short gasps that reminds me of my own.

But perhaps the most atypical thing about MC Frontalot is that he is not ashamed to admit that he fronts. A lot. This is not something that most rappers would readily concede: to "front" means to adopt a fake pose, and anyone deemed to be fronting risks losing his reputation in the credibility-obsessed world of hip-hop. But MC Frontalot has no problem with this. "I am so not a cool rap guy," he tells me. "It's like, for me to pick up a microphone and press 'record,' I have to front so hard. Just to hold a mike up to my mouth. Most people don't have to front that much all day."

In short, MC Frontalot is a geek. If he weren't, he probably wouldn't be where he is right now, mobbed by admirers at the 2005 Penny Arcade Expo at a convention center in Bellevue, Washington. Until about three weeks ago, I had never heard of the Penny Arcade Expo, a confab hosted by and named after a Web site for video-game enthusiasts, but apparently that's just because I am not a big enough geek, a word that here has lost its stigma and become a prideful expression of self-identification. The Web site draws 250,000 geeks every day, who log on to check out the latest snarky game review or esoteric comic strip. (One recent punchline: "The guild needs a level 60 priest and you need to cowboy up.") Nine thousand geeks have convened here, traveling from such far-flung locales as New Zealand and Japan, and they have turned the Meydenbauer Center into Geek Central. They mill around the "free play" zone on the first floor, where they plug into consoles, hunch forward with their elbows on their thighs, and silently battle their way through *Mario Tennis* or *Halo 2*. Those who favor more regimented gameplay head up to the fourth floor, where they can join a *Super Smash Brothers* or *Tekken 5* tournament. Others check out the exhibition hall, where they can take a spin in a spherical virtual-reality machine, or try the latest military recruitment device, a game called *America's Army*. Should their endurance flag, they can head up to a table by the fourth-floor escalators and pick up a free can of a highly caffeinated energy drink called Bawls.

And right now, many of them are hovering around a table on the mezzanine floor where MC Frontalot presides. Tomorrow night, MC Frontalot—who uses his government name, Damian Hess, when working at his regular job as a freelance web and print designer—will perform in concert in front of many of these people, but for now he's sitting behind a pile of T-shirts and a stack of *Nerdcore Rising* CDs, his newly minted self-published full length debut, pressing the somewhat oily-looking flesh of his many fans, most of whom do not look all that different from MC Frontalot. The overwhelming majority of them are not just white but downright translucent, possessed of the wan, slick look of people who have spent more time maintaining their online profiles than their corporeal ones, and they are people around whom MC Frontalot looks supremely comfortable. He grins and shrugs when one rotund individual castigates him for not carrying enough XXXL-sized T-shirts. He gamely plays along when another fan begs him to leave an outgoing message on his voicemail. When any of his fans buy a CD, he encourages them to roll his two twenty-sided Dungeons & Dragons dice; a roll of thirty-nine or forty wins them a copy of his rare demo CD ("It's a tough roll," Frontalot concedes). And he beams with astonishment when a starstruck younger fan approaches his table. "Are you MC Frontalot?" the nineteen-year-old asks. "I've been listening to your stuff since ninth grade."

"Wow," MC Frontalot responds, with what sounds like genuine bewilderment.

But perhaps he should not be so surprised. After all, MC Frontalot is something of a legend here. His big break came in

2001, when the Penny Arcade site linked to one of his songs, "Yellow Lasers," about a sexual escapade at a Star Wars convention. The resulting crush of traffic provided MC Frontalot with the bulk of his fan base. Today, MC Frontalot enjoys the title of Penny Arcade's official rapper, a distinction that led him to record a theme song for the Web site. The chorus, "L-shift-O-to-the-quote and then dollar," is a reference, he tells me, to "the beginning of the syntax for loading a directory off of a disk on a Commodore 64." Other MC Frontalot songs address such pressing geek concerns as spam e-mail and Internet porn.

Frontalot is also credited with coining the phrase "nerdcore hip-hop," a term that describes a new and burgeoning genre of rap in which unabashedly geeky MCs forego tales of crime and aggression to rhyme about such topics as computer programming, science fiction, civil engineering, and the second law of thermodynamics. Frontalot came up with the "nerdcore" name in 2000, a year after he began recording hip-hop tracks on his desktop. "It was just sort of a goof," he says. "I was sitting there, rapping by myself in front of the computer, and I was like: 'This is nerdcore. Who's as nerd as this? Just me.'"

It turns out, though, that it was not just he. Two tables to Frontalot's left sits mc chris, a former animator of the Cartoon Network who left his job in 2004 to pursue his rapping full-time (and makes his iconoclasm apparent by insisting on keeping all the letters of his handle lower-case). Today, he runs neck and neck with Frontalot for the title of Most Popular Nerdcore Rapper. This is saying something; the world of nerdcore rap is expanding almost as inexorably as the universe according to Hubble's Law. In addition to Frontalot and mc chris, there is MC Hawking, who delivers his rhymes via a talking computer, in the style of the famous physicist Stephen Hawking. Ytcracker refers to himself as a "digital gangster" and waxes nostalgic about his early coding days: "Every time

I wrote a GOTO, bitch, I had that baby looping." MC Plus+ boasts on his Web site that he is "to [computer science] gangsta rap what a blue screen is to Windows" and dedicates his art to "all the grad students in the struggle." By now, the tradition is so established that self-described "second-generation" nerdcore rappers have begun to appear, such as Ultraklystron, twenty-one, who calls himself an "open-source lyricist."

mc chris rejects the "nerdcore" label as he rejects any attempt to categorize his music, other than as "crap." But it is hard to think of a more apt description. mc chris's best-known song is "Fett's Vette," an ode to Boba Fett, a minor character in the *Star Wars* movies, but his other hits include a song about overdosing on Robitussin, and another about playing *Super Mario Brothers* in an effort to "get Mario laid." He tours almost constantly; he's already scheduled to perform at two more conventions this year, Atlanta's Dragon Con and Chicago's Wizard World. Physically, he is the Oliver Hardy to MC Frontalot's Stan Laurel: not fat, but short and pug-doggish. Behind him hangs a banner that reads FAKE RAP FOR REAL PEOPLE. When I ask him what the slogan means, he tells me, "Everyone's living vicariously through 50 Cent. I thought, why not put the mirror up and be like, 'We're pretty awesome as we are'? It's kind of a self-empowerment thing. Especially with nerds, who feel like they're losers and like to run away into these imaginary video-game landscapes where they can be the handsome seven-foot-tall warlord. I'm saying, you can be the warlord in real life, too."

That is a message that has resonated strongly with the crowd here at the Penny Arcade Expo. Most of us tend to associate hip-hop with the code of the streets, not the code of computer programmers. But MC Frontalot and mc chris's geeksta-rap has proved wildly popular to a certain population who don't feel comfortable listening to Tupac Shakur or Jay-Z. "This is the first time I thought I could rap about various things I was into," says Ultraklystron, whose real name is Karl Olson. "I wasn't a hip kid. I had a periodic table in my binder when I was in second grade. I have *manga* [Japanese comic books] in my backpack *right now*. But in some ways, this is very true to hip-hop's roots, because we're talking about day-to-day life. It's just day-to-day life for a kid who's living in the suburbs and spending two to eight hours every day on the Internet."

"This lets me enjoy a kind of music that I never had any claim to in the past," says one MC Frontalot fan, a college student wearing a T-shirt that depicts an old Nintendo controller over the slogan KEEP IT REAL. "Now I actually have a style of music that is hip-hop and cool and urban, or whatever you want to call it. And I can say, 'This is my brand of hip-hop.'"

Nerdcore is just the most striking example of a trend that has been escalating since the dawn of the millennium: hip-hop without the blackness; white performers singing in front of almost entirely white audiences about topics and themes that are familiar to their own, white, lives. This goes beyond geeks. Although the hip-hop magazines and pop charts are still dominated by black musicians, the underground rap scene is rife with white MCs, many of whom have fan bases that contain hardly a drop of melanin. Today there are white rappers whose concerts primarily attract white heavy-metal listeners (Non Phixion), white bookish palindrome fanatics (MC Paul Barman), white collegiate students of Joycean obscurantism (Aesop Rock), white tortured-poet types (Sage Francis), and white would-be class warriors (Vinnie Paz of Jedi Mind Tricks). Welcome to the age of white-on-white rhyme.

"I don't think in the history of hip-hop there's ever been this many white rappers," says the hip-hop journalist Gabriel Alvarez. "Groups like 3rd Bass had to constantly refer to their whiteness, and they constantly had to explain themselves and make reference to their being nonblack. Now I think up-and-coming rappers don't have to deal with that anymore."

Not only don't they have to deal with it, they exist in their own hermetic subcultures where white kids can interact with hip-hop without interacting with blackness. "I lived in Boston from 1991 to 1994," says Erik "Mr. Eon" Meltzer, the white MC who heads up the underground Philadelphia rap duo High & Mighty. "It's kind of a racially charged town, and I remember performing at parties and I was the only white dude there. And I'd get the mike snatched from me. Black people now are obviously used to seeing white people rapping, but this was a time when it was like, 'Get the fuck off the stage! You're white!' Now it's a completely different world. There's so many white MCs. In the underground, people who sell ten thousand to seventy-five thousand units, all the big groups are white. I know one hundred fifty white MCs in the underground. And their audiences are all nerdy, or they feel like outcasts, or they're into skateboarding. All these different kids are going to these shows, and I don't know, man. I don't like a lot of the underground stuff. The culture of it is that of a seventeen-to-twenty-four-year-old white dude who's in college."

This is quite a change from the post–Vanilla Ice era of the early to mid-1990s, when hip-hop was so tied to blackness that almost every white rapper draped himself in Wegro self-consciousness and scrambled to identify himself as somehow nonwhite, and white listeners depended on urban black audiences to help them distinguish dope from wack. Just when, exactly, did it become okay for white people to stop worrying and drop lyrical bombs?

An early indication of the coming thaw occurred in 1992, when the Beastie Boys released their third album, *Check Your Head*, a hodgepodge of hardcore punk songs, amateurish funk instrumentals, and the group's classic adenoidal rhyme style. The album returned the Beastie Boys to national prominence, although it splintered the black-white coalition that had formed their audience for *Licensed to Ill*. Members of the traditional hip-hop community may have respected the album, but they largely ignored it. The writer Touré summed up the air of grudging respect the group received from some hip-hoppers with his 1998 four-star *Rolling Stone* review of the group's album *Hello Nasty*: "See all those stars up there?" he wrote. "That means I can't walk down my block for a whole month. For a black man, championing the Beasties is like being down with Madonna or rooting for the Utah Jazz." Instead, the Beasties tapped into, and helped create, a new force: white kids who combined rap's attitude with skater style to create their own version of hip-hop culture. This was the precursor to white-on-white rhyme, but for years it represented a sui generis anomaly.

The real breakthrough occurred in June 1999, when the highly respected hip-hop magazine the *Source* published an approving six-page profile of the rap world's latest superstar, a white kid from Detroit named Marshall Mathers III but better known as Eminem. Before Eminem, it was assumed that a white person could never become a truly great rapper. Although a handful of white MCs had received a modicum of credibility—the Beastie Boys; MC Serch; underground up-and-comers such as El-P and the hardcore shock-rapper R.A. the Rugged Man—none of them were seen as possible entrants among the ranks of hip-hop legends. But Eminem's breakthrough album, 1999's *The Slim Shady LP*, for the first time raised the specter of a white boy who could truly compete, who could signify with the best of the black guys, and whose complex rhyme structures and smooth delivery approached those of such revered figures as Rakim and The Notorious B.I.G. Furthermore, Eminem's appeal extended beyond the hard-core hip-hop heads. His humor, good looks, outrageous persona, and—as Eminem himself would often admit—his white skin appealed to even the most sheltered of teeny-bopper mallrats, kids who may never have picked up a rap CD before in their lives. This was a white guy who was talented *and* commercial, an exciting but threatening prospect.

The *Source*'s article, headlined "Fear of a White Rapper," addressed the hip-hop community's mixed emotions. Several sidebars flanked the Eminem feature. One, titled "White-Out Alert," asked whether the rise of a successful white rapper foretold a future in which "rap cease[s] to live up to its subtext as the Blackest music around? Or will hip-hop be refashioned, over the next few years, into music that is primarily performed by, bought by, and enjoyed by white people?" Professor Michael Eric Dyson contributed a column on the phenomenon of white rap fans who feel entitled to use the word "nigga." A two-page spread investigated "the past and present contributions of white MCs to hip-hop" and determined that—all complications aside—"to imagine you can racially limit hip-hop's growth or negate the cultural contributions white folks have made by incorporating hip-hop into other forms and styles of music would be wrong." But the package's centerpiece, the Eminem profile, seemed to settle the issue once and for all with its conclusion that, whatever your beliefs or fears about the impact that he would have, you could not question Eminem's talent and passion. The piece ended with a three-word sentiment that pointed to a new frontier for hip-hop: "Color be damned."

If you listened carefully, you could hear almost two decades of failed white MCs and nervous white fans all crying as one: "How did he do it?" How did Eminem, who represented the greatest threat to hip-hop's black identity, win the respect and imprimateur of one of the industry's most discriminating gatekeepers? Of course, some of it had to do with his undeniable talent and skill. Some of it had to do with the fact that he had paid his dues, proving himself in freestyle battles instead of being plucked from obscurity by label executives seeking the next Great White Hope.

OTHER PEOPLE'S PROPERTY

Eminem could also boast a seal of approval from his mentor and producer, Dr. Dre, the former member of N.W.A. whose solo album, *The Chronic*, became one of the most beloved gangsta-rap albums ever. Unlike some other white rappers, Eminem's top priority seemed to be winning over the respect of the hip-hop community rather than climbing the pop charts. Furthermore, Eminem grew up poor, recalling in songs and interviews his life of economic hardship: how his father abandoned him when he was six months old; the time he hid his family's welfare cheese under a piece of lettuce where his friends wouldn't see it; getting fired from his minimum-wage job right before Christmas, with a baby girl to support. The fact that Eminem came to hip-hop as a troubled, alienated child seeking an outlet instead of a pampered dilettante looking for the next cool thing impressed the *Source* enough for the magazine to conclude that Eminem represented a broadening of the definition of the hip-hop nation to one based more on class than on race: "Rap music is the language of the disenfranchised, a slang speech of outrage and anger (and joy and love) from a people who don't have more mainstream ways of articulating themselves. And some of those people are white folks. Poor white folks."

But perhaps most important, Eminem didn't front; he was unabashedly white. Listen again to *The Slim Shady LP*. You won't hear any Ebonics or roughneck posing or racial politics. He drops references to such white pop-culture icons as the Spice Girls, Pamela Anderson Lee, and Nine Inch Nails. Instead of attempting to blacken his image with baggy clothing or gruff vocals, Eminem keeps it real white: platinum-blond hair, nasal delivery, cheeky lyrical comparisons to previous white MCs such as Miilkbone and the Beastie Boys' Mike D. All those ghetto signifiers that defined traditional rap are replaced by symbols of trailer-park depravity. Instead of drinking forty-ounce bottles of malt liquor, Eminem raps about taking speed. Rather than singing about hypermasculine pimps, Eminem describes a pathetic, guilt-wracked episode of statutory rape. While N.W.A.'s "Dopeman" was told from the perspective of a crack dealer, the salesman in Eminem's "I'm Shady" offers a different selection: mushrooms, LSD, and aspirin. And while Tupac Shakur rapped reverently of his noble, long-suffering mother, Eminem excoriates his mother, accusing her of everything from drug abuse to neglect to (weirdly) breastlessness.

Eminem's reliance on such white subject matter won him more than "keep-it-real" points from the hip-hop community; it also won him a huge fan base of white kids who could see themselves more readily in his rhymes than in those of his black counterparts. "He's talking to them, too" Mark Kempf, the head of a Detroit music label, told the *Metro Times*, "about going to school and being white and getting picked on and stuff that white kids can relate to."

That's pretty much how Euc Pereyra felt the first time he heard Eminem. Pereyra is MC Frontalot's hype man, a sidekick who performs onstage with him under the name Gelatinous Cube, yelling at the crowd to keep them energized and acting as a comical counterpart to the (already comical) main attraction of Frontalot. Pereyra looks like his fellow Penny Arcade geeks in most ways—he's got glasses and a smattering of curly facial hair and a plump body—but he stands out in one sense: his skin color. Pereyra is Dominican, but he tells me that he identifies more with geek culture than with his own racial heritage: "I'm a geek, first and foremost." And although he listened to some rap as a kid, he grew disenchanted with the genre as gangsta rap overtook it. Occasionally he'd hear something that sparked his interest. Eminem for instance. "I had no idea who this guy was," he says. "I just heard these songs that were ridiculously good." He recites a couple of lines from the chorus of "My Fault," in which Eminem apologizes for giving a young woman an overdose of psychedelic mushrooms. "I'm like, I've been that girl! And I've been that guy! You know: 'Sorry about that; I guess we shouldn't have done that much.'"

That feeling of identification is also what drew Pereyra and other die-hard nerdcore fans to Frontalot's music. Finally, someone was rapping about something they knew and cared about, something that didn't make them feel uncomfortable or alienated, as they usually did when they listened to hip-hop. Several fans recount for me a scene from the movie *Office Space* in which a very geeky, white computer programmer listens to a song by the rapper Scarface during his morning commute. He has the music turned up loud, and is furiously rapping along to the hard-core rhymes, until he notices a black man selling flowers by the side of the road. Instantly, he locks his doors, turns down the music, and stops rapping until he has safely passed, at which point he resumes his driver-seat performance just as forcefully as before. I've seen the film, and I remember laughing at the scene. It seemed a perfect critique of drive-by rap fans, whose attempts to connect with blackness are undone by their own irrational anxieties. I always assumed that the solution to the programmer's dilemma was to get out of the car, to meet actual black people, to use his interest in rap music as a jumping-off point to come to terms with his fear. But most people here at the Penny Arcade Expo reached a different conclusion: that guy should never have been listening to hip-hop in the first place.

"I saw that and I totally knew people like that," one Frontalot fan tells me. "They have these stupid little desk jobs and they have these songs that are all foul-mouthed and hard-core, and they're like 'Yeah! I'm bad-ass!'"

The solution, nerdcore fans tell me, is to listen only to music

that speaks to your direct experience. "I'm not a big rap fan," says
Steve, a heavyset man who could have been the model for the
comic-book shopkeeper on *The Simpsons* and who traveled all the
way from Austin just to catch the MC Frontalot concert. "It doesn't
do much for me. I don't know much about bling and bitches. It's
not my world and so I don't identify with it. But MC Frontalot raps
about computers, and that's what I do."

As he tells me this, I think back to a conversation I had with
Jeff Chang. Chang, the author of the hip-hop history *Can't Stop
Won't Stop*, founded a Bay Area record label called SoleSides and
served as organizer of the National Hip-Hop Political Convention,
a nonprofit aimed at mobilizing the hip-hop generation. He shared
with me his vision of hip-hop as a culture that takes people outside
their comfort zones and forces them into difficult or uncomfortable challenges. "It's not something that you should feel that because it's available to you, it's yours," he said. "There's a certain
level of humility with which you have to take this. Just because
you can go home and use [computer software] to make beats, and
you can put rhymes together in an interesting way, that doesn't
mean that you don't have to go out and earn your spot in the cipher," the competitive circle where breakdancers or MCs test one
another's skills in battle.

But when I mention this notion to some of the nerdcore rappers, they look at me as if I had suggested they trade in their desktop computers for garage-sale Tandys. "I can't imagine anybody
who's spent their whole musical upbringing chasing the regular
hip-hop ideals of being 'real' about everything ever feeling anything but antagonism towards MC Frontalot," MC Frontalot says.

"I'm not a member of the hip-hop community. I don't pretend that I could walk into a battle scenario," says mc chris. "When
I was a kid I really was picked on a lot and made fun of a lot, so I
don't see why in my right mind I would put myself in a situation

where I *know* I'm going to get made fun of. Not only that but to a beat and in front of a hundred people? Why would I put myself in that situation? I don't get respect from the other hip-hop players because I don't do that? That's fine. They shouldn't respect me."

The conundrum that the nerdcore rappers raise—is it possible for them to keep it real without keeping it all-white?—is one that white rappers of all stripes face. The issue comes up again when I speak with Hot Karl, a geeky white rapper who is not so terrified of battle rapping. Hot Karl is a bespectacled native of a Los Angeles suburb and a graduate of the University of Southern California's creative writing department who has nursed an obsession with hip-hop since his early childhood. In 2000, he won the attention of record labels after successfully dispatching more than one hundred consecutive opponents in a call-in freestyle contest on a popular radio station. It was not the first time Karl—birth name: Jensen-Gerard Karp—had the opportunity to pursue a rap career. When he was thirteen, he was managed by the Rhyme Syndicate, the rapper Ice-T's posse-cum-record-label, as a member of the mixed-race kid-rap duo X-tra Large. When it came time to shoot photographs for their press kit, they trekked out to post-riot South Central, where they posed menacingly among the rubble. "It never felt comfortable," he says, "and then when it failed, I was even more mad. Like, 'Fuck, I just failed and I wasn't even being myself.' And that bothered me the most."

This time Hot Karl wanted to do things differently. "I had meetings with record executives who were like, 'I see you rapping like a pimp.' I had to make a decision. Do I want to just sell out, and go rhyme like Cam'ron [a popular black rapper]? Or do I act like myself and do what I want to do?"

Hot Karl ended up signing with Interscope, the label that had turned Eminem into a star, in part because its executives seemed most willing to let him follow his vision of recording songs that recounted the pain of growing up in the wealthy suburbs, where parents buy their daughters breast jobs and kids pick on classmates who can't afford fancy cars. But as Hot Karl worked on his album he worried that the label's attempts to endear him to the hip-hop audience were damaging the integrity of his record. He felt a twinge of unease when Interscope paid two respected rap stars, Redman and Fabolous, to perform cameo verses. "I don't know these guys," he remembers thinking. "It feels weird giving someone fifteen thousand dollars that you know is basically for street credibility." He was annoyed when his managers kept asking him to contribute a single that wouldn't sound out of place on the street-level mixtape circuit, the underground network where most hip-hop stars are discovered. He also fought to preserve a lyrical reference to Ralph Wiggum, a minor character on *The Simpsons*, when his manager worried that hip-hoppers would miss the joke. In 2003, after Interscope had delayed his album's release, Hot Karl decided that he wanted out of the deal. He used his advance and publishing money to purchase an art gallery and set to work recording a separate debut for an independent label, Headless Heroes, that seemed more comfortable letting him be as suburban as he wanted to be. The result, 2005's *The Great Escape*, came without any club bangers or mixtape fodder or credibility-burnishing celebrity cameos. It also failed to win over many fans within the hip-hop world. Today, Karl says, his fan base is tiny, and most of its members are white, with backgrounds similar to his own.

"Basically, I put out the record I wanted to put out," he concludes. "I knew I was getting into something where I wasn't going to sell a lot of copies. Basically, it was just for my soul. I'm not hanging my hat on being a huge hip-hop sensation."

If Hot Karl is at all crestfallen at his failure to become a rap star, it doesn't come across. He is, after all, in very good company. In Eminem's wake, scads of white rappers were unleashed onto the record-buying public, each of them hoping to emulate his success. But despite the concerns of the *Source*, none of the next generation of white boys succeded at winning over the hip-hop audience's hearts and minds. Not hick-hoppers Bubba Sparxxx and Haystak, who tried to do for the rural South what Eminem had done for trailer park Detroit: equate its poverty and marginalization with that of inner-city black people. Not Everlast, the former House of Pain front man who reinvented himself as Whitey Ford, a guitar-wielding bard of lower-class America. Not Poverty, a native of Portland, Maine, who was homeless until he signed his record deal. Not Jojo Pellegrino, an Italian American who fashioned himself "The Rap Tony Soprano." Not Sarai, a female MC whose label sold her as "Feminem." And not MC Paul Barman, a protégé of De La Soul's producer, Prince Paul, whose erudite rapping included references to such high-minded personages as Susan Faludi, Krzysztof Kieslowski, and Chuck Close. Hip-hop's borders, it seemed, remained secure, a nation dedicated to primarily black voices protected by its gatekeepers, an amorphous collection of disc jockeys, music-video programmers, marketers, magazine editors, critics, record-label executives, mixtape aficionados, and the buying public.

This helps to explain why most white rappers thrive only within the white-on-white underground. Eminem's success didn't allow them unquestioned entry into the hip-hop nation, but it did inspire the founding of a number of different nations, hip-hop-inflected subcultures that interacted only glancingly with rap's traditional audience or concerns. The first of these nations was made up of "mooks," a word used to refer to testosterone-fueled white guys who liked their music macho and aggressive. The mooks' house bands—Limp Bizkit, Korn, and Kid Rock—had been around for years, but it wasn't until 1999 that they amassed enough momentum to become a movement. Their music was a punk-funk mash-up of phat beats and monster riffs, their rapped lyrics expressing metalhead angst rather than urban blight. Hip-hoppers tended to dismiss their simplistic rhymes and tractor-pull following, but that didn't deter the music's fans: in 1999, Limp Bizkit and Korn's albums both topped sales charts the weekends they were released. Although the mook, and the musicians he championed, is today a faint pop-culture memory, the phenomenon of white-on-white rhyme lives on.

"In a way, it makes sense. I'd much rather hear a white rapper bitching about his mom putting him on a curfew and being in the suburbs and eating French fries at the mall and crying because his girlfriend left him, rather than trying to front like he's a gangster," journalist Gabriel Alvarez says. "But at the same time, are people in Inglewood or in Harlem really pumping that? I'm going to bet that they're not."

It's Saturday night at the Penny Arcade Expo—actually, Sunday morning, around one A.M.—and MC Frontalot has finished his set. I'm exhausted, but the rest of the three-thousand-strong crowd, hopped up on adrenaline and free Bawls energy drink, shows no sign of fatigue. It's impossible not to notice the sense of communal euphoria in the air, as if for just this one night they have entered a fantasy realm where the model of the car you drive or the clothes you wear isn't nearly as telling as the number of hours you've logged playing *World of Warcraft*. I've felt this electricity all weekend. Last night, concertgoers listened respectfully to Martin Leung, a classically trained musician who showed up in a tux, sat behind an immense piano, and played a series of video-game theme songs for the crowd. Nobody smirked or laughed or in any way indicated that there was anything humorous or ironic about the performance. This was, quite simply, their music, and they listened to it with all the reverence of an Upper West Side doyenne taking in a

Mahler symphony at Lincoln Center. After the final song, a blind-folded rendition of the *Super Mario Brothers* theme, they granted Leung a unanimous standing ovation.

The crowd is a bit more raucous tonight. Perhaps their fervor has been stoked by the preshow hoop-jumping: before the concert, for reasons unclear, everyone with a ticket was asked to leave the convention center and file up outside. When I joined the line it had already slinked around the block and begun to stretch toward the I-405 on-ramp. After entering the concert hall, we watched rival geeks face off over *Karaoke Revolution*, a video game in which players sing into a microphone that records their pitch, and scores them on the basis of their tonal accuracy. By the time MC Frontalot took the stage—with a shout of "Nerd ho!"—the crowd was amped. Frontalot was bedecked in his finest, geekiest apparel, a short-sleeved button-down shirt, orange tie, and pocket protector, and although he announced that he felt a bit intimidated ("If you decided to tear me to shreds right now, I'd have little to no chance of survival") he had little reason to worry. The audience cheered as he introduced their favorite songs—"This is about a PBS special I saw"—and responded to Front's attempts at old-school call and response: "Did any of you play *Magic: The Gathering* today?"

Frontalot's set was followed by another crowd favorite, mc chris. It's hard to tell who is more beloved; Frontalot may be the sentimental favorite, but mc chris can boast a more pugnacious stage presence, carrying himself like a mix of Spanky from *The Little Rascals* and Benito Mussolini. And he is certainly raunchier, with cutting, sarcastic wit. "This is the part of the show where you hear the word 'cunt' a lot!" he announced as he took the stage. "Do we have any nerds or losers in the house tonight?" he asked later and, after the roar of approval subsided, deadpanned, "That is very surprising to me."

Now, about halfway through his performance, he has decided

that it is time to get political. "If you guys are nerds like me, then you can understand me when I say that my people have been persecuted!" he yells, to the roar of the crowd. "Fuck those Abercrombie and Bitch motherfuckers! What the fuck gives them the right to treat us like shit, just because they can catch a football, and put a penis in a vagina, and vote for Bush!" The cheers get louder. "What do you say after the show we go find ourselves a frat house and burn that fucker down?" The room feels close to eruption. "Now put your motherfucking hands in the air like we're the Black Panthers but we got small dicks." Hundreds of fists fill the air.

"Nerd power!" mc chris shouts.

"NERD POWER!" the crowd responds, and mc chris rides the momentum into his next song, which begins "Stop picking on me because I'm a geek."

This is a theme that mc chris has been developing of late. He tells me that the poster for his next tour, called Revenge of the Nerd, will show a bespectacled geek standing atop a pile of dead football players. MC Frontalot's forays into identity politics aren't quite as explicit; the closest he comes to rabble-rousing is a chorus that urges, "The nerdcore could rise up if you get elevated." But his girlfriend, Emily Epstein, a twenty-seven-year-old student at Georgetown Law School, tells me that nerdcore's music and culture is inherently empowering. "A lot of rap grew out of a sense of otherness, a sense of oppression, a sense of needing to be heard and not being accepted by the mainstream," she says. "Nerds aren't financially disempowered—in fact, a little bit the opposite—but they are definitely socially shunned. . . . And I think it's interesting, because if you put a stereotypical rapper next to a nerdcore rapper on the playground, probably the nerdcore rapper is going to get beat up. So maybe this is laying their own claim to a culture that they feel threatened by or nervous about. For someone who's experienced that fear of being ostracized, this is taking on the ultimate cool thing, the thing that the people who are beating them up are listening to."

It takes me a few minutes to sort out the Möbius strip at the center of this argument. Nerdcore fans respond to hip-hop because the culture represents a rebellion against those forces that would subjugate them. And for geeks, those forces are . . . people who listen to hip-hop.

I start to get a bit dizzy, until I realize that this is the basic argument that underlies Eminem's biopic, *8 Mile*, in which the rapper uses hip-hop to prove wrong those forces keeping him down: black people who say he has no place in hip-hop. *8 Mile* met with a rapturous response when it was released in 2002. Before his film debut, Eminem was viewed by polite middle-class society as the latest manifestation of a by now familiar hip-hop archetype: the moral scourge. Parents and politicians and op-ed columnists decried Eminem's rampant homophobia and misogyny, and worried that his pop prominence presented an even greater danger than N.W.A., Ice-T, or any of the other hip-hop bad boys who came before him. Even the *Village Voice*'s Richard Goldstein referred to Eminem as a "celebrity bigot."

Yet with the release of *8 Mile*, Eminem's role shifted almost instantaneously, from the honky you love to hate to defanged heartthrob. The rumblings of Eminem's impending crossover began soon before the film's release. "For the rock 'n' roll generation," wrote Paul Slansky in the *New York Observer*, "Eminem, né Marshall Mathers III, is the most compelling figure to have emerged from popular music since the holy trinity of Dylan, Lennon and Jagger." But once *8 Mile* debuted, even the fustiest bastions of high society became enamored of the vanilla-thug life. A cartoon in the *New Yorker* depicted a woman confiding in her friend, while her middle-aged husband read a newspaper nearby, "I cannot believe the things I've heard coming out his mouth since he started listening to Eminem." In a piece headlined "The Boomers' Crooner," Maureen Dowd, a middle-aged columnist for the *New York Times*, wrote that her girlfriends all harbored crushes on Eminem, and wondered what the impact of their affection would be: "[Y]o, dawg, our suffocating yuppie love has turned Mashall Mathers into Jerry Mathers. Eminem is now as cuddly as Beaver Cleaver."

Eminem's newfound respectability may have been startling, but it was all part of the plan. *8 Mile*'s producer, Brian Grazer, told the *New York Times Magazine* that the very idea for the movie was based on the rapper's untapped crossover appeal, and Eminem's manager, Paul Rosenberg, said that he hoped to create "the same sort of cultural phenomenon as *Saturday Night Fever*." Yet even industry insiders were shocked when the film pulled in a remarkable $51.2 million in its opening weekend. Even more surprising, almost one third of the audience members were over twenty-five years old.

On one level, the film's appeal is obvious. *8 Mile* tells the story of Jimmy "B-Rabbit" Smith Jr., a poor white kid who lives in a trailer park with his irresponsible mother, holds down a miserable job at a metal-stamping facility, and is screwed over by friends and girlfriends, until he channels all of his pain into a blistering performance at a freestyle-rap competition. It is a classic triumph-of-the-underdog tale, a hip-hop version of *Rocky*, *Flashdance*, or any of a thousand other crowd-pleasing rags-to-riches allegories. And the film also hints at the exciting possibilities of a racial realignment: the movie's title refers to the road that separates mostly black Detroit from its mostly white suburbs, and draws an implicit connection between the ghetto upbringing recounted by many rap stars and the malaise that enveloped many members of the white underclass.

But for white middle-class rap fans, the film also suggested something else: how we, too, could be down. The central dilemma that B-Rabbit faces is whether he, a white guy, can win over the approval of an all-black rap audience. The film's opening scene, in which Eminem listens to Mobb Deep on his headphones while rapping into a hip-hop club's bathroom mirror, looks familiar to any number of suburban hip-hop heads. So does the anxiety he feels when, after a knock on the door, he leaves the bathroom and enters the hostile black world of the rap club. First, black dudes stare menacingly at him, asking "Who the fuck is you, nigga?" Then the club's bouncer refuses to let him backstage, until B-Rabbit's black friend, mentor, and protector vouches for him. "That fuckin' guy's obviously got something against me!" B-Rabbit complains. What white rap fan hasn't felt that same feeling of powerlessness, angry that he's been made to feel so unwanted and out of place, simply because he happens to be white?

The hints of reverse racism only escalate as B-Rabbit takes the stage to participate in the film's first freestyle battle. The crowd begins rooting against him as soon as he steps on the stage, and his first opponent shreds him with a series of race-based insults: "They don't laugh at you because you're white, they laugh because you're white with a mike." Within forty-five seconds, B-Rabbit is told he doesn't belong in hip-hop, called a tourist and a wigger, jeeringly compared to the white rapper Everlast, teased for having a small penis, and commanded to return to his rightful home in the suburbs. B-Rabbit freezes, staring out at every white rap fan's nightmare, a crowd full of black people laughing at him, chanting "Choke! Choke! Choke!" and demonstrating, once and for all, that he can never be down. The movie's central message—we should not be judged on the color of our skin, but the content of our character—is familiar, if couched in a neat reversal: this time, it is a white person who is unfairly victimized by racial prejudice. Is it a coincidence that, after leaving the club, B-Rabbit is shown alone in the back of a public bus, while an elderly bespectacled black woman who sits toward the front and looks just a little bit like Rosa Parks stares back at him sympathetically?

If it is flattering for white fans to compare themselves to unfairly oppressed civil rights leaders, the film's conclusion is only
more cathartic. B-Rabbit has spent the previous ninety minutes
facing insults and beat-downs, most of them at the hands of the
ironically named all-black posse, Leaders of the Free World. A
white friend of B-Rabbit's, Cheddar Bob, fares even worse. His
own friends deride him for defending the Beastie Boys and for living in the 810 area code (as opposed to the downtown 313), and
then, in an altercation with Leaders of the Free World, he shoots
himself in the crotch with his own gun, demonstrating once and
for all that white boys who mess around with black culture should
prepare to be emasculated.

So what white rap fan—or any white person who was intimidated or confused by hip-hop culture—could help but feel energized when, at the end of the film, B-Rabbit wins over his black
audience, not by demonstrating his sensitivity or prostrating himself to racial politics but by asserting his whiteness and refusing to
apologize for it? The movie's climax is a mirror image of its opening sequence. Again, we start with B-Rabbit in the club's bathroom, but this time he isn't listening to headphones and trying to
emulate Mobb Deep; he is his own man. The knock at the door
this time comes not from impatient black club goers but from
Cheddar Bob, who tells his friend that the stage is ready for him.
B-Rabbit marches down the hallway, the same one that the bouncer
previously tried to block him from, and heads to the stage, staring
down all of the hostile black faces who are still taunting him over
the previous week's failure to perform. But this time, B-Rabbit
isn't fazed by the antiwhite rhetoric. When his first opponent tells
him to "take your white ass back across 8 Mile," B-Rabbit bests
him by dropping his pants, proudly showing off that same white ass
to the crowd. His second opponent comes out swinging, announcing from the start, "I spit a racial slur, honky," and referring to him

as "that dude from *Leave It to Beaver*." B-Rabbit turns the slur around by asking, after another strong showing, "You see how far them white jokes get you?" And in his final showdown, B-Rabbit anticipates every conceivable insult and beats his rival to the punch, admitting that, yes, okay, he *is* white, but that nobody in the crowd can judge him or know what he's been through. "I'm a piece of white trash," he concludes. "I say it proudly." B-Rabbit wins his final showdown—and, by extension, the approval of the hip-hop community—not through any deep understanding of black culture, but by taking pride in his own white identity.

Nerd pride has proven a similarly powerful message. The big question facing the nerdcore rappers these days is: How far can this thing go? MC Frontalot put his design clients on hold for eight months while he worked up to fourteen hours a day completing his *Nerdcore Rising* CD. He tells me he has a three-year plan to perform and promote his music, just to see what happens. And at that point, he'll likely leave hip-hop behind. "I'll probably get a job doing something really boring with a steady paycheck, and I'll assume a mortgage and have children," he says with a grin. mc chris has slightly greater ambitions for his work. He says that he already makes about eight times as much money as he did working at the Cartoon Network. ("I know you're not supposed to brag about how much money you make, but I'm a rapper.") He tours almost constantly. "I have my own business," he says. "I'm on my friends' label, and they get me press and into magazines, and I've got managers and booking agents. We're not just on the Internet now."

In fact, there are signs that the world might be ready for nerdcore hip-hop. Chris Parnell and Adam Samberg, a pair of white *Saturday Night Live* cast members, rose to national prominence with a rap-parody video called "Lazy Sunday." The song features Parnell and

Samberg enthusiastically rapping about such non-hip-hop exploits as eating cupcakes, using MapQuest, and catching a matinee of the fantasy film *The Chronicles of Narnia*. In the ten days after its airing, the video was downloaded 1.2 million times from the video-sharing Web site YouTube, and before long it inspired a string of lame "answer" tracks from other un-hip white kids detailing the dork life in Los Angeles and Muncie, Indiana. The *New York Times* wrote that the clip's success showed that the best road to Internet fame might come from "being as nerdy as possible."

But if nerdcore—or any other breed of white-on-white rhyme—represents the future of hip-hop, not everyone will be pleased. Sacha Jenkins, the editorial director of *Mass Appeal* magazine and a cocreator of the *ego trip* series of books and television specials about hip-hop and race, worries what will happen if today's white underground artists grow into the next generation of rap stars. "In ten years, it's entirely possible that mainstream rap is 80 percent white. There is a real danger in white kids taking over hip-hop and not knowing where this shit comes from. I'm concerned about that," he says. He shares with me a conversation he had with an aspiring white rapper who was proudly ignorant of hip-hop's black roots. "He told me, 'I don't need to know about black stuff. Hip-hop is for everyone.' Well, so is rock and roll. It wasn't always. It was black. It's for everyone now. That's what America has a tendency of doing, especially when it comes to [the culture of] people of color. At first it's really scary and dangerous. Of course white kids are fascinated by it. They share it with their friends, and so on and so on, and time passes, and then all of a sudden it's not so scary anymore. And it's not a black thing anymore. It's an American thing. And I think when it becomes an American thing, black people lose interest. What's that going to mean in ten years?"

For his part, mc chris does not expect to become hip-hop's next breakout superstar. He recognizes his limits, doesn't fight them, sees no reason to reach beyond them, and sounds almost grateful for them. "We're keeping it small. We're not trying to become a humongous success story. We don't want to fizzle out after a huge explosion. We're just making crazy amounts of money—from deep nerd pockets—that we can stockpile and then pour back into the business," he says. "My music is not going to be placed next to [that of rappers such as] KRS-One or Talib Kweli. But I think white kids deserve to have a good time, too."

CHAPTER EIGHT
Selling Down: The Marketing of the Hip-Hop Nation

Yo, Blood . . . You want fresh? Be a playa—first of your posse in da hood to have your tricked out wearin' dubs? If you want da bling, ya gotta have da juice. Talkin' cheddar here, boo . . . crisp Benjamins. Lots of 'em. Then your rims be kickin'.

Yeah, if you wanna be da bomb . . . that's jiggy to you neophytes . . . the tire of choice for the ride of choice has become the color of cool: a big, black Pirelli. Bigger the better.

At least, that's what Pirelli Tire North America Inc. execs are saying.

—Sigmund J. Mikolajczyk, "Hip-Hop Help?"

Tire Business, **November 8, 2004**

I tend to grow paranoid when I think about advertising and marketing. Can you blame me? It is an industry that seems to thrive by tapping into our deepest fears, insecurities, anxieties, and aspirations. Edward Bernays—Sigmund Freud's nephew, who is considered the father of modern public relations—drew on his uncle's theories of the subconscious to craft his marketing campaigns. In his 1928 book, *Propaganda*, he wrote that "the true ruling power of our country" belonged to those who could practice "the conscious and intelligent manipulation of the organized habits and opinions of the masses." Almost thirty years later, in his 1957 book *The Hidden Persuaders*, Vance Packard argued that some advertisers were "systematically feeling out our hidden weaknesses and frailties in the hope that they can more efficiently influence our behavior." Today, consultants promise marketers that they can use psychological techniques to uncover consumers' subliminal desires. One of the most successful marketing consultants, a former child psychiatrist named Clotaire Rapaille, told a reporter that his company excels at tapping into our "reptilian brain." "Most of the time, people have no idea why they're doing what they're doing," he said. "It's fascinating to try to understand, to break the code."

But my paranoia reached new levels when I saw a recent television advertisement for T-Mobile, a cell-phone company, that seems to crack my own personal code and tap directly into my reptilian brain. The ad begins in a bowling alley, where a tall, attractive African American man is engaged in a cell-phone conversation. From the snippet that we can hear ("So, you want me to come over tonight? That's cool"), he sounds as if he has just secured some big-time sexual guarantee. Just then, with a samurai scream, a small Asian man wearing a powder-blue jumpsuit runs across the screen and wraps himself around the black man's thigh. He is, it turns out, a representative from Poser Mobile, the cell phone company the black guy is using, and he's joined by six others, all of them nonblack (they appear to be white, Latino, and Asian), and all dressed in ridiculously oversized and out-of-date hip-hop fashions. "Poser Mobile says you're out of prepaid minutes, yo!" the Asian man announces, and when the black guy protests, he shouts back, "Fees, shorty! Fees!" But his obvious inauthenticity makes it hard to take him seriously, and the protagonist just grins and calls the gang "clowns." The Poser Mobile team stares silently for a second before breaking into a painfully cacophonous and arrhythmic bout of beatboxing. Eventually, the black man leaves to pick up a phone from T-Mobile To Go, which lets him avoid the hidden fees—and fake posturing—of Poser Mobile. "Straight up prepaid," the ad closes.

I suppose that I am meant to identify with the black guy, a cool customer under siege from clueless marketers hoping to tap into his preferred lifestyle in order to sell him products. But I don't. I identify with the Poser Mobile guys. They remind me of my own embarrassing attempts to prove myself as a full-fledged member of the hip-hop community. Whether T-Mobile's marketers intended to or not, they have brought up a long series of uncomfortable memories: the time I realized that everybody at the Third World Center at my college was laughing at my dancing; the time that the Digable Planets dismissively referred to me and my friends as "devils"; the time that guy laughed at my Malcolm X hat; the palpable anxiety and self-doubt I felt so many times when I had to interact with a black person and I couldn't help but think, *Is this working? Are they buying it? Am I a poser?* But apparently, all of that unease and despair wasn't the product of history or race or guilt or frustration or inequity. I just wasn't using the right cell-phone service.

One of hip-hop's most powerful and elusive promises is that it will help us come to terms with, understand, and maybe even participate in blackness. That we can change ourselves through our listening, make ourselves better and more comfortable and more accepting and accepted than we are. That through hip-hop, we can become down—completely and utter comfortable with, and de facto members of, the black community. And because down is one of those unattainable states of grace that we can asymptotically approach but never actually achieve—like supreme self-confidence or utter peace or Zen-like enlightenment—we keep coming back over and over again.

We all know that marketers thrive by exploiting urges and desires that can never be satisfied, and at long last it seems that, knowingly or not, they have stumbled upon our never-ending quest to be down. Hip-hop has always tossed up rapper-approved signifiers, commodities that promised to grant down status to anyone that consumes them—Adidas sneakers, Cross Colours sweatshirts, Cazal glasses, basketball jerseys, the music itself. Now marketers have enlisted hip-hop to extend that promise to a mind-boggling array of products, reaching deep into the heart of mainstream America. White kids seeking a hip-hop stamp of approval are encouraged to buy slacks at JC Penney, which used Black Sheep's "The Choice Is Yours" to score a recent ad campaign. They can go back-to-school shopping at Target, which repurposed Sir Mix-A-Lot's "Baby Got Back," an infamous ode to the black female form, as "Baby Got Backpacks." Virtually any footwear white kids care to select can offer them a shot of hip-hop credibility: they can pick up Ludacris-endorsed Pumas, or Jay-Z–approved Reeboks, or "Hurricanes," sneakers designed by the gangsta-rap sensation The Game. If they don't feel like getting a T-Mobile phone, they can grab one from Boost Mobile, a Nextel brand with an ad campaign that features such luminaries as Fat Joe and Eve, and a tagline—"Where You At?"—that positively drips with hip-hop attitude. "For better or worse, for good or evil, hip-hop has become a weapon of choice for marketers," says Rob Schwartz, executive director of the Los Angeles office of TBWA\Chiat\Day, an advertising agency.

Of course, part of hip-hop's appeal is that it is impenetrable to exactly the kind of people who tend to run stodgy major corporations. Fortunately for the captains of industry, there are now dozens of boutique marketing, advertising, and public-relations firms dedicated to guiding big businesses through the sometimes forbidding landscape of the urban marketplace. In 2001, the performer then known as P. Diddy created Blue Flame Marketing+Advertising to help corporations tap into the next wave of tastemakers. Steve Stoute, a former manager of the acclaimed rapper Nas, formed

Translation, an agency that has helped link brands such as Crest and Reebok to high-profile hip-hop stars. The Web site for Burrell Communications, an advertising firm, promises that it can "make your logo the next hot ankle tattoo," while describing the African American market as the firm's "specialty of the house." Morris L. Reid, the managing director of Westin Rinehart, a Washington, D.C., public affairs firm that works with multinational businesses and government agencies, describes the service that urban marketers provide thusly: "I'm the person that can tell you what's going on in the 'hood, and I can also come into your boardroom and not scare anyone."

It is not hard to see why corporations would turn to hip-hop as a marketing platform. First and foremost it is overwhelmingly popular, the culture of teenage America, and this makes it the lingua franca that any lifestyle marketer must speak. Furthermore, compared to other social movements, hip-hop seems to lend itself particularly well to marketing messages. From its early days, it has blurred the distinction between art and advertising: graffiti writers splashed their tags across subway trains as a way of creating rolling billboards for themselves; the first MCs acted as pitchmen who existed solely to praise the DJ's skills and get the crowd riled up (today that role is played by the appropriately-named "hype man"); and rappers turned themselves into superhero icons, giving themselves new names, creating logos, and adopting certain verbal tics—for instance, the early-nineties rap duo Das EFX's fondness for dropping "iggidy" into the middle of words—to define themselves as entertainers. "More than anything else, hip-hop has been about marketing," Jameel Spencer, the president of Blue Flame Marketing + Advertising, told the *New York Times* in 2004. "You're creating a brand for yourself." Nelson George has written that hip-hop arose as a way of "announcing one's existence to the world." Could there be any better definition of the goals of marketing?

But if hip-hop rose to power as the voice of the streets, what does it mean that one of those streets is now Madison Avenue? In my crustier moments, it is easy for me to conclude that hip-hop has gone from black people's CNN to everybody's Home Shopping Network. And these moments have been coming faster and crustier. I have one almost every time I turn on MTV and find myself wondering whether the iPods and Sidekicks and Hummers that pop up in every hip-hop video are paid plugs. I have one when I log on to *Business Week*'s Web site and read about a conference put together by the youth-marketing division of McCann-Erickson, in which a group of rappers took the stage in front of fifty brand representatives of corporations including Wendy's, L'Oréal, and Verizon Wireless to tell them "what kind of sponsorships and marketing deals they would be interested in." I had another one when I learned about American Brandstand, a survey by a San Francisco marketing firm, Agenda Inc., that tracks the number of times that brand names are mentioned in the songs that make up the *Billboard* Top 20.

Why does this bother me so much? Partly because I'm clinging to some pretty quaint notions of artistic purity. Blame the Romantics. They're the ones who, in the nineteenth century, came up with the idea that artists had a duty to oppose the compromises and corruptions of mainstream society. And that's been a hard attitude to shake. It led to the idea of the counterculture, which held that the only true enlightenment could come from living on society's margins. The counterculture has given us Giacomo Puccini's *La Bohème* and Ralph Waldo Emerson's and Henry David Thoreau's retreats back to nature. After World War II, the counterculture became a defining element of American life, underlying the promise of the beatnik, folk, hippie, rock, and punk movements. In fact, one of the great ironies of the counterculture is that its ideals of nonconformity and independence are so widespread that they have become integral parts of the mainstream society that the counterculture was created to counter. It was these ideals that drew me to hip-hop in the first place. Who could imagine that music so difficult, so aggressive, so *black*, would one day be used to sell backpacks?

If this makes me a curmudgeon, at least I am not alone. "I think what made hip-hop compelling to white kids is that it seemed to exist outside the corporate-driven suburban monotony," says Douglas Rushkoff, a social theorist and writer of a *Frontline* documentary, "The Merchants of Cool," about youth marketing. "The function of hip-hop in the early days was to galvanize its audiences around certain kinds of values—of pride, of racial unity, of urban creativity. It was relatively hard to listen to 'The Message' and not go, 'Whoa. There's something happening here.' But now, when I listen to hip-hop, I think, 'Is this going to stay at number two? Is this going to be on a commercial? Are those diamonds in his teeth real?' That's a very different set of questions."

But hip-hoppers tend not to share my mistrust of corporate culture. Indeed, in hip-hop America, marketing is the sincerest form of flattery. Witness the response to Sprite's mid-1990s "Obey Your Thirst" advertising campaign, one of the most influential and successful of the decade. Between 1994 and 1997, Sprite produced television advertisements featuring some of hip-hop's most respected stars, including A Tribe Called Quest, Grand Puba, Large Professor, Pete Rock, C.L. Smooth, KRS-One, MC Shan, Nas, AZ, Eve, and Missy Elliott. By the end of the campaign Sprite, previously a distant second to 7-Up, held a dominating lead in the lemon-lime category. The campaign also proved that, unlike other musical movements that gestured toward ideological purity and authenticity, hip-hop's fans would not necessarily object to their culture's commercialization. Far from being shunned as an exploiter, which is how many Beatles fans responded to Nike when the company used the group's "Revolution" to score a sneaker ad, Sprite was enthusiastically welcomed as a full-fledged member of the hip-hop community.

OTHER PEOPLE'S PROPERTY

"Back in 1994, hip-hop artists did not have big budgets with which to market themselves," Darryl Cobbin, one of the executives credited with creating the Sprite campaign, tells me. "You did not have major companies platforming the culture. You had a couple of them that were dabbling in jingles, but not truly understanding the culture. We began to create a platform for those rappers that were most authentic and credible to talk about their culture, and to use 'Obey Your Thirst' as a vessel to fill with the creativity that is hip-hop. And that helped hip-hop . . . This is what the best companies do. Find a way to help advance the culture and you will be rewarded."

"It sounds cartoonish that people were big-upping [praising] products for using hip-hop," Alan Light, the former editor in chief of *Vibe*, says. "But at the time there was so much fear, so much resistance [to hip-hop from mainstream and corporate America], that it meant something."

It doesn't mean that much anymore. Now, almost every youth marketer recognizes the power and appeal of hip-hop. And while it would be nice to conclude that today's massive corporate investments are coming about as a result of a sincere desire to help spread the culture—or even a desire to sell product to the inner-city black customers who constitute hip-hop's core audience—it's far more likely that big business sees hip-hop as a means to a more familiar end: the wallets of all those white kids out there. Black kids are what are known in the industry as "influencers," a group of consumers who have an inordinate impact on the tastes and behaviors of the rest of the country. As Ivan Juzang, the head of a Philadelphia firm that specializes in marketing to urban youth, told a reporter: "If you don't target the hard-core, you don't get the suburbs." And so corporations go after the urban market because they've realized the truth of what the editor-in-chief of *Frontera* magazine triumphantly concluded in an opinion piece that ran in the *Daily News of Los Angeles* back in 1997: "Middle American teens and twentysomethings don't want to buy products pitched by suburban kids who look just like them."

Not everybody views this as something to celebrate. Harvard University's Douglas Holt and Juliet B. Schor—marketing researchers who, it is safe to say, are no fans of hip-hop—have argued that the street image "has proven to be a potent commodity because its aesthetic offers an authentic threatening edginess that is very attractive both to white suburban kids who perpetually re-create radical youth culture in relation to their parents' conservative views about the ghetto, and to urban cultural elites for whom it becomes a form of cosmopolitan radical chic."

But Darryl Cobbin, the creator of the Sprite campaign, who is African American and a lifelong hip-hop fan, sees different forces at work. He tells me that hip-hop succeeds as a marketing platform because it connotes values that people simply cannot help but respond to. "What's more honest than an MC describing what's happening in his neighborhood?" he says. "Who is more stylish than a b-boy rocking his block on a piece of cardboard? 'Obey Your Thirst' means trust your instinct, be true to yourself and others, and operate with confidence and swagger. That for us represented what hip-hop culture is all about." As he tells me this, I can't help but notice that all of these adjectives—honest, stylish, instinctive, true, confident, swaggering—pretty neatly describe all the characteristics that, in my younger days, in the deepest reaches of my subconscious, I always felt that I lacked and that I assumed those mysterious, authentic black folks possessed in abundance.

Honesty and authenticity are particularly crucial and difficult attributes for marketers to capture. Let's face it, they are running a pretty fundamentally inauthentic game: spending untold billions of dollars to convince us to spend even more billions of dollars on their products. They face two great challenges: (1) getting us to notice their messages, and (2) getting us to believe them. Naomi Klein, the antibranding crusader, has said that marketers view consumers as cockroaches. We keep growing resistant to their efforts, and so they need to keep building stronger sprays to take us down.

This helps explain the success of street promotion, a concept that originated in the world of hip-hop but that has since become a de rigueur tactic throughout corporate America. *New York* magazine has referred to street promotion as "everything they don't teach you at Harvard Business School." What that means operationally is that street marketers simply do anything possible, no matter how crass, to raise awareness of their products: handing out posters and fliers at playgrounds and barbershops, glad-handing DJs and club bouncers, carpet-bombing every blank wall with stickers, sending vans ostentatiously plastered with advertising through busy city streets. Street marketing is a natural outgrowth of hip-hop's by-any-means-necessary entrepreneurial spirit—the culture is filled with stories like that of Master P, a New Orleans rapper-producer whose path to riches began when he started selling his CDs out of the trunk of his car—but it wasn't codified until 1993, when Steven Rifkind, the head of Loud Records, used similar tactics to create buzz for one of his label's acts, the Wu-Tang Clan. When the group's first album, *Enter the Wu-Tang (36 Chambers)*, went platinum despite a complete lack of radio airplay, other businesses began to pay attention. Before long companies such as Nike, Pepsi, and Coors were enlisting his services. "Corporations realized there was a huge untapped urban market," Rifkind told a reporter, "that it had a huge influence on the country as a whole, and that it took its cues from hip-hop. I'd been promoting hip-hop records to that market for ten years. It wasn't hard to go from that to sneakers."

But if street teams aren't aggressive enough for you, check out the Web site of a Washington, D.C., firm called Maven Strategies. It may not look like much at first—the site is filled with the sort of Madison Avenue corporatese that is almost as hard to decipher as the latest hip-hop jargon. The company promises to "develop high value brand solutions to triumph over extreme clutter and under-performing message vehicles" and to leverage its "experience with the creation and execution of fully integrated entertainment, prod-uct placement, sponsorship, and event marketing platforms." But here is what that means: In addition to its other services, Maven Strategies can get your product mentioned in a rap song.

This is not an insignificant promise. Sales of Grey Goose shot up in 2001 after the rapper 8Ball dropped a reference to the vodka in "Stop Playin' Games." In the song "Hey Ya," OutKast's request for female audience members to "shake it like a Polaroid picture" helped "raise the profile of our brand and was a positive influence on it," ac-cording to a company spokesman, Skip Colcord. And, in one of the best-known examples, Busta Rhymes and Puff Daddy's single "Pass the Courvoisier Part II" helped boost the cognac's sales by 4.5 per-cent, leading the vice president for corporate communications for Courvoisier's parent company to refer to hip-hop name-drops as "the holy grail of marketing."

Part of the reason these endorsements are so successful is that they are not seen as advertisements. If, as Naomi Klein says, mar-keters see consumers as cockroaches, then we have become almost entirely immune to the bug spray that is traditional advertising. Between the advent of TiVo, enabling us to fast-forward through commercials, and our ever-increasing sophistication, the traditional thirty-second spot has lost much of its persuasive power. "We have seen a lot of big companies get much more interested in alternatives to advertising—product placements, merchandising, and events," says Laura Ries, a partner at Ries & Ries Focusing Consultants, a marketing firm, and the coauthor of *The Fall of Advertising and the*

OTHER PEOPLE'S PROPERTY

Rise of PR. "There's too much advertising, but using entertainment is one way to get people to watch the advertisement without ignoring it." Everyone has his favorite example of this. In 2001, the novelist Fay Weldon published *The Bulgari Connection* after receiving an undisclosed fee from the eponymous jeweler. The same year, BMW introduced its on-line film series "The Hire," in which eight acclaimed directors created shorts that featured its automobiles. And of course there's the grandpappy of them all, MTV, which fashioned what was essentially record-label advertising into music videos, an art form in its own right. Small wonder then that product plugs in hip-hop tracks would be so attractive to marketers: the practice completely demolishes the line between promotion and entertainment.

To be sure, some folks became upset in 2005 when reports surfaced that, through Maven Strategies, McDonald's had quietly offered to pay rappers to mention Big Macs in their song lyrics. In the past—at least according to the official tales—MCs mentioned brands that were meaningful to them, and only later formed professional relationships. Even Adidas didn't sign an endorsement deal with Run–DMC until they saw the rappers perform "My Adidas" in concert. Openly paying in advance for a product plug destroyed its power, which stemmed from the perceived honesty and incorruptibility of the messenger. After the story broke, McDonald's discontinued its efforts. "It seemed that they were trying to become authentic in a way that's fundamentally inauthentic," said Lucian James, whose company, Agenda Inc., compiles the American Brandstand list. "They were caught and they were right to be caught."

Which suggests the next question: Who isn't getting caught? When we hear a product name mentioned in a song, how do we know that it came about as a product of the rapper's honest enthusiasms, and not as the result of some under-the-table deal? James can't answer that question, and points out that even if there isn't a deal, rappers may very well mention a brand in the hopes of securing one in the future. "It's pretty impossible in this day and age to mention a brand and not wonder if you're going to get something," he says. "I don't know where that line gets drawn. It's the gray area of rappers understanding their power and realizing they can get free stuff, and not seeing rapping about Cadillac vehicles as an impediment to their creativity."

But I'm not sure anyone would have much cared even if the McDonald's deal had gone through. Nobody seemed too bothered in 2004 when a rapper named Petey Pablo announced at the end of his song "Freek-A-Leek" that he was obligated to announce his fealty to Seagram's Gin, because "they're paying me for it." The old Romantic ideal of the separation of art and commerce appears to have been abandoned finally and irrevocably. It has been a long time going. Pop artists such as Andy Warhol, James Rosenquist, and Roy Lichtenstein have blurred the distinction between art and marketing for a while, eagerly incorporating logos and advertisements into their work. John Seabrook, writing in the *New Yorker* in 1999, coined the term "Nobrow" to describe a world in which the binary opposition of "lowbrow" commercial culture and "highbrow" elite culture was no longer relevant: "In Nobrow," he wrote, "the challenge that élite institutions such as the major museums face is how to bring commercial culture into the fold—how to keep their repertoire vibrant and solvent and relevant without undermining their moral authority, which used to be based, in part, on keeping the commercial culture out." On October 31, 2004, music critic Kelefa Sanneh railed in the *New York Times* against "rockists," those raggedy music lovers who spend their time quaintly "grousing about a pop landscape dominated by big-budget spectacles and high-concept photo shoots, reminiscing about a time when the charts were packed with people who had something to say, and meant it, even if that time never actually existed." Today, Agenda Inc.'s Lucian James tells me, the most successful rappers consider themselves "businesspeople first and artists second. And that's a big change."

And to hear marketers tell it, that's not the only big change. By now, most of us are familiar with the concept of "branding." A Madison Avenue buzzword, it describes the practice of imbuing a product or company with emotional resonances so that potential customers will be drawn to purchase not just the product but a feeling, an identity that they see in it. "People, whether they're joining a cult or brand, do so for the same reasons," an advertising strategist, Douglas Atkin, has said. "They want to belong, and they want to create meaning." The strategy has been working. In her 2004 book, *Born to Buy*, Juliet B. Schor finds that children are more brand-aware than ever. She reports that $15 billion is spent every year on advertising and marketing directed at kids. "Kids can recognize logos by eighteen months, and before reaching their second birthday, they're asking for products by brand name," she writes. "By three or three and a half, experts say, children start to believe that brands communicate their personal qualities." It may just be that brand-spouting MCs simply understand the rules of engagement—and of modern life—in a more honest way than their critics. Maybe those of us who object to the corporate intrusion of hip-hop are like the doddering writing professors that David Foster Wallace describes in his 1990 essay "E Unibus Pluram," pointlessly objecting to students who reference television or popular culture in their writing. Maybe rappers are just realisticly depicting a brand-obsessed, marketing-saturated world as it is, not as some of us might wish it to be.

And maybe this is the final joke on those of us who expected the music and culture of black folks to provide us with some escape from the confines of contemporary white society: we were looking to them to provide us with a way out, not realizing that they were looking to us to provide a way in. One early autumn evening, I wangle a free ticket to see Kevin Liles speak. Liles is the executive vice president of Warner Music Group, and as if that weren't enough, he has opened up a side business as a motivational speaker, a kind of hip-hop Tony Robbins (or, as Liles himself would put it, "my good friend Tony Robbins"). The small lecture hall in midtown Manhattan is stuffed with hundreds of eager young hustlers—most of them black, all of them comfortably ensconced within the loosey-goosey "urban" psychographic—hoping to learn the keys to success in the business world. Liles's presentation is powerful, if filled with the standard-issue motivation advice: believe in yourself, push hard, don't listen to naysayers. He closes his speech by announcing that he dedicated his just-released autobiography to hip-hop, to "the struggle against people who tell you that you can't be what you want to be, and you can't do what you want to do."

And I realize, listening to him, that one of those people might be me; I prefer my rappers to be angry and resistant, even if it means that they must stay broke to do so. I think back to the Hush Tour I took of the South Bronx, and hearing LL Cool J rap about his desire to leave the ghetto even as we white tourists paid seventy-five dollars to file into it for a few minutes. It feels like a good metaphor for the feedback loop that is hip-hop marketing. Inner-city black kids, seeking a modicum of respect and financial security, created a point of entry into the commercial world that had ignored them for so long. We white kids, drawn to the implicit escape that their music and lifestyles represented, bought it. Hip-hop is where we meet, we on our way out of the system, they on their way in. Is hip-hop a door that swings open between our two cultures, letting us mix freely with each other, or is it a revolving door, endlessly spinning, allowing us to pass in opposite directions without ever actually touching?

★ ★ ★

OTHER PEOPLE'S PROPERTY

Maybe this paradox helps to explain why so many white people are drawn to what's become known as "conscious" rap, a genre of hip-hop whose practitioners continue the tradition of Afrocentrism and political awareness launched by Public Enemy in the early 1990s. The movement began to take shape in 1994, when a rapper called Common Sense (now called Common), released "I Used to Love H.E.R.," a song that compared hip-hop to a wayward girl-friend who, overcome by gangstaism and commercialism, had lost her sense of direction. Today, fans look to conscious rappers to pro-vide an alternative to what they see as the hopelessly corrupted world of mainstream hip-hop. Its most devoted adherents view it not only as music, but as a mix of entertainment, spiritual quest, and social mission, and see in their favorite performers almost unimpeachably pure moral arbiters.

I witness this firsthand when I attend a conscious hip-hop concert one late-winter evening at Toad's Place, a concert venue in New Haven, Connecticut, located next to the Yale University cam-pus. I know it is a conscious concert, because in the show's first twenty minutes, the white people in the audience throw their fists in the air no fewer than three times. They do it when tonight's mas-ter of ceremonies, a zaftig, full-throated poet named Amir Su-laiman asks them if they are "ready to get free." They do it again when the opening act, a Somali rapper named K'Naan, leads them in a call-and-response chant, exhorting them to shout "Freedom!" to his repeated question, "What do we want?" And they do it again when K'Naan announces, "The revolution is here."

But there are at least twelve fists in this crowd that do not find their way into the air, and those belong to the six marketers who are circulating through the audience. This concert—in fact, the whole tour of twenty-odd cities, which goes by the name "Breed Love Odyssey"—is sponsored by Sony PlayStation Portable, a video-game console better known as the PSP. As concertgoers trickle in the front door tonight, they are met by a chipper young couple in Sony T-shirts who hand out coupons for free song downloads from the company's online music store. Once inside, they are likely to run into at least one of the six members of the PSP street team, who mill through the crowd while tethered to PSP devices via a utility belt or leg brace. Actually, the street team members might more accurately be dubbed a "perfume-counter team," because that better describes their appearance and strategy: the well-scrubbed twenty-somethings hold out their PSP's invitingly, smilingly approach their marks, and ask whether they'd care to give the device a try. They stand by as concertgoers take a test run of some of the PSP's games. If there are any questions, the street marketers try their best to remember some of the information they were hurriedly given in a three-minute tutorial they received before the concert.

When I called Sony to ask if I could tag along with the street team, I assumed that I would be hanging out with a group of hip-hop fanatics eager to make a few bucks while catching the show. But I was mistaken. Tonight's street-team members hold no particular affection for any of the evening's performers—nor for Sony, for that matter—but are here for extra cash or résumé padding. Most of them found out about the concert only this morning, as they made their daily visit to Craig's List, an online bulletin board, to see what jobs were available tonight. New Haven is a small market, which leads to a lot of overlap in such temporary gigs, so it's not surprising that two of the street-team members have worked together before; they wave and grin when they see each other. One of them, a high-energy blonde named Dara DeCroce, estimates that she does over twenty of these a week; earlier today she was at a retirement home, leading a Walgreen's-sponsored seminar to explain the new Medicare prescription-drug benefit to senior citizens. Between them, tonight's street-team members have also worked at Bacardi parties and Geico events and something called The Dunkin' Donuts Ice Lounge tour.

If the prospect of Sony street marketers at a conscious hip-hop concert starts feeling a bit vertiginous and sinister, you might derive some comfort from reading a recent essay by Mackenzie Eisenhour called "Counterculture vs. Big Business: The Chase Is On." Published in the winter of 2005, the article presents a short history of corporate attempts to absorb the language and styles of independent trendsetters, from the Sex Pistols to skateboarders. It also addresses the question of "selling out," and concludes, comfortingly enough, that "sometimes it can be good": "While there can never be a fool-proof formula for maintaining independence and legitimacy, the important thing is a mutual respect between all parties."

Reading this piece did not actually make me feel much better, because it was published in *Scion* magazine, an "advertorial" product designed to promote the Toyota Scion, a line of low-priced cars targeted to hip-hop lovers. Scion's marketing is headed up by a company called the Rebel Organization. The Rebel Organization was founded in 1999 as a marketing offshoot of *URB* magazine, a publication devoted to underground hip-hop and electronic culture. When I asked Josh Levine, the head of the Rebel Organization, if any members of the hip-hop underground, his target market, have shown skepticism toward Scion's involvement, he assured me that the opposite was the case. "The overwhelming majority is open to it," he says. "I think the stereotypes of people being hypersuspicious of any corporation, that's really the minority. Most people, especially younger ones, have accepted as a fact of life that marketing is part of their everyday experience. And they want something in it for themselves."

Still, even knowing all of this, it is hard not to be a bit taken aback during my conversation with Jimmy Smith, the executive creative director at the advertising agency BBDO. Smith created Nike's 1994 "Freestyle" ad campaign, another spot that, with its merging of basketball stunt-dribblers and rap beats, helped prove the power of hip-hop marketing. He turned the commercial into a video, which was run on MTV, and worked on a hip-hop magazine called *You Don't Stop* with articles written by hip-hop legends. One was by the famed underground DJ Bobbito; in it he listed the twenty-five greatest shoes of all time. (Smith says that the list contained only Nikes.)

But Smith also tells me about a campaign that was created before his time, a Nike spot that featured KRS-One singing Gil Scott-Heron's "The Revolution Will Not Be Televised." The original song, a spoken-word precursor to modern hip-hop, argued that when the revolution for racial equality does arrive, it will not be "brought to you by Xerox" or "make you look five pounds thinner" or "go better with Coke," but will be led by black people in the street. "There was a big brouhaha because they used that song, and it really put the question out there: Is there going to be a line that we can't cross?" he says. "Some heavy hitters came out in defense of it. KRS-One was the voice. Gil Scott-Heron gave the approval rights. And then Missy Elliott came out and said it was cool. And after that, there was no line."

This is not the first time the language of revolution has been used to sell products. In the 1960s, Bill Bernbach's agency, Doyle Dayne Bernbach, famously used the language of the counterculture and its ideals of rebellion and individuality to sell everything from El Al Airlines to American Tourister luggage. The firm's influential ads for Volkswagen tapped into mistrust of the automobile industry, pitching the car as an honest alternative to Detroit's corporate behemoths. It even turned suspicion of advertisers into grist for the advertising mill. A headline for a 1964 magazine ad for

Chivas Regal screamed "Don't bother to read this ad" above columns of crossed-out copy. In his book, *The Conquest of Cool*, Thomas Frank writes that Bernbach "was the first adman to embrace the mass society critique, to appeal directly to the powerful but unmentionable public fears of conformity, of manipulation, of fraud, and of powerlessness, and to sell products by so doing. He invented what we might call antiadvertising: a style which harnessed public mistrust of consumerism—perhaps the most powerful cultural tendency of this age—to consumerism itself."

DDB's tactics quickly became standard advertising procedure. A 1965 magazine ad for Booth's House of Lords gin—"the nonconformist gin from England"—encouraged its readers to "tell us your beef against society in 25 words or less," and even included a form for them to fill out: "I hate conformity because ____." In 1968, a magazine ad for Columbia Records showed seven men in a jail cell under the slogan "But the Man can't bust our music." In 2003, *Adbusters*, a magazine that had devoted its four-year existence to stamping out commercialism, introduced a line of "subversive" running shoes called Blackspots, a development that the writers Joseph Heath and Andrew Potter say proves that "cultural rebellion, of the type epitomized by *Adbusters* magazine, is not a threat to the system it *is* the system." A recent television ad for Sprint shows a fat-cat industrialist gleefully boasting to his underling that his new cell phone represents his way of "sticking it to the Man." When the employee sheepishly points out that his boss is, in fact, the Man, and asks if he isn't therefore sticking it to himself, the boss doesn't blink. "Maybe," he says. Which, when you think about it, is a kind of triple-hairpin double-flip: satirizing advertisers that appeal to our desire to stick it to the Man, and in so doing, encouraging us to stick it to *them* by buying a cell phone.

Still, Smith's conclusion that there is no line whatsoever between revolutionary rhetoric and the marketing forces it explicitly condemns pushes these age-old contradictions into high relief. How can there really be no line between art and marketing? How can there be no line between resistance and co-optation? Is there really no message that cannot be twisted into an advertisement? Smith shrugs. "White rockers are always like, 'No! No! Keep it pure!'" he says. "I think hip-hop realized that none of it's pure. If you're signed to Epic Records, or whatever, you're in business."

Certainly, Sony's marketing efforts here at Toad's Place don't seem to be ruffling too many feathers. It is near the end of K'Naan's set, and Lisa Erb, one of the PSP street-team members, approaches yet another concertgoer to see if he would be interested in giving the video-game system a whirl. Erb does not seem to be enjoying the show very much—earlier in the evening, she referred to one of Amir Sulaiman's poems as "perverted," although she declined to expand on this when I asked her what she meant—but she is twenty-three and blonde and what you could call perky and not unattractive, and the crew-cut, rugby-shirt-wearing white guy she comes up to seems thrilled to win her attention for a few minutes. He asks her to hold his beer and, as he begins to play one of the machine's games, performs for her a little bit. "Oh, I missed him!" he shouts as he jerks his body to one side. Erb giggles. On stage, K'Naan introduces his next song: "This is for the struggle."

By the time Mos Def, the show's headliner, takes the stage, the club is mobbed with his fans. I count myself one of them. Not only is Mos Def talented and charismatic, he also seems to possess such uncompromised righteousness that I can imagine him tossing all of us into a sack and carrying us into a promised land of sheer authenticity. The crowd tonight enthusiastically bobs along to their favorite songs. They listen respectfully to "Katrina Klap," released after Hurricane Katrina, that calls for new political leadership, urges audience members to donate money to the rebuilding effort, and chastises Bono, U2's do-gooder front man, for not paying more attention to the residents of the inner city. They sing along to "Mathematics," in which Mos criticizes a world that creates young black men who exhibit more skill at Sony PlayStation than they do at spelling. And they chant along with him as he leads a call-and-response number: "We are," he begins, and the crowd shouts back "so ghetto." Throughout his performance, my eye keeps wandering to the image projected against a wall to the right of the stage: Mos Def's face beaming out of the screen of a Sony PSP.

The place is now packed. I haven't seen the street-team members for about fifteen minutes, and I've given up hope of catching up with them. I am at the edge of an impenetrable mass of people, and it takes me a good ten minutes to move five feet. Maybe they've found their way into the lounge behind the stage, which is called the Budweiser Tropical Rain Forest and which is marked by a banner that advertises itself as the "home of the original Wednesday & Saturday night dance party!!!" Or perhaps they're standing near the concession stand by the front door, where you can buy Toad's Place–branded T-shirts or plastic cups. Maybe they're taking a break outside the club, next to the street sign covered in stickers, most of them advertising seat-of-the-pants college bands, but one touting STA Travel, the discount-travel agency for college students, which urges its audience to "travel like you mean it." And probably a couple of them are still gamely trying to wend their way through the crowd, hoping to find some concertgoers willing to spare a few minutes to try out the PSP, turning their attention from the stage to the small, glowing screens in their hands.

CHAPTER NINE
Lose Yourself: A Conclusion

When we act, we create our own reality.
—Bush administration official, quoted in Ron Suskind,
"Without a Doubt," *New York Times Magazine*,
October 17, 2004

I have to confess that I enjoy karaoke. I try not to make a habit of it, but I've sung my fair share. I've stood on stages in sloppy bars and crooned the Clash's "London Calling" and the Barbra Streisand part of "You Don't Bring Me Flowers" and Don McLean's "American Pie." (I think everybody's sung "American Pie.") Part of the thrill comes from the simple act of performance—the opportunity to get up in front of a group of strangers and belt out the hits. But the *real* pleasure comes from the obvious artificiality of the entire enterprise: the sappy, unconvincing instrumental tracks; the misspelled lyrics on the teleprompter; the bizarre videos of sultry Asian women and lush, sandy beaches projected on a screen to distract the audience from the terrible singing; the casual, tongue-in-cheek renditions of such emotional material. Karaoke is a little bit fun because we can pretend it is real, but it is mostly fun because it is so obviously not real. (Exhibit A: Have you ever been to a karaoke bar with someone who sincerely believes that he is a good singer, and who solemnly tries to hit every note with accuracy and emotion? Those performances are always excruciating, because those people miss the point of karaoke. The singers who know they can't sing and who enthusiastically embrace their shortcomings are always more fun to watch.)

But hip-hop karaoke is a different matter. All of the hallmarks of artificiality that mark the traditional karaoke performance no longer apply; the performance is, essentially, real. While standard karaoke goers sing over synthetic re-creations of the original instrumentation, hip-hop karaoke performers sing over the *exact same* instrumental tracks that their heroes do (and these usually are synthetic recreations and amalgamations of previous songs themselves). Hip-hop's lyrics are so densely packed that if you stutter or fall behind, there's no catching up. There are no teleprompters or cheesy, distracting videos. Just you, up on stage, with a microphone and a lyric sheet, a DJ behind you spinning a beat, and hundreds of hip-hop fans staring at you. Hip-hop karaoke may still be a simulation, but it is one that so closely approximates a real hip-hop performance that there is virtually no operational difference.

Hip-hop karaoke is not yet a national phenomenon. In fact, as far as I know, there's only one place that it exists: a dive bar on Manhattan's Lower East Side called Rothko, which hosts the event once a month. It was created by three white hip-hop fans—two music-booking agents and one Wall Street equity researcher—because, in the words of one of its founders, "I thought people would have fun if they could act out the role of their favorite emcee." I spent much of the week before I attended the event deciding which song I would sing, practicing it over and over and over. Even though it was just karaoke, I felt the need to get my shit together. Somewhere in the recesses of my mind I was still haunted by that fear familiar to so many white rap fans: a room of dedicated (black?) hip-hop fans, pissed off at my substandard rendition, chanting "Choke! Choke!" at me, like the crowd that taunts Eminem's character at the beginning of *8 Mile*.

But as I step into Rothko, a red-walled closet of a bar, I see that I may have overprepared. I don't know why I'm still surprised by this, but a full 85 percent of the crowd falls comfortably within the white-hipster-and/or-frat-boy demographic. As the first acts take the stage—a tubby, bespectacled white guy who leads the crowd in a group chant of the Beastie Boys' "Paul Revere"; another white dude wearing a skull-and-crossbones T-shirt who recites a flat, interminable version of DJ Jazzy Jeff & the Fresh Prince's crossover hit "Parents Just Don't Understand"—my confidence swells. I am going to kill this.

About a half hour into the performances, two guys take the stage to present their rendition of Dr. Dre and Snoop Doggy Dogg's classic, "Nuthin' but a 'G' Thang." They are a pretty good summation of this evening's uneasy mix of reverence and irreverence. They are both white. One of them is wearing a black T-shirt that reads, in a formal calligraphic font, DON'T HATE THE PLAYER, HATE THE GAME, an early-nineties slogan encouraging those who would judge pimps and gangsters to instead turn their critical eye on the country that created them. I will bet any amount of money that he intends this to be an ironic statement. His singing partner is wearing an off-white fedora. They both appear more nervous than their cocky wardrobes would suggest, a fact that they try to mask behind an array of smirks. I put them in their early twenties, which would mean that they were less than ten years old in 1993, when I was in college and the video for this song became an MTV staple. So maybe they don't feel the racial dissonance that I do: this music was always part of their lives; it is not something that they had to grow into or process or work to understand. Still, when the chorus comes, the pair changes the words ever so slightly, referring to themselves as "two loc'ed-out brothers" rather than "two loc'ed-out niggas," which answers the question that I'm sure everyone here was silently asking. You can almost hear the room exhale.

And then it is my turn. I run up onto the stage and grab the microphone. I've chosen Cypress Hill's "How I Could Just Kill a Man," and when the whippersnappers in the audience hear the first telltale samples, they roar. This song was an enormous hit in 1992, my senior year of high school, and it has been a pleasure to spend the week listening to it, reminiscing about a time when hip-hop still seemed new and strange and exciting and scary and something that I could never fully comprehend.

Actually, that's what the song is about—how the listener at home cannot ever understand the life that Cypress Hill sings about—and I dutifully recite the lyrics, which detail stoned drive-bys, cop killings, and car jackings. At some point, as I furiously rip through the verses attempting to simulate the lead rapper B-Real's nasal, syncopated style, my rapping becomes almost unconscious. I have recited these lyrics so many times, not just in the previous week but ever since I first heard them in high school, that I feel myself relying on a kind of muscle memory, as if a voice is moving through my body without any effort or will on my part. I am no longer the outsider looking in that I have been for most of my life. Now, looking out at the youngsters in the crowd, hearing the familiar beat behind me and the vocals swelling out through my chest, I am the guide. I reach the last verse and seamlessly glide through B-Real's excoriation of his comfortable white audience; I announce that my listeners, in their relatively luxurious homes, can't know what it's like for a guy like me, forced to scrounge and kill and risk my hide for a quick buck. I inform them that they have to live my life to understand it, that it is not the sort of thing that they can grasp merely by listening to a rap song, not even this one. The crowd is jumping as I reach the final chorus. I close my eyes and shout into the microphone. I tell them that no matter how hard they try, they can never, ever, ever understand. Then

I hold the microphone out toward the audience, and they joyously holler back, "How I could just kill a man!"

Let's pretend that you are a hip-hop DJ. You are standing behind two turntables and a crossfader, a switch that lets you toggle between records to determine which one plays over the speakers. The left record plays a looped drum beat, a simple pattern repeating over and over. The right record contains a song with a long horn stab. While the left record plays, you move the right record slowly with your right hand. On the downbeat, you slap the crossfader to the right and then back to the left, inserting a shot of horn into the mix. As the music continues you repeat the procedure, dropping the sample in and out in coordination with the beat. This scratch is one of hip-hop's foundational techniques. It is called the transformer.

Hip-hop has always celebrated transformation. One of its most beloved credos is derived from an old Rakim lyric—"It ain't where you're from, it's where you're at"—implying that our present selves will always overcome our past. Hip-hop's founder, Clive Campbell, handily illustrates the theory: first, the Jamaican immigrant lost his accent; then he changed his name to DJ Kool Herc; and then he created a new kind of music by extending prerecorded musical snippets into the backbones of new songs. As hip-hop historian Jeff Chang writes, "He was in the process of reinventing himself." By now, thousands of MCs, DJs, graffiti writers, and breakers have used hip-hop to create new selves and lives, complete with matching nicknames and personalities. When I asked Fab 5 Freddy, the Brooklyn-born graffiti writer who first introduced hip-hop to the white denizens of downtown Manhattan, why he used a pseudonym, he told me that he and his fellow writers were inspired by comic books, in which a seemingly mild-mannered and overlooked shmoe transformed into a superhero. "The whole idea of being this other person, of having this alter ego or persona that could do these things, that was at the root of it all," he told me.

Could there be any more purely American urge? From the Pilgrims who landed in Massachusetts to forge a new world to the immigrants who decided to cast off some of their ethnic or national identities and redefine themselves as Americans, this country's inhabitants have always celebrated the belief that they can, with one fell swoop, remake their world. One of the reasons that the African American experience of slavery continues to provoke such raw emotions is that it flies in the face of this national mythos of self-reliance. We are a nation of strivers, citizens obsessed with the promise of social mobility and personal reinvention, always reaching toward the next iteration of ourselves in the hopes that it will be better, truer, realer, than the ones we're currently stuck inside. "The truth was that Jay Gatsby, of West Egg, Long Island, sprang from his Platonic conception of himself," wrote F. Scott Fitzgerald of Jay Gatz, his fictional impoverished North Dakotan who grew up to surround himself with the trappings of wealth and sophistication. "[H]e invented just the sort of Jay Gatsby that a seventeen year old would be likely to invent, and to this conception he was faithful to the end." That's America in a nutshell. That's hip-hop.

It may seem ironic that hip-hop, a culture so obsessed with transformation, would so fetishize authenticity. "Keeping it real" has become more than an ethos—it is a downright cliché, reflecting the widespread belief that the only legitimate rappers are the ones who live through the street drama they depict in their rhymes. Some observers, as I've tried to show throughout this book, have found themselves drawn to or repulsed by hip-hop because they see in it an unfiltered truth, a documentary immediacy. But this is, I think, a misreading of the term and of the culture. Ice-T, one of the smartest and most quotable observers of hip-hop, once remarked, "Rap is really funny, man, but if you don't see that it's funny, it will scare the crap out of you." Not everyone gets the joke. Here's the thing: we hip-hop fans know that N.W.A. didn't kill and rape all the people they rapped about killing and raping. Nobody believes that the members of the Wu-Tang Clan have mastered the kung-fu art of "Shaolin shadowboxing" (at least not when their first album dropped in 1993; maybe by now they've hired some tutors). Rap fans don't swarm to Young Jeezy's tales of crack peddling because they want to know what life is like as a drug dealer; they like his superheroic persona, his "snowman" logo, his world-conquering swagger, his self-fulfilling prophecy of success in the face of adverse conditions. "Keeping it real" means acknowledging the artifice and artistry in our everyday lives. It means being true to our fantasies, not simply listing the details of our reality.

Maybe this is the only form of authenticity that still means anything. The notion of an immutable inner core—a pure "self" that we must remain "true" to—has not held up well over the last couple of decades. We have learned that we can manipulate our genetic code, once thought of as the immutable building blocks of being, to create clones or transgenic crops. The stigma once attached to plastic surgery, that it is a vain attempt to deny the aging process or to artificially tweak our God-given features, now seems trite; television programs such as *Extreme Makeover* posit that cosmetic surgery can uncover a new, truer self, not artificially mask an old one. Psychopharmaceuticals are no longer seen as threats to our true personalities; instead, we use them to treat conditions that prevent us from being the person that we want to be, and thus the person that we really *are*. Even the notion of an objective truth—a fundamental reality that journalists seek to uncover and explain—feels outdated, as partisans endlessly debate how reporters' biases impact our perceptions of reality and politicians argue that the way events are covered have more of an impact than the events themselves. Small wonder that the French philosopher Jean Baudrillard has become newly popular, thanks to his impact on the *Matrix* films. Back in 1981, he argued that the old distinction between "simulation" and "reality" no longer held, for the simple reason that our reality had become an enormous act of simulation. There was no more fundamental reality to remain true to. "Disneyland exists in order to hide that it is the 'real' country, all of 'real' America that is Disneyland," he wrote. "Disneyland is presented as imaginary in order to make us believe that the rest is real, whereas all of Los Angeles and the America that surrounds it are no longer real, but belong to the hyperreal order and to the order of simulation."

So maybe Anthony Bozza is correct when he writes, in his biography of Eminem, that the white rapper "represents the current paradigm of race consciousness in America, whereby skin color is almost of secondary consequence to one's racial identity, where racial association seems to be more defined by behavior than color." Bozza quotes the journalist Farai Chideya: "What Eminem demonstrates clearly is that race now is not just about the color of your skin, it's also about your psychology. It's about you positioning yourself. It is a mix of conscious and unconscious factors that situate you in a demographic which your skin color might even deny. It's a fact today and it took hip-hop to make this fact manifest."

(If this sounds familiar, it may remind you of a quote from the Young Black Teenagers' Kamron, back in 1990: "We're taught that all Afro-Americans are black and all Caucasians are white. That's a generalization. People should start to individualize.")

Well, why not? Race is, after all, a social construction. If science can help us renegotiate such seemingly essential characteristics as our genetic code, our brain chemistry, and our breast size, why can't culture help us renegotiate our race? Can we simply decide that we no longer wish to be white, in the way that we can take a pill and decide that we no longer wish to suffer from attention deficit disorder?

And are black people free to make those same decisions? Our national obsession with racial difference survived two and a half centuries of slavery, the Civil War, Reconstruction, the civil rights movement, the black separatist movement, the Black Panthers, and affirmative action. Does that history no longer matter? Can the legacy of race so simply, so naturally, so smoothly waft away from us merely because we all want it to? Could this problem have been solved long ago if we'd only known how to correctly "position" ourselves? Is this what Eminem really meant when he told us to "Lose Yourself"?

That's one of the questions I asked former Def Jam publicist Bill Adler. By way of an answer, he recounted the first time he watched *The Jerry Springer Show*, ten years earlier. "I was completely stunned," he said, "because the guests on the show never addressed the racial particulars of their situation. Over and over again it was a black man and a white woman or a white man and a black woman. There was beef in the household, but it was never about race. They were beyond it. It was always, 'What!? You fucked my best girlfriend?' Not, 'You triflin' nigga' or 'You scheming white bitch.' Never. Never! It was literally beneath discussion. When I saw that, I thought to myself, 'Wow, maybe this is how some people are really living today.' In effect, these are people who are living in a postracial society, people who have already 'lost themselves.' I love that [Eminem] metaphor. And it begs the question: Have they really lost themselves, or have they found themselves? To me, they've lost something old, but they've found something new—a new paradigm for a new society, one that's less uptight about race. We've got new things to worry about."

The evidence of our new society is everywhere. On February 28, 2006, the Smithsonian announced that it was launching a new initiative for its National Museum of American History: "Hip-Hop Won't Stop: The Beats, the Rhymes, the Life." At a press conference,

Afrika Bambaataa, legendary b-boy Richie "Crazy Legs" Colon, Grandmaster Flash, Ice-T, and Russell Simmons all celebrated the museum's decision to present hip-hop artifacts alongside such iconic American objects as Alexander Graham Bell's telephone, Dizzy Gillespie's trumpet, and a Kermit the Frog puppet. Simmons, the king of crossover, told the crowd that his first thought upon hearing the Smithsonian's plan was, "The party's over." "The idea of hip-hop is that it's from the underbelly, it's from people who've been locked out and not recognized," he said. But he changed his view over time. "It's not a signal to the end of hip-hop," he told the Associated Press. "We know it will be a lasting fixture. And it should be. All over the world, hip-hop is an expression of young people's struggles, their frustrations, and their opinions."

Five days later, at the 2006 Academy Awards, another nation-defining moment is taking place. The members of Three 6 Mafia, the Atlanta rap group, stand on the stage of the Kodak Theatre, giving the Academy Awards audience its first hip-hop performance. (Eminem declined the offer to perform "Lose Yourself" in 2003.) They are singing "It's Hard Out Here for a Pimp," a track they wrote for the film *Hustle & Flow*, about a pimp who dreams of becoming a rap star. The set is a staged re-creation of that movie's ramshackle scenery: a small cube of a room decorated with strings of Christmas lights and eggshell cartons that have been stapled to the walls in an attempt at makeshift soundproofing. In front of the rappers, a gaggle of dancers embody some of the film's characters— luscious prostitutes (much more glamorous than the ones in the actual film), well-dressed johns, hard-scrabble street fighters who battle one another with immaculately choreographed moves. In contrast, the members of Three 6 Mafia seem nonchalant in their T-shirts and sneakers as they effortlessly chant their song's lyrics. At the end of the performance, Taraji P. Henson, the actress from the film who sings the song's chorus, walks downstage. She is wearing a glimmering white dress and extravagantly strapped high-heel shoes. The orchestra's strings swell behind her as she brings the song to its conclusion. "You know it's haaaaaaaaaard," she belts, and then pauses before continuing. "Out heeeeeeere." Her voice gets slightly quieter as she sings "for a," but then she blasts out the last word, long and proud, shaking her head slowly side to side as the orchestra climaxes and the final syllable pours out of her: "PIIIIII-IIIIIIIIIIIIMP!" The tuxedoed film-industry bigwigs in the seats of the Kodak Theatre applaud politely.

But if that moment seems strange, it is nothing compared to what comes next. Queen Latifah, the hip-hop star who has gone on to a successful acting career in films such as *Chicago* and *Bringing Down the House*, takes the podium to announce the winner for Best Original Song. "And the Oscar goes to . . ." she says, opening the envelope. She looks down at the winner's name. She can't speak. She laughs. And then she sings that chorus: "It's hard out here for a pimp." "Oh my God!" she says, and that seems to be the general consensus. The members of Three 6 Mafia, who are watching from offstage, jump into the air and run onto the stage. They approach Latifah, who covers her mouth in shock. In the audience, John Singleton, the director of *Boyz N the Hood* and one of *Hustle & Flow*'s producers, stands and applauds, his face cracking into an expression of pure joy. The Three 6 Mafia approach the microphone. They are giddy. They thank Jesus, their choreographer, the Academy, and George Clooney (for some reason). The camera flashes on Jamie Foxx. Last year, he was one of four black nominees up for an acting award and took home the prize for his performance in *Ray* (Chris Rock, the 2005 Awards host, quipped that the event was "kinda like Def Oscar Jam"). Now he's beaming and pumping his fist in the air.

After the Three 6 Mafia exit stage right and the excitement dies down a bit, host Jon Stewart takes the podium. He claps a few times. He chuckles. He works his tongue around his mouth as he thinks of what to say. He puts his head down and *cackles*. He's got it. He lifts his head again. "You know what?" he says. "I think it just got a little easier out here for a pimp."

He's joking, of course. But one of the reasons the joke works is because it so seamlessly taps into one of the underlying myths of hip-hop: that somehow our consumption of the culture reflects and impacts the way we live. That there is some connection between what we listen to and who we are. That through watching breakdancing movies, or listening to Public Enemy, or wearing baggy jeans, or buying a Boost Mobile phone, we are, ever so subtly, changing ourselves and our world. Hip-hop lets us create a fantasy space in which the old categories of race can be renegotiated, and where we can finally take another step closer to living up to our color-blind ideals. A world in which our recognition really does make it a little easier out here for a pimp.

But fifteen days after the Oscars, the *New York Times* offers a new snapshot of what has happened to the young, inner-city black men whose images and narratives we have entertained ourselves with for the last two decades. It turns out that, even as hip-hop has made them more visible and their culture and voices a greater part of America's definition of itself, their real lives have grown far, far worse. The front-page article, "Plight Deepens for Black Men, Studies Warn," reports that "the huge pool of poorly educated black men are [*sic*] becoming ever more disconnected from the mainstream society, and to a far greater degree than comparable white or Hispanic men." In the inner cities, more than half of black men do not finish high school. A full 72 percent of these dropouts are without jobs, up from 43 percent in 1980. More black high school dropouts in their late twenties are in prison (34 percent) than working (30 percent). "If you look at the numbers, the 1990s was a bad decade for young black men," says Harry J. Holzer, a Georgetown University economist.

It is sobering to think that the situation has deteriorated so much even since the early 1990s, a decade that began with gang wars, the Rodney King verdict, and the ensuing unrest. Whatever the cause, one thing is clear: while white rap fans' racial attitudes may have improved, the economic reality of being black and poor in America has not. We may have changed the way we think about race, and we may have changed the way we think about ourselves. We may be better individuals. But we have not helped create a better society for those that hip-hop was created to represent. Maybe that's not surprising. "Consumers are not the people who make social movements," Jeff Chang, the author of *Can't Stop Won't Stop*, told me. "That's not how it gets done."

White rap fans live in the world of representation, identity, culture, mirrors, and windows. We project our own ideals and beliefs and images of ourselves: through breakdancing performances, where individual effort always overcomes obstacles; on hip-hop radio stations that gerrymander an image of unthreatening diversity; at dance parties, where our musical taste and libertine values trump race, economics, or history; in gangsta-rap cliques that tell us how dangerous we are; at nerdcore concerts in which we bestow upon ourselves the mantle of victimhood; and in advertisements that promise us that we can become that down, comfortable, aware person we always knew we could be. We point to our self-conceptions, and we hope that is enough. We look to our music and our movies and our television programs—the "dream life of our nation," to borrow a term from film critic J. Hoberman—to tell us who we are. And if we squint at what they show us hard enough, it almost becomes real.

One afternoon, my wife takes off on a getaway with an old college roommate, leaving me alone for the weekend. I use the opportunity to borrow an XBox video-game system from a friend of mine and space out for a couple of days. I buy some beer and some snacks, settle into the couch, and slide a copy of *Grand Theft Auto: San Andreas* into the console. I have wanted to play *San Andreas* for a while now. I am not much of a video-game guy, but friends have shown me the previous couple of installments of the wildly popular Grand Theft Auto series, *Grand Theft Auto III* and *Grand Theft Auto: Vice City*, and I was amazed. These were huge, open-ended games, digital cities in which I was free to roam around, get lost, rob cars, and shoot random passersby. They were also pretty hilarious and knowing send-ups of pop-culture tropes. *Grand Theft Auto III* placed players in the middle of a *Goodfellas*-like gangster flick. *Vice City* presented a sun-soaked crime drama, a mix of *Miami Vice, Carlito's Way*, and *The Godfather, Part II*.

San Andreas updates the franchise. This time, instead of inhabiting the character of Tommy Vercetti, an Italian mobster, I am CJ, a black man who flies home for his mother's funeral and gets caught up in the gang violence that he thought he had left behind. I take a few minutes to drive around my new neighborhood, which looks suspiciously like Rodney King–era South Central Los Angeles. I say this not from personal experience, of course—I've never visited the place—but from the hours that I spent during the early 1990s watching *Boyz N the Hood, Menace II Society*, and other films that purported to document the grim life of that neighborhood's African American residents. The makers of this game have clearly studied those movies; everything from the sun-bleached cinematography to the low-rider bicycles could have been cribbed from a director's-cut DVD. They have also studied their gangsta rap. My character's sidekicks bear striking resemblances to Eazy-E and Ice Cube, the two most outspoken members of N.W.A. As I play the game I go through experiences that feel oddly familiar; it's almost as if I've lived them before. I am harassed by the fucking cops. I am chased by rival gang members. I call my sidekicks "nigga," and they call me "nigga" in return. I drive slowly past a fast-food restaurant, and as I do so my friends lean out the car windows and spray gunfire at our enemies. Whenever I hop into a car, I flip through the radio stations, listening again and again to old-school gangsta-rap classics by Compton's Most Wanted and Above the Law.

It takes me a few minutes to grow familiar with the game's controller, but once I do, the connection between me and the black body on the screen becomes nearly unconscious. I think "Move left," and my black avatar moves left. I think "Steal that car," and my black avatar steals that car. I think "Shoot that bitch," and my black avatar shoots that bitch. The distance between my thoughts and his actions is minuscule, barely existent. Together, we go to the barbershop and get our Afro trimmed. Together, we go to a department store and pick up a red, black, and green Africa pendant. Together, we go to the gym to bulk up our shared black body. After a few hours, my own body may as well not exist. I have been sitting on the couch since two P.M. and I have not scratched my nose nor shifted my weight nor, as far as I can tell, breathed. I have not been aware of a single physical impulse.

Because I was not raised on a steady diet of video games, I haven't built up the Herculean tolerance of some of my friends, and after five hours of steady playing my eyes dry out and my head starts to throb. I stagger outside into the deepening navy evening to take a walk around the block and grab a few gasps of oxygen. In my groggy vision, the Brooklyn landscape appears pixellated, like the colliding planes of the virtual world I have just spent the bulk of the day within. My ears are still throbbing with the aftershocks of my afternoon's gangsta-rap soundtrack. My addled brain can't quite make sense of my surroundings. Every car looks like it is waiting for me to steal it. Every one of my neighbors could be a racist police officer or a rival gang member. And I, I could be anything. Short or tall. Weak or strong. Real or virtual. Black or white. It is an overwhelming moment. What could be more thrilling, more noble, more fulfilling, more terrifying, than living in somebody else's skin?

NOTES

To write this book I drew on a number of previously written hip-hop histories. I owe a particular debt to Jeff Chang's *Can't Stop Won't Stop: A History of the Hip-Hop Generation* (St. Martin's Press, 2005). I also drew heavily on *The Vibe History of Hip Hop*, edited by Alan Light (Three Rivers Press, 1999), for historical information and context; and on the essays collected in *That's the Joint!: The Hip-Hop Studies Reader*, edited by Murray Forman and Mark Anthony Neal (Routledge, 2004), for fresh perspectives.

PREFACE

x **"Finally, something white people can't steal"**: Anthony Bozza, *Whatever You Say I Am: The Life and Times of Eminem* (Three Rivers Press, 2003), 175.

x **"Hip-hop will not be consumed"**: The writer was John Leland. *Spin* revisited the quote in its fifteenth-anniversary issue. "Quote Unquote," *Spin*, April 2000.

xi **Today we remain separated:** National Urban League, "State of Black America 2006." The study found a "high level of residential segregation between blacks and whites which in most cities has created a dual housing market whereby demand for homes in black neighborhoods is limited to black home seekers." Quote from Lance Freeman's abstract "Black Homeownership: A Dream No Longer Deferred?" available on the National Urban League's Web site—www .nul.org/stateofblackamerica.html, under "abstracts."

xii **"black America's CNN"**: At least this is how Alan Light reprints the quote in his essay "About a Salary or Reality? Rap's Recurrent Conflict," in Murray Forman and Mark Anthony Neal, editors, *That's the Joint! The Hip-Hop*

Studies Reader (Routledge, 2004), 141. Others remember the quote as "black people's CNN," or, simply, "the black CNN." I was unable to locate the original reference.

CHAPTER 1—WHITE LIKE ME: AN INTRODUCTION

3 **"benign neglect":** Jeff Chang, *Can't Stop Won't Stop: A History of the Hip-Hop Generation* (St. Martin's Press, 2005), 14.

3 **"urban renewal":** Ibid., 11.

3 **"Young white listeners' genuine pleasure and commitment to black music":** Tricia Rose, *Black Noise: Rap Music and Black Culture in Contemporary America* (Wesleyan University Press, 1994), 5.

4 **"[H]istory repeats itself":** Minister Paul Scott, "The Hip Hop Hatin' That Hate Produced," *The Final Call*, online edition, July 24, 2002.

4 **"We've got to remember where we came from":** Nekesa Mumbi Moody, "Feud Between Eminem and *The Source* Magazine Wounds on Both Sides," Associated Press, February 2, 2004.

4 **In 1923 the cultural critic Gilbert Seldes declared:** Michael North, *The Dialect of Modernism: Race, Language, and Twentieth-Century Literature* (Oxford University Press, 1994), 154.

5 **"White folks tend to worry":** Bill Adler, in-person interview, May 10, 2005.

6 **A poll taken by the *New York Times* in 2000:** Kevin Sack and Janet Elder, "Poll Finds Optimistic Outlook but Enduring Racial Division," *New York Times*, July 11, 2000.

6 **According to the U.S. Census:** Per data available at www.census.gov /popest/national/asrh/NC-EST2005-srh.html. I derived these figures by dividing the total population by the number of people categorized as "one race" "not Hispanic or Latino" white, and the number of people categorized as "race alone or in combination" black.

6 **a study by Harvard's Civil Rights Project:** Gary Orfield and Chungmei Lee, "Racial Transformation and the Changing Nature of Segregation" (The Civil Rights Project at Harvard University, 2006), 9.

6 **The Lewis Mumford Center:** John Logan, "Ethnic Diversity Grows, Neighborhood Integration Lags Behind," report (Lewis Mumford Center, State University of New York–Albany, April 3, 2001).

NOTES

7 **"Yeah, hip-hop has brought people closer together"**: Gabriel Alvarez, telephone interview, February 9, 2005.

8 **"listened to the rumbling underground"**: Jack Kerouac, *The Subterraneans* (Grove Press, 1958), 10.

14 **"the nigga you love to hate"**: Ice Cube, "The Nigga Ya Love to Hate," *AmeriKKKa's Most Wanted* (Priority, 1990).

14 **" 'cause you cannot be it"**: Black Sheep, "To Whom It May Concern," *A Wolf In Sheep's Clothing* (Mercury, 1991).

17 **"the greatest of the corporate rappers"**: Kelefa Sanneh, "Gettin' Paid," *New Yorker*, August 20, 2001.

17 **"becoming more Wall Street"**: Guy Trebay, "Maturing Rappers Try a New Uniform: Yo, a Suit!" *New York Times*, February 6, 2004.

19 **"At least they're not fucking niggers or Puerto Ricans"**: Adam Heimlich, "Vice Rising: Why Corporate Media Is Sniffing the Butt of the Magazine World," *New York Press*, October 1, 2002.

CHAPTER 2—TOURING THE 'HOOD: HUNTING FOR REALITY IN NEW YORK CITY

I drew on a number of sources in this and subsequent chapters for background in hip-hop's early history. In addition to the specific citations listed below, the following sources were immensely helpful: *And It Don't Stop*, edited by Raquel Cepeda (Faber and Faber, 2004); *Style Wars*, a film directed by Henry Chalfant and Tony Silver (Public Broadcasting Service, 1983); *Can't Stop Won't Stop*, by Jeff Chang (St. Martin's Press, 2005); *Hip Hop Files*, by Martha Cooper (From Here to Fame, 2004); *The New Beats*, by S. H. Fernando Jr. (Anchor Books, 1994); *That's the Joint!*, edited by Murray Forman and Mark Anthony Neal (Routledge, 2004); *Yes Yes Y'All*, by Jim Fricke and Charlie Ahearn (Da Capo, 2002); *Hip Hop America*, by Nelson George (Penguin, 1998); *The Freshest Kids*, a film directed by Israel (QD3 Entertainment, 2002); *The Vibe History of Hip Hop*, edited by Alan Light (Three Rivers Press, 1999); *Bring the Noise*, by Havelock Nelson and Michael A. Gonzales (Harmony Books, 1991); *And You Don't Stop: 30 Years of Hip-Hop*, a documentary series produced by Dana Heinz Perry and Bill Adler (VH1 Television, 2004); and *Black Noise*, by Tricia Rose (Wesleyan University Press, 2004).

25 **"personal bastion against society"**: Kenneth T. Jackson, *Crabgrass Frontier: The Suburbanization of the United States* (Oxford University Press, 1985), 47.

25 **"a safeguard against the moral slide":** Ibid., 48.

26 **"horrible noise"** . . . **"whizz that decapitates":** Lester Bangs, "A Reasonable Guide to Horrible Noise," in *Psychotic Reactions and Carburetor Dung: The Work of a Legendary Critic* (Random House, 1987), 301–2.

26 **"the most godforsaken bathroom in Christendom":** Rob Kemp, club review, *New York Magazine*, available online at newyorkmetro.com/listings/bar/cbgb/.

26 **"as offensive as possible":** Legs McNeil and Gillian McCain, *Please Kill Me: The Uncensored Oral History of Punk* (Grove Press, 1996), 299.

27 **"In Detroit, if you were a white kid":** Ibid., 48.

27 **"punks are niggers":** interview in *New Musical Express*, quoted by Dick Hebdige, *Subculture: The Meaning of Style* (Routledge, 1979), 62.

27 LAST OF THE WHITE NIGGERS: McNeil and McCain, *Kill Me*, photo insert.

28 **"Never in Pazz & Jop history":** Robert Christgau, "Funkentelechy vs. the Placebo Syndrome," *Village Voice*, February 22, 1983.

29 **"People hated that record":** David Samuels, "The Rap on Rap," *New Republic*, November 11, 1991.

31 **"In the Bronx's new hierarchy of cool":** Jeff Chang, *Can't Stop Won't Stop: A History of the Hip Hop Generation* (St. Martin's Press, 2005), 82.

33 **"I was reading some early articles":** Fab 5 Freddy, telephone interview, June 8, 2005.

34 **"insecure cowards":** Jeff Chang, *Can't Stop Won't Stop*, 134.

34 **"We were aware of the art world":** Patti Astor, telephone interview, March 23, 2005.

35 **"the bunker where the action truly headquarters":** Rene Ricard, "The Pledge of Allegiance," *Artforum*, November 1982.

38 **That is how history is made:** In addition to the sources listed at the beginning of this chapter's footnotes, this account of the Sugarhill Gang was informed by Steven Daly, "Hip-Hop Happens," *Vanity Fair*, November 2005.

38 **"didn't really represent what MCing was":** S. H. Fernando Jr., "Back in the Day: 1975–1979," in Alan Light, ed., *The Vibe History of Hip Hop* (Three Rivers Press, 1999), 21.

38 **"We said, 'Who the hell is this'":** Daly, "Hip-Hop Happens."

39 **"[i]f civilization is to blame":** Joseph Heath and Andrew Potter, *Nation of Rebels: Why Counterculture Became Consumer Culture* (HarperCollins, 2004), 254.

NOTES

39 "As more visitors pile into [an] area": Ibid., 271.

40 "As soon as these guys started stabbing me in the back": Astor interview.

40 "disillusioned": Bill Stelling, telephone interview, March 30, 2005.

40 "Pretty early on": Lady Pink, telephone interview, March 31, 2005.

40 "There was a lot of 'Oh, look!' ": Zephyr, e-mail interview, March 2005.

41 "There's a new wave of galleries": David Howard, director, "New York's East Village Art Scene," *David Howard's ArtSEEN*, video series (Visual Studies, 1985).

41 YANKEE GO HOME: Martha Cooper, *Hip Hop Files* (From Here to Fame, 2004), 159.

41 "They were young, unreliable, and always broke": Elizabeth Hess, "Graffiti R.I.P.: How the Art World Loved 'Em and Left 'Em," *Village Voice*, December 22, 1987.

41 "Mention the word 'graffiti' these days": Ibid.

41 "By 1984, it's over": Carlo McCormick, telephone interview, March 16, 2005.

42 "Nobody talks about the East Village any more": Liza Kirwin, "East Side Story," *Artforum*, October 1999.

CHAPTER 3—SPIN CONTROL: A HISTORY OF BREAKDANCING IN THE SUBURBS

This chapter's writing on Ronald Reagan was influenced by Haynes Johnson's *Sleepwalking Through History: America in the Reagan Years* (Anchor Books, 1991); *Culture in an Age of Money*, edited by Nicolaus Mills (Ivan R. Dee, 1991); Gil Troy's *Morning in America: How Ronald Reagan Invented the 1980s* (Princeton University Press, 2005); and Garry Wills's *Reagan's America: Innocents at Home* (Penguin, 2000).

48 "a competitive, warlike dance": Martha Cooper, *Hip Hop Files* (From Here to Fame, 2004), 92.

49 "Back then, we had something to prove": Richie Williams, telephone interview, May 15, 2005.

51 "head wax": "Analysts Skeptical About Breakdancing," *USA Today*, September 19, 1984.

51 "It was wreckage": Henry Chalfant, telephone interview, May 15, 2005.

54 **"When I wanted to do shows":** Michael Holman, telephone interview, June 2, 2005.

54 **"My idea was to bring the street onto the stage":** Ruthe Stein, "Kids Break into Show Business," *San Francisco Chronicle*, January 23, 1984.

54 **"take it from the streets to Carnegie Hall":** Miles White, "Street Steps Break into the Big Time," *USA Today*, January 11, 1984.

55 **the nation's subconscious "dream life":** J. Hoberman, *The Dream Life: Movies, Media, and the Mythology of the Sixties* (New Press, 2003), xvii.

55 **"United before the same vision":** Ibid., xi.

55 **Between 1979 and 1983, the percentage of Americans living below the poverty level:** Data from www.census.gov/hhes/www/poverty/histpov/hstpov2.html.

55 **Almost half of African Americans under the age of eighteen, 46.6 percent:** www.census.gov/hhes/www/poverty/histpov/hstpov3.html.

56 **a film that "can change the impressions people may have of the South Bronx":** Gene Siskel, " 'Street': Political and Social Commentary for Harry Belafonte," *Chicago Tribune*, May 27, 1984.

56 **"Harry bought my script":** Steven Hager, e-mail interview.

57 **Golan once referred to their domestic box office receipts as "gravy":** Sandra Salmans, "Cannon's Box-Office Respect," *New York Times*, April 26, 1983.

57 **"a sadistic, bloody, foul-mouthed action movie":** Lawrence Van Gelder, "The Screen: 'Revenge of the Ninja,' " *New York Times*, September 8, 1983.

57 **"I got the script":** Timothy Solomon, telephone interview, May 20, 2005.

59 **"street dance's first matinee idol":** Kevin Grubb, "Shabba-Doo: Street Dance's First Matinee Idol," *Dancemagazine*, October 1984.

59 **"Every morning all these street dancers congregate on my front lawn":** Ibid.

59 **"hit the heartland":** Cathleen McGuigan, "Breaking Out: America Goes Dancing," *Newsweek*, July 2, 1984.

59 **a radio station canceled a breakdancing contest:** Associated Press, "Nothing Moves Before 5,000 Dancers," April 20, 1984.

59 **Watkins's "official breakdance dictionary":** William H. Watkins, *Breakdance!* (Contemporary Books, 1984), 5–7.

59 **Sartorial "essentials":** Ibid., 9–11.

NOTES

60 **Louisiana's JPSO Hot Rock Express:** James A. Perry, "Break Dancers Strut Their Stuff," *Times-Picayune*, June 3, 1984.

60 **"I used to be a snob about music":** Elaine Lembo, "Breakin' Out All Over," *Washington Post*, August 3, 1984.

60 **"It came originally from African Americans":** Tim Danczuk, telephone interview, May 16, 2005.

60 **"intimidated and obstructed shoppers":** Kevin Grubb, "Banning Break Dancing—Another Farenheit 451?" *Dancemagazine*, June 1984.

60 **"affluent, upper-middle-class, white-as-Wonder-Bread":** Bob Greene, "Full-Tilt-Boogie Trendsetting," *St. Louis Post-Dispatch*, June 30, 1984.

61 **"Frankly, I miss the old style of dancing":** Lewis Grizzard, "Give Me a Break!" *Houston Post*, April 17, 1984.

61 **"go through her teenage years without knowing":** Shirley L. Larsen, "When My Daughter Moonwalks," *Christian Science Monitor*, September 11, 1984.

61 **"Breakdancer's Pulmonary Embolism":** S. Tiu et al., "Breakdancer's Pulmonary Embolism," *Clinical Nuclear Medicine*, June 1986.

61 **"Differential Diagnosis of Scrotal Pain After Break Dancing":** R. E. Wheeler and R. A. Appell, "Differential Diagnosis of Scrotal Pain After Break Dancing," *Journal of the American Medical Association*, December 28, 1984.

61 **"I had this whole mentality":** Greg Selkoe, telephone interview, May 16, 2005.

62 **"breakdancing will go away as quickly as it came in":** "Analysts Skeptical."

63–64 **funding for food stamps and Aid to Families with Dependent Children was cut by 13 percent . . . training programs was cut by 35 percent:** Robert Pear, "Reagan Has Achieved Many Goals, but Some Stir Opposition," *New York Times*, August 20, 1984.

64 **1981 budget cuts alone pushed 560,000 people, including 325,000 children:** Hobart Rowen, "Who's Better Off?" *Washington Post*, August 16, 1984.

64 **black unemployment rate rose to 15.1 percent:** Peter T. Kilborn, "4 Years Later: Who in U.S. Is Better Off?" *New York Times*, October 9, 1984.

64 **"pockets of poverty [that] haven't caught up":** Ibid.

64 **"patronizing socialism":** George Gilder, "But What About Welfare's Grim Side?" *New York Times*, April 22, 1984.

64 $25,000 dress that the new first lady wore: Nina Hyde, "Reagan Regalia: Nancy's $25,000 Inaugural Wardrobe," *New York Times,* January 19, 1981.

64 the deficit balloon to $208 billion in 1983: Congressional Budget Office data, available online at www.cbo.gov/budget/historical.pdf.

64 "You can will your way out of trouble": Edwin M. Yoder Jr., "Come On and Level with Us," *Washington Post,* January 27, 1984.

65 "spirit of can-do, can-work, can accomplish": Gil Troy, *Morning in America: How Ronald Reagan Invented the 1980s* (Princeton University Press, 2005), 152.

65 "A lot of people who are poor are poor through no fault of their own": Milton Coleman and David S. Broder, " 'Fairness' Issue Loses Potency," *Washington Post,* October 7, 1984.

66 "It was like anything when you're a kid": Matt Zimmerman, in-person interview, September 19, 2005.

66 "They took breaking away from us": Israel, director, *The Freshest Kids,* DVD (QD3 Entertainment, 2002.)

67 "This new series is not about a black middle-class family": Arthur Unger, " 'Bill Cosby Show'—Earmarks of an Enduring Hit," *Christian Science Monitor,* September 20, 1984.

67 "no longer qualifies as black enough to be an Uncle Tom": quoted in William Raspberry, "Cosby Show: Black or White?" *Washington Post,* November 5, 1984.

67 in 1986, the percentage of black people earning more than $35,000 a year: Richard Bernstein, "20 Years After the Kerner Report: Three Societies, All Separate," *New York Times,* February 29, 1988.

67 "white America understands that blackness": Raspberry, "Cosby Show."

67 "If blacks aren't making it, that's their fault": Deborah Hastings, "Study Finds 'Cosby' Left a Mixed Legacy," *Chicago Sun-Times,* May 20, 1992.

68 third-highest mean income: Available online at money.cnn.com/best/bplive/topten/earners.html.

CHAPTER 4—CROSSOVER: HIP-POP HITS THE AIRWAVES

Nelson George's *The Death of Rhythm & Blues* (Penguin, 1988) was very influential in my reading of radio history. Also helpful were William Barlow's *Voice Over: The Making of Black Radio* (Temple University Press, 1998); Susan J. Douglas's *Listening In: Radio and the American Imagination* (University of Minnesota Press, 1999); and

NOTES

Mark Newman's *Entrepreneurs of Profit and Pride: From Black-Appeal to Radio Soul* (Praeger, 1998). Information on Def Jam and the Beastie Boys comes from Stacy Gueraseva's *Def Jam, Inc.: Russell Simmons, Rick Rubin, and the Extraordinary History of the World's Most Influential Hip-Hop Label* (One World, 2005); Alan Light's *The Skills to Pay the Bills: The Story of the Beastie Boys* (Three Rivers Press, 2006); Alex Ogg's *The Men Behind Def Jam: The Radical Rise of Russell Simmons and Rick Rubin* (Omnibus Press, 2002); and Ronin Ro's *Raising Hell: The Reign, Ruin, and Redemption of Run-DMC and Jam Master Jay* (Amistad, 2005).

74 **in 1990 the city had only 453 black residents:** www.census.gov/prod/cen1990/cp1/cp.1.51.pdf.

74 **In 2000 there were about 1,400:** http://quickfacts.census.gov/qtd/states/55/5531000.html.

74 **it remains almost 86 percent white:** Ibid.

75 **contributed thirteen of the country's thirty most-played songs:** Available online at http://www.billboard.com/bbcom/yearend/2005/charts/hot100.jsp.

75 **"Radio stayed away from hip-hop":** Raphael George, telephone interview, June 30, 2005.

76 **"proceeds as if music by and for blacks is alien":** Jon Parcles, "Who Decides the Color of Music?" *New York Times*, May 17, 1987.

76 **"[A]t its best it is an impulse to wholeness":** Greil Marcus, *Mystery Train: Images of America in Rock 'n' Roll Music*, 4th ed. (Plume, 1990), 97.

76 **"The explosion of rap music":** Quincy McCoy, telephone interview, July 25, 2005.

76 **"You can call hip-hop 'ethnic music'":** Dusty Hayes, telephone interview, August 15, 2005.

76–77 **"has no place in our society":** Christopher Connell, "Quayle Demands That Rap Record be Yanked," Associated Press, September 22, 1992.

77 **"If you never compromise, your core audience":** Russell Simmons and Nelson George, *Life and Def: Sex, Drugs, Money + God* (Three Rivers Press, 2001), 82–83.

77 **"commercial pap" and "that raw ghetto sound":** Boogie Down Productions, "Ghetto Music," *Ghetto Music: The Blueprint of Hip-Hop* (Jive, 1989).

78 **"the culture industry":** Theodor Adorno, *The Culture Industry* (Routledge, 1991).

78 "fundamental characteristic of popular music" was "standardization": Theodor Adorno, "On Popular Music," in Simon Frith and Andrew Goodwin, eds., *On Record: Rock, Pop, and the Written Word* (Routledge, 1990), 302.

78 "wholly antagonistic to the ideal of individuality": Ibid., 305.

78 "obedience to the social hierarchy": Max Horkheimer and Theodor W. Adorno, translated by Edmund Jephcott, *Dialectic of Enlightenment: Philosophical Fragments* (Stanford University Press, 2002), 305.

78 "mass deception": Ibid., 94.

78 "lot of fools": Elvis Costello, "Radio, Radio," *This Year's Model*, reissue (Rykodisc, 1993).

79 "coke-sniffing DJs": Janine Coveny, "Philly: The Home of Brotherly Radio? Battle Between R&B Stations Gets Hostile," *Billboard*, April 11, 1998.

79 "too often, research plays 100% of the role in decision making": Steve Warren, *Radio: The Book: For Creative, Professional Programming*, 4th ed. (Elsevier Focal Press, 2005), 78.

82–83 70 percent of a record's sales had to come from white listeners: William Barlow, *Voice Over: The Making of Black Radio* (Temple University Press, 1998), 200.

83 In 1971, an in-house study conducted by CBS Records: Nelson George, *The Death of Rhythm & Blues* (Penguin, 1988), 136.

83 "The disco backlash": Sean Ross, telephone interview, June 30, 2005.

83 "We resisted it": Donnie Simpson, telephone interview, July 25, 2005.

84 "It's just difficult for listeners over twenty-five to accept": Dan Stuart, "The Rap Against Rap at Black Radio: Professional Suicide or Cultural Smokescreen"? *Billboard*, December 24, 1988.

84 "The stations that were completely vehement": Bill Stephney, telephone interview, June 8, 2005.

84 "The bourgeois people in black radio": Yvonne Olson, "Meet Tackles Tough Topics in Black Broadcasting," *Billboard*, June 11, 1988.

86 "aimed more at disarming listeners than challenging them": Robert Hilburn, "Run-DMC Wins in a 'Walk,' " *Los Angeles Times*, January 3, 1987.

86 "At least in Detroit, I don't recall that record": Jay Dixon, telephone interview, August 3, 2005.

86 "hillbilly bullshit"; "that rap-rock shit too far"; "trying to ruin us":

NOTES

Ronin Ro, *Raising Hell: The Reign, Ruin, and Redemption of Run-DMC and Jam Master Jay* (HarperCollins, 2005), 136.

87 "American rock 'n' roll": Stacy Gueraseva, *Def Jam, Inc.: Russell Simmons, Rick Rubin, and the Extraordinary Story of the World's Most Influential Hip-Hop Label* (One World Books, 2005), 101.

87 "one of rock's hottest new acts": Jim Miller and Bill Rapkin, "Hymning the Joys of Girls, Gunplay, and Getting High," *Newsweek*, February 2, 1987.

88 "[A]s long as they talked about white boys and beer": Alan Light, *Skills to Pay the Bills* (Three Rivers Press, 2006), 60.

88 particularly its "big rock drums" and "real Top Forty cheesy rock sound": Gueraseva, *Def Jam, Inc.*, 82.

89 "You don't have to be from a certain background": Glenn Collins, "Rap Music, Brash and Swaggering, Enters Mainstream," *New York Times*, August 29, 1988.

90 "There's a lot of anger. A lot of social energy in it": Mark Steyn, "No Lie: Kerry's Just a Wannabe," *Chicago Sun-Times*, April 4, 2004.

92 "escape the mechanized work process": Horkheimer and Adorno, *Dialectic of Enlightenment*, 109.

93 "spend a lot of time studying and figuring out ways to seduce": Transcript and audio of David "Davey D" Cook's lecture of May 2005 available at democracynow.org.article.pl?sid=05/05/23/1339234.

95 "When we first put Power 106 on the air": Rick Cummings, telephone interview, August 1, 2005.

95 "Two stations could play the exact same things": Kevin Ross, telephone interview, July 2005.

96 "Right now there are only four markets": Sean Ross interview.

CHAPTER 5—GREAT WHITE HOPES: WEGROES SHED THEIR SKIN

In researching the white fascination with transcendence of racial categories through pop culture, I was greatly aided by Susan Gubar's *Racechanges* (Oxford University Press, 1997); John Leland's *Hip: The History* (HarperCollins, 2004); and Greg Tate's *Everything but the Burden* (Harlem Moon, 2003).

103 "the dawning of a new reality of race in America": Bakari Kitwana, *Why White Kids Love Hip-Hop: Wangstas, Wiggers, Wannabes, and the New Reality of Race in America* (Basic Civitas, 2005), xii.

104 commissioning a portrait, called *A Prediction*: John Leland, *Hip: The History* (HarperCollins, 2004), 83–84.

104 "not only loved those colored boys, but I was one of them": Mezz Mezzrow and Bernard Wolfe, *Really the Blues* (Citadel Press, 1946), 18.

104 "I felt black": quoted in Ken Emerson, *Always Magic in the Air: The Bomp and Brilliance of the Brill Building Era* (Viking, 2005), 7.

105 "a simultaneous drawing up and crossing of racial boundaries": Eric Lott, *Love and Theft: Blackface Minstrelsy and the American Working Class* (Oxford University Press, 1995), 6.

105 They described themselves as "original Negroes" and "the very pinks of negro singers": Ibid., 20.

105 "I was the first white man they had seen who sang as they did": Ibid., 50.

106 drove the crowd to "near abandon": Melvin Patrick Ely, *The Adventures of Amos 'n' Andy: A Social History of an American Phenomenon* (Free Press, 1991), 62.

106 "Thus, what blackface entertainers attempted to annihilate was white responsibility": Susan Gubar, *Racechanges* (Oxford University Press, 1997), 56.

106 "stammering, terrified dialogues": James Baldwin, "White Man's Guilt," in *Black on White: Black Writers on What It Means to Be White*, edited by David Roediger (Schocken Books, 1998), 322–23.

107 "I began to wonder whether Negrophilia and Negrophobia": Mezzrow and Wolfe, *Really the Blues*, reissue (Carol Publishing, 1991), 390.

107 "melanin-lacking hip-hop party": Michelle Garcia, "Deejay's Appeal: 'Kill the Whiteness Inside'; In Brooklyn, a Club Following Feels the Irony," *Washington Post*, August 26, 2005.

111 "music's worst nightmare": Alan Light, "About a Salary or Reality?—Rap's Recurrent Conflict," in Murray Forman and Mark Anthony Neal, *That's the Joint! The Hip-Hop Studies Render* (Routledge, 2004), 141.

111 "the Black Panthers of Rap": Richard Harrington, "Public Enemy's Assault on the Airwaves," *Washington Post*, July 31, 1988.

111 "jam[ming] urban tension and black anger into the foreground": Jon Pareles, "Rap with a Fist in the Air," *New York Times*, July 24, 1988.

111 "the biggest college hit of 1989": David Samuels, "The Rap on Rap," *New Republic*, November 11, 1991.

NOTES

112 "The difference was, trees and houses": Chuck D, telephone interview, March 8, 2005.

113 "We were these working- to middle-class black kids": Bill Stephney, telephone interview, March 8, 2006.

113 "We had a recording contract": Chuck D interview.

114 "the majority of wickedness that goes on across the globe": David Mills's original *Washington Times* article was unavailable. I found it referenced in Richard Harrington, "The End of Public Enemy?," *Washington Post*, June 28, 1989.

115 "P-Dog the militant": Paris, "Panther Power," *The Devil Made Me Do It* (Tommy Boy, 1991).

115 "the whole damn government": Ibid.

115 "Beware, devil man": Brand Nubian, "Drop the Bomb," *One for All* (Elektra, 1990).

115 "Originally, *Check Your Head* wasn't going to have any hip-hop on it": Light, *Skills*, 144–5.

116 "We were the whole antithesis": Chuck D interview.

116 "These kids come from places like Kansas": quoted in Playthell Benjamin, "Two Funky White Boys: Judging 3rd Bass by the Standards of the Street," *Village Voice*, January 9, 1990.

116 "I didn't think I was white": MC Serch, telephone interview, December 8, 2005.

117 "the real deal": Benjamin, "Two Funky White Boys."

117 "Trying too hard": David Mills, "Another Round of White Rappers in Search of 'Black Authenticity,'" *Washington Post*, August 30, 1992.

117 "Dolph Lundgren meets James Dean": Susan Wloszczyna, "Vanilla Ice Melts Hearts, Charts," *USA Today*, November 1, 1990.

118 "Celtic rebels": House of Pain, "One for the Road," *House of Pain* (Tommy Boy, 1992).

118 "Irish intellect": House of Pain, "Danny Boy, Danny Boy," *House of Pain* (Tommy Boy, 1992).

118 "here to keep rap raw": David Mills, "It's a White Thing: Is It Serious Hip-Hop, or a Pale Imitiation?" *Washington Post*, July 14, 1991.

118 "born to the establishment": Chilly Tee, "Krisis of Identity," *Get Off Mine* (MCA, 1993).

118 "stuck in the struggle": Chilly Tee, "Just Do It," *Get Off Mine* (MCA, 1993).

119 "We're taught that all Afro-Americans are black": Greg Kot, "Rap Masters: New SOUL Label Has a Definite 'Street' Beat," *Chicago Tribune*, October 28, 1990.

119 "Calling them Young Black Teenagers": Hank Shocklee, telephone interview, June 23, 2005.

120 "deep, deep blackness": X-Clan, "Verbs of Power," *To the East, Blackwards* (Fourth & Bway, 1990).

120 W. E. B. DuBois called it "a blow in the face": Mark Helbling, "Carl Van Vechten and the Harlem Renaissance," *Negro American Literature Forum*, Summer 1976, 39–47.

120 dismissed the book as "an insult to the race": Robert F. Worth, "*Nigger Heaven* and the Harlem Renaissance," *African American Review*, Autumn 1995, 461–73.

CHAPTER 6—WIGGAZ4LIFE: WHITE GANGSTAS IN THE BUBBLE

Todd Boyd's *Am I Black Enough For You?* (Indiana University Press, 1997); Michael Eric Dyson's *Holler If You Hear Me* (Basic Civitas, 2002); and Ronin Ro's *Gangsta* (St. Martins, 1996) all helped me understand the complexities of gangsta-ism.

128 "ear wigger," a term used by confidence men: D. W. Maurer, "The Argot of Confidence Men," *American Speech*, April 1940.

128 "I do records for black kids": Ice Cube, quoted in Todd Boyd, *Am I Black Enough for You?* (Indiana University Press, 1997), 15.

128 "Wigger" entered the common parlance in the late 1980s: John Algeo and Adele Algeo, "Among the New Words," *American Speech*, Autumn 1991.

130 "wishing I were a Negro": Jack Kerouac, *On the Road* (Penguin, 1957), 179–80.

130 "Knowing in the cells of his existence that life was war": Norman Mailer, "The White Negro," *Advertisements for Myself* (Harvard University Press, 1959), 341.

131 "I'm happy being white emulating black": Laura Blumenfeld, "Black Like Who? Why White Teens Find Hip-Hop Cool," *Washington Post*, July 20, 1992.

131 "the tragic-magical displays of virility": Greg Tate, *Everything but the Burden: What White People Are Taking from Black Culture* (Harlem Moon, 2003), 9.

NOTES

134 "If I had a chance": Josie Newman, "In Toronto, New Crime-Fighting Tactics," *Christian Science Monitor*, December 27, 2005.

134 a member of the Detroit group Blakkattakk: Tom Godfrey, "Rapper: I'm Target of Border Unit; Checked 117 Times Entering Canada," *Toronto Sun*, November 29, 2005.

135 I stole this idea from, among others, Henry Louis Gates Jr.: See Henry Louis Gates Jr., "2 Live Crew, Decoded," *New York Times*, June 19, 1990.

137 "encourages violence against and disrespect for the law officer": Dave Marsh and Phyllis Pollack, "Wanted for Attitude," *Village Voice*, October 10, 1989.

137 "alert local police to the dangers they may face": Ibid.

137 Officers arrested two teenagers in Omaha: "Judges Reach Different Conclusions About Rap Song," Associated Press, March 31, 1989.

137 "underground street reporters": David Mills, "Guns and Poses; Rap Music Violence: Glorifying Gangsterism or Reflecting Reality?" *Washington Times*, August 17, 1989.

138 the state of California was home to an estimated eighty thousand gang members . . . the Vietnam conflict . . . war-zone-like setting: Scott Armstrong, "Gang-Drug Violence Grows in L.A.," *Christian Science Monitor*, November 21, 1989.

138 "selling crack everywhere they go": Patricia Nealon, "Boston Gang Members Making Suburban Forays; City Youths Increasingly Seen in Randolph, Brockton," *Boston Globe*, August 6, 1989.

138 "My son took to using words that I knew were used by gang members": Rod Bernsen, "A Police Officer–Parent Praises a Crackdown That Snared His Son," *Los Angeles Times*, June 25, 1989.

139 "The music is enticing": Bob Sipchen, "Call of the Wild; In the Upscale Suburbs, a Teen Fascination with Gang Life Creates Fears, Challenges for Adults," *Los Angeles Times*, June 25, 1989.

139 "Whatever happened to the idea that rock and roll would make us free?": Jerry Adler, Jennifer Foote, and Ray Sawhill, "The Rap Attitude," *Newsweek*, March 19, 1990.

140 "Sixteen-year-olds are wearing tie-dyed T-shirts": Jonathan Yardley, "The '60s Revival: Echoes from an Empty Decade," *Washington Post*, July 20, 1987.

140 adolescent patients wished they had been born twenty years earlier:

Patricia Leigh Brown, "Once Was a Time: Sharing the 60's," *New York Times*, July 11, 1987.

141 "We'll be demonstrating and going to jail, just like we did in the sixties": Danyel Smith, "House of Pain," *Rolling Stone*, April 7, 1994.

141 "backward baseball caps turn me off ": Bill Maxwell, "The Cleavers Offer a Refuge in a Troubled World," *St. Petersburg Times*, January 1, 1995.

143 "When rap came out of L.A., what you heard initially was my voice yelling about South Central": Quoted in Alan Light, "L.A. Rappers Speak Out," *Rolling Stone*, June 25, 1992.

144 "Perhaps more than any other rapper, Tupac tried to live the life he rapped about": Michael Eric Dyson, *Holler If You Hear Me: Searching for Tupac Shakur* (Basic Civitas, 2001), 15.

146 "You would go to these parties": Luke Buffum, telephone interview.

CHAPTER 7—WHITE-ON-WHITE RHYME: *8 MILE*, NERDCORE, AND MOOKS

Some of my thinking on Eminem's authenticity was influenced by Edward G. Armstrong's article in the October 2004 issue of *Popular Music and Society*, entitled "Eminem's Construction of Authenticity"; Anthony Bozza's *Whatever You Say I Am: The Life and Times of Eminem* (Three Rivers Press, 2003) was also helpful.

157 "I don't think in the history of hip-hop": Gabriel Alvarez, telephone interview, February 9, 2005.

158 "I lived in Boston from 1991 to 1994": Erik Meltzer, telephone interview, January 6, 2006.

159 "See all those stars up there?": Touré, untitled review, *Rolling Stone*, July 9, 1998.

160 One, titled "White-Out Alert": Christopher John Farley, "White-Out Alert," *The Source*, June 1999.

160 Michael Eric Dyson contributed a column: Michael Eric Dyson, "Niggas Gotta Stop," *The Source*, June 1999.

160 "the past and present contributions": Dalton Higgins, "White Boy Shuffle," *The Source*, June 1999.

160 "Color be damned": Scott Poulson-Bryant, "Fear of a White Rapper," *The Source*, June 1999.

NOTES

161 **"Rap music is the language of the disenfranchised"**: Ibid.

162 **"He's talking to them, too"**: quoted in Nate Cavalieri, "Gangsta Surprise," *Metro Times*, May 1, 2002.

164 **"It's not something that you should feel"**: Jeff Chang, telephone interview, May 24, 2005.

165 **"It never felt comfortable"**: Hot Karl, telephone interview, January 21, 2006.

167 **whose label sold her as "Feminem"**: Jim Farber, "The Changing Face of Hip-Hop," *Daily News*, April 17, 2003.

168 **"In a way, it makes sense"**: Gabriel Alvarez interview.

171 **"celebrity bigot"**: Richard Goldstein, "Celebrity Bigots: Why Hate Is Hot," *Village Voice*, July 12, 2000.

171 **"For the rock 'n' roll generation"**: Paul Slansky, "Guess Who Thinks Eminem's a Genius? Middle-Aged Me," *New York Observer*, June 3, 2002.

172 **"The Boomers' Crooner"**: Maureen Dowd, "The Boomers' Crooner," *New York Times*, November 24, 2002.

172 **8 Mile's producer, Brian Grazer**: Frank Rich, "Mr. Ambassador," *New York Times Magazine*, November 3, 2002.

172 **pulled in a remarkable $51.2 million**: Anthony Breznican, "Eminem Raps Competition as *8 Mile* Debuts Atop Box Office," Associated Press, November 11, 2002.

176 **was downloaded 1.2 million times**: Dave Itzkoff, "Nerds in the Hood, Stars on the Web," *New York Times*, December 27, 2005.

176 **"being as nerdy as possible"**: Ibid.

176 **"In ten years, it's entirely possible"**: Sacha Jenkins, in-person interview, March 8, 2006.

CHAPTER 8—SELLING DOWN: THE MARKETING OF THE HIP-HOP NATION

My study of the nexus between commerce and culture was greatly aided by Thomas Frank's *Conquest of Cool* (University of Chicago Press, 1997) and by Joseph Heath and Andrew Potter's *Nation of Rebels* (HarperCollins, 2004). The PBS *Frontline* documentary "The Persuaders," directed by Barak Goodman and Rachel Dretzin, was also very helpful.

178 "the true ruling power of our country": Edward Bernays, *Propaganda* (Ig Publishing, 1928), 37.

179 "systematically feeling out our hidden weaknesses and frailties": Vance Packard, *The Hidden Persuaders* (Pocket Books, 1957), 2.

179 "Most of the time, people have no idea why they're doing": Barak Goodman and Rachel Dretzin, directors, "The Persuaders," *Frontline*, PBS, November 9, 2003.

181 "For better or worse": Telephone interview with Rob Schwartz, November 7, 2005.

182 "I'm the person that can tell you": Telephone interview with Morris L. Reid, November 14, 2005.

182 "More than anything else, hip-hop has been about marketing": Nat Ives, "Hip-hop Admen: Walk This Way, Shop This Way," *New York Times*, August 9, 2004.

182 "announcing one's existence to the world": Nelson George, *Hip Hop America* (Penguin, 1995), 14.

183 "what kind of sponsorships and marketing deals they would be interested in": David Kiley, "Hip Hop Gets Down with the Deals," businessweek.com, May 16, 2005.

184 "I think what made hip-hop compelling": Douglas Rushkoff, telephone interview, June 10, 2005.

185 "Back in 1994, hip-hop artists": Darryl Cobbin, telephone interview, December 1, 2005.

185 "It sounds cartoonish": In-person interview with Alan Light, January 30, 2006.

185 "If you don't target the hard-core, you don't get the suburbs": Marc Spiegler, "Marketing Street Culture," *American Demographics*, November 1996.

186 "Middle American teens and twentysomethings don't want to buy": Yvette C. Doss, "Locating 'Where It's At,' " *Daily News of Los Angeles*, January 24, 1997.

186 "has proven to be a potent commodity": Juliet B. Schor, *Born to Buy: The Commercialized Child and the New Consumer Culture* (Scribner, 2004) 48–49.

187 marketers view consumers as cockroaches: Goodman and Dretzin, "Persuaders."

NOTES

187 "everything they don't teach you at Harvard Business School": Zev Borow, "Living Out Loud," *New York*, May 24, 1999.

187 "Corporations realized there was a huge untapped urban market": Ibid.

188 "raise the profile of our brand": Stephen Kiehl, "Cashing in on the Pop and Hip-Hop Name-Drop," *Baltimore Sun*, August 22, 2004.

188 "the holy grail of marketing": William Chipps, "Luxury Life: Hitching Brands to the Stars," *Billboard*, August 21, 2004.

188 "We have seen a lot of big companies": Laura Ries, telephone interview, November 2005.

189 "It seemed that they were trying to become authentic": Lucian James, telephone interview, November 1, 2005.

190 "In Nobrow": John Seabrook, "Nobrow," *New Yorker*, September 20, 1999.

190 "grousing about a pop landscape dominated by big-budget": Kelefa Sanneh, "The Rap Against Rockism," *New York Times*, October 31, 2004.

191 "People, whether they're joining a cult or brand": Goodman and Dretzin, "The Persuaders."

191 "Kids can recognize logos by eighteen months": Schor, *Born to Buy*, 19.

191 doddering writing professors that David Foster Wallace describes: David Foster Wallace, "E Unibus Pluram: Television and U.S. Fiction," in *A Supposedly Fun Thing I'll Never Do Again* (Little, Brown, 1997), 21–82.

195 "The overwhelming majority is open to it": Josh Levine, telephone interview, October 31, 2005.

196 "There was a big brouhaha": Jimmy Smith, telephone interview, November 10, 2005.

196–97 In the 1960s, Bill Bernbach's agency, Doyle Dayne Bernbach; A headline for a 1964 magazine ad for Chivas Regal; "I hate conformity because____.": Thomas Frank, *The Conquest of Cool: Business Culture, Counterculture, and the Rise of Hip Consumerism* (University of Chicago Press, 1997).

197 Bernbach "was the first adman to embrace the mass society critique": Ibid., 35.

197 "But the Man can't bust our music": John Leland, *Hip: The History* (HarperCollins, 2004), 287.

197 "cultural rebellion, of the type epitomized by *Adbusters* magazine":

Joseph Heath and Andrew Potter, *Nation of Rebels: Why Counterculture Became Consumer Culture* (HarperCollins, 2004), 1.

CHAPTER 9—LOSE YOURSELF: A CONCLUSION

201 "I thought people would have fun": Mary Huhn, "Karaoke Gettin' a Good Rap: Where You Can Find Your Inner Eminem," *New York Post*, March 7, 2005.

204 "It ain't where you're from": Eric B & Rakim, "In the Ghetto," *Let the Rhythm Hit 'Em* (MCA, 1990).

204 "He was in the process of reinventing himself ": Jeff Chang, *Can't Stop Won't Stop* (St. Martin's Press, 2005), 73.

204 "The whole idea of being this other person": Fab 5 Freddy, telephone interview, June 8, 2005.

205 "The truth was that Jay Gatsby": F. Scott Fitzgerald, *The Great Gatsby* (Scribner, 1925), 104.

205–06 "Rap is really funny, man": Chang, *Can't Stop*, 331.

207 "Disneyland exists": Jean Baudrillard, *Simulacra and Simulation* (University of Michigan Press, 1994), 12.

207 "represents the current paradigm": Anthony Bozza, *Whatever You Say I Am: The Life and Times of Eminem* (Three Rivers Press, 2003), 172.

207 "What Eminem demonstrates": Ibid., 194.

208 "I was completely stunned": Bill Adler, in-person interview, May 10, 2005.

209 "The idea of hip-hop": David Segal, "At the Smithsonian, Hip-hop Is History," *Washington Post*, March 1, 2006.

209 "It's not a signal to the end of hip-hop": Marcus Franklin, "Hip Hop Relics," Associated Press, February 28, 1996.

211 "the huge pool of poorly educated black men": Eric Eckholm, "Plight Deepens for Black Men, Studies Warn," *New York Times*, March 20, 2006.

212 "Consumers are not the people": Jeff Chang, telephone interview, May 24, 2005.

ACKNOWLEDGMENTS

It took a nation of millions to write this book. Well, okay—dozens.

My agent, Paul Bresnick, first suggested that I could tackle this topic, and provided assistance and encouragement along the way. Big up to everyone at Bloomsbury, especially Kathy Belden and Yelena Gitlin, who have been consistent in their enthusiasm and wisdom.

Thanks to Charles Eisendrath, Birgit Rieck, and the rest of the staff at the University of Michigan's Knight-Wallace Fellows program. Thanks also to the many University of Michigan faculty members who offered their advice and ideas, including Nicholas Delbanco, Nadine Hubbs, Lucia Saks, and Richard Tillinghast.

Dan Goodgame and the staff of *Fortune Small Business* magazine were flexible and understanding through the entire book-writing process.

Early conversations with Gabriel Alvarez, Jeff Chang, John Leland, and Oliver Wang helped me get my shambling thoughts in order. Bill Adler was generous with his time, insight, and contacts. I am indebted to everyone who agreed to be interviewed, especially those who let me intrude in their lives for hours or even days at a stretch. I'm particularly grateful to the members of AR-15, whose lyrics subconsciously inspired my title. ("Rich folks got O.P.P.: other people's property.")

This book is the end result of a lifetime of bullshitting about hip-hop and race; thanks to Jimmy Kim, Daniel Spirn, and especially to Lukas Hauser, for the mixtapes and conversations. Thanks as well to everyone who read sections of the manuscript and offered their sage advice: Cynthia Barnett, Jennifer C. Lena, David Nadler, and Ron Stodghill. Brandi Stewart provided invaluable last-minute research. Special thanks to Alan Light, whom I've long admired and who shared so much of his knowledge, time, energy, and goodwill.

I am so lucky to have such warm and supportive in-laws in Diane and Richard Cante. And Rich Cante, my brother-in-law, was a great fellow traveler.

My parents and sister have never offered me less than their wholehearted encouragement and confidence in me. They gave me the strength to believe that I could write a book. I cannot thank them enough for a lifetime of love and support.

Ultimately, this book belongs to my wife, Denise. We were married just as I began the proposal. She encouraged me to take an unpaid leave from work. She read every page of every draft of my manuscript, offering painfully honest but always correct critiques. She endured my late-night unburdenings with unwavering love, optimism, and patience. Marrying Denise has given me more than a wife, more than a best friend, more than a brilliant editor. It has given me a new part of myself. That's the part that wrote this book.

INDEX

INDEX

INDEX

INDEX

INDEX

INDEX

INDEX

INDEX

A NOTE ON THE AUTHOR

Jason Tanz's work has appeared in the *New York Times*, *Fortune*, *Spin*, and *Time Out New York*, among other publications. He lives in Brooklyn, New York.